Mandela's World

The International Dimension of South Africa's Political Revolution 1990–99

Other books
By James Barber

Rhodesia the Road to Rebellion Oxford University Press (For Institute of Race Relations) 1967
Imperial Frontier: Relations between the British and the Pastoral Tribes of NE Uganda, East African Publishing House 1968
South Africa's Foreign Policy 1945–1970 Oxford University Press 1972
European Community: Vision and Reality (Editor) Open University Press 1973
The Nature of Foreign Policy (Editor) Open University Press 1974
Who Makes British Foreign Policy? Open University Press 1976
The Uneasy Relationship: Britain and South Africa Heinemann (For Royal Institute of International Affairs) 1983
South Africa's Foreign Policy: The Search For Status and Security 1945–1988 (With John Barratt) Cambridge University Press 1990
The British Prime Minister Since 1945 Blackwell 1991
Forging the New South Africa Royal Institute of International Affairs 1994
South Africa in the Post Cold War World South African Institute of International Affairs 1996
South Africa in the Twentieth Century: In Search of a Nation State Blackwell 1999

Mandela's World

The International Dimension of South Africa's Political Revolution 1990–99

James Barber

James Currey
OXFORD

David Philip
CAPE TOWN

Ohio University Press
ATHENS

James Currey Ltd
73 Botley Road
Oxford OX2 0BS
www.jamescurrey.co.uk

Ohio University Press
Scott Quadrangle
Athens
Ohio 45701
www.ohioedu/oupress

David Philip Publisher
An imprint of New Africa Books (Pty) Ltd
99 Garfield Rd
Claremont 7700, Cape Town

First published 2004

1 2 3 4 5 08 07 06 05 04

ISBN 0-85255-877-5 (James Currey cloth)
ISBN 0-85255-876-7 (James Currey paper)
ISBN 0-8214-1565-4 (Ohio University Press cloth)
ISBN 0-8214-1566-2 (Ohio University Press paper)

British Library Cataloguing in Publication Data

Barber, James, 1931–
Mandela's world : the international dimension of South Africa's political revolution 1990–99
1.South Africa – Politics and government – 1989–1994
2.South Africa – Politics and government – 1994– 3.South Africa – Foreign relations 1989-1994 4.South Africa – Foreign relations – 1994–
I.Title
968′.064

Library of Congress Cataloging-in-Publication Data available on request

Typeset in 10/12pt Monotype Plantin
by Avocet Typeset, Chilton, Aylesbury, Bucks
Printed and bound in Great Britain by
Woolnough, Irthingborough

Contents

Acknowledgements

In writing this book I have received valuable help, advice and support. Among those I should particularly like to thank are Professors John Barratt, Deon Geldenhuys, Maxi Schoeman and Jack Spence; the staff of the South African Institute of International Affairs – especially Dr Greg Mills, Mrs Pauline Watts and the library staff; Deputy Minister Aziz Pahad and Abdul Minty; the publisher James Currey; and, as always, my wife June, who has helped me in numerous ways.

James Barber
Cambridge 2003

Abbreviations

AAM	Anti Apartheid Movement
ACP	Africa, Caribbean and Pacific
ADB	African Development Bank
ADFL	Alliance of Democratic Forces for the Liberation of Congo-Zaire
ANC	African National Congress
APM	Anti Personnel Mines
APLA	Azanian People's Liberation Army
Armscor	Armaments Corporation of South Africa
ASAS	Association of Southern African States
AWB	Afrikaner Weerstandsbeweging
CAAA	Comprehensive Anti Apartheid Act
Codesa	Convention for a Democratic South Africa
Comesa	Common Market for Eastern and Southern Africa
Consas	Constellation of Southern African States
Cosatu	Congress of South African Trade Unions
CP	Conservative Party
Dexsa	Defence Exposition of South Africa
DFA	Department of Foreign Affairs
DP	Democratic Party
DRC	Democratic Republic of the Congo
DTI	Department of Trade and Industry
EAC	Economic Advisory Council
EC	European Community
ECOSOC	Economic and Social Council
EPG	Eminent Persons Group
EU	European Union
FF	Freedom Front
FLS	Front Line States
Frelimo	Frente de Libertação de Moçambique
GATT	General Agreement on Trade and Tariffs
GDP	Gross Domestic Product
Gear	Growth, Employment and Redistribution
GNU	Government of National Unity
GNP	Gross National Product
IAEA	International Atomic Energy Authority
IEA	Independent Electoral Authority
IFP	Inkatha Freedom Party
ILO	International Labour Organisation
IMF	International Monetary Fund
IOR-ARC	Indian Ocean Rim-Association for Regional Co-operation
ISDCS	Inter-State Defence and Security Conference
LDC	Lesotho Congress for Democracy
MK	Umkhonto we Sizwe
MPLA	Movimento Popular de Libertação de Angola
NAM	Non Aligned Movement
Nato	North Atlantic Treaty Organisation
NCACC	National Conventional Arms Control Committee
NGO	Non Governmental Organisation
NP	National Party
NPT	Non Proliferation Treaty
OAU	Organisation of African Unity
OPDS	Organ for Politics, Defence and Security (Organ)
PAC	Pan Africanist Congress
Pafmeca	Pan African Movement for East and Central Africa
PLO	Palestine Liberation Organisation
PRC	People's Republic of China
PTA	Preferential Trade Area
RDP	Reconstruction and Development Programme
RECAMP	*Renforcement des capacités africaines de maintien de la paix*

Renamo	Resistência Nacional Moçambicana
RMA	Rand Monetary Area
SACBL	South African Campaign to Ban Landmines
SACP	South African Communist Party
SACU	Southern African Customs Union
SADC	Southern African Development Community
SADCC	Southern African Development Co-ordination Conference
SADF	South African Defence Force
SANDF	South African National Defence Force
SAP	Structural Adjustment Programme
SSC	State Security Council
Swapo	South West African Peoples Organisation
TDCA	Trade, Development and Co-operative Agreement
TEC	Transitional Executive Council
UDF	United Democratic Front
UDI	Unilateral Declaration of Independence
UN	United Nations
UNCHR	United Nations Commission on Human Rights
UNCTAD	United Nations Conference on Trade and Development
Unesco	United Nations Educational, Scientific and Cultural Organisation
UNHCR	United Nations High Commission for Refugees
UNHRC	United Nations Human Rights Commission
Unicef	United Nations (International) Childrens (Emergency) Fund
Unita	União Nacional para a Independência Total de Angola
Unomsa	United Nations Observer Mission to South Africa
WHO	World Health Organisation
WTO	World Trade Organisation
ZANU(PF)	Zimbabwe African National Union (Patriotic Front)
ZAPU	Zimbabwe African Peoples Union

1
Setting the Scene

The end of apartheid had long been predicted, but not the timing or the means by which it was achieved. Before 1990 the prevailing assumptions had been that the struggle would stretch over many years and the white regime would only be overthrown after further major conflict and bloodshed. Yet, while violence was not absent, South Africa's political revolution – by which white minority rule was replaced by a democratic regime – was in the end achieved by multi-party negotiations leading to an election and the installation of the new government.

The formal process that led to the final settlement started on 2 February, 1990, when F.W. de Klerk, the State President and leader of the National Party (NP) government, addressed parliament. It was a defining moment in South Africa's history. De Klerk declared his intention to set the country on the road to fundamental change. The alternative, he stated, was 'growing violence, tension and conflict'. He spoke of initiating negotiations to achieve a new political dispensation in which 'every citizen will enjoy equal rights, treatment and opportunity'. To that end he announced the release of political prisoners, the removal of emergency regulations, and the lifting of existing bans on all political parties – including the African National Congress (ANC), the Pan Africanist Congress (PAC) and the South African Communist Party (SACP). De Klerk called on all South Africans to put aside past divisions and 'build a broad consensus about the fundamentals of a new, realistic and democratic dispensation'. Our country and its people, he stated, have been embroiled in conflict and struggle for decades. 'It is time for us to break out of the cycle of violence and break through to peace and reconciliation' (De Klerk 1991: 34–46).

Conscious that he was also speaking to an international audience, de Klerk said that he was aware of the part 'the world at large has to play in the realisation of our county's national interests'. That, he said, would be helped by the recent and welcome collapse of 'the Marxist economic system in Eastern Europe', which had opened up opportunities for South Africa to break the international shackles that had been imposed upon it. He laid special emphasis on improving relations in Africa, where 'hostile postures have to be replaced by co-operative ones; confrontation by contact; disengagement by engagement' (De Klerk 1991: 34–5).

In pursuing his ends de Klerk seized the opportunity provided by the presence in the country of a large body of international journalists. Later he explained: 'We had prepared a comprehensive media strategy to ensure that the speech received maximum favourable publicity ... The scene was set for a massive marketing exercise.' The content of the speech was, therefore, kept secret until immediately before it was delivered. Copies were then handed to the journalists, but, to ensure its full impact was not lost through leaks, they were locked in a briefing room until de Klerk had finished speaking (De Klerk 1998a: 164–5).

Nine days after de Klerk's speech an even larger body of the world's media assembled outside Victor Verster prison, near Cape Town, to witness the release of Nelson Mandela. Mandela, the most famous of political prisoners, had been incarcerated for twenty-seven years. Later he described the scene on his release. 'Reporters,' he wrote, 'started shouting questions; television crews began crowding in; ANC supporters were yelling and cheering. It was a happy, if slightly disorientating, chaos.' Eventually, after much confusion, Mandela was driven to the City Hall. There, from the balcony, he addressed 'a boundless sea of people cheering, holding flags and banners, clapping and laughing. I raised my fist to the crowd ... "Amandla" I called out. "Ngawethu" they responded. "iAfrika" I yelled. "Mayibuye" they answered' (Mandela 1994: 553–5). Then, after thanking those South Africans who had supported the ANC during the long years of struggle, and after describing de Klerk as a 'man of integrity', Mandela spoke of the world community's contribution to the anti-apartheid struggle. 'Without your support,' he stated, 'our struggle would not have reached this advanced stage.' He made special mention of the neighbouring black states (the Front Line States), which had stood firm against apartheid. However, Mandela emphasised that his release and lifting bans on the parties was not the end of the struggle. With that in mind, he called on the international community to retain sanctions and continue to isolate the apartheid regime. 'To lift sanctions now,' he said, 'would be to run the risk of aborting the process towards the complete eradication of apartheid.' Meanwhile, he called on South Africans to return to the barricades and intensify the struggle (Clark 1993: 23–9).

In the event there was little need to return to the barricades. South Africa's political revolution was largely achieved by negotiation not armed force – the 'miracle' was in the means as well as the end. Although the negotiations that followed de Klerk's speech and Mandela's release were conducted against a backcloth of conflict – involving covert government forces, white extremists and 'black on black' violence – the transformation was achieved not on the field of battle by troops in camouflage jackets, but rather by men in dark suits, who met publicly in conference halls and privately in back rooms. Yet the path of negotiation was often rough. From time to time the process broke down and the threat of major conflict was never far away, but the determination of the political leaders to succeed through negotiation was reinforced by their fear that failure would lead to civil war. Succeed they did. Eventually they hammered out agreement for a five-year, interim constitution, together with the principles on which a permanent constitution would be fashioned during those first five years.

Based on that agreement, just over four years after de Klerk's speech, the country's first democratic election was held in April 1994. It was a time of great emotion as South Africans – irrespective of colour, creed or ideology – cast their votes, most of them for the first time. The high turn-out of voters and their patience in waiting in long queues fostered new hope where previously there had only been despair. Based on strict proportional representation, the electorate returned a parliament with a large ANC majority (63%), followed by de Klerk's NP (20%) and the Inkatha Freedom Party (IFP) of Chief Mangosuthu Buthelezi (11%). Within the terms of the interim constitution, a Government of National Unity (GNU) was formed from the three major parties, for the five years of the interim constitution.

The new South Africa was ceremonially born on 10 May 1994, when princes, presidents and prime ministers from all corners of the world assembled before the Union Buildings in Pretoria, to celebrate the installation of Mandela as the country's first black head of state, with Thabo Mbeki and de Klerk as his Deputy Presidents. As those in Pretoria paid their personal tributes, so television cameras beamed the ceremony to millions around the globe. The distinction of the audience and the media attention demonstrated the intensity of attention that had been given to South Africa in the past and the high hopes that were entertained for its future. The collapse of the apartheid state and the arrival of a democratic government were greeted in triumph not only in South Africa, but throughout the world community. The installation of Mandela was seen as the fulfilment of a prolonged international campaign against apartheid.

When the new government came to power, South Africa's international status changed dramatically – rejection gave way to acceptance; criticism to praise; the old pariah was embraced as the prodigal that had returned, the sinner that had repented. International organisations eagerly opened their doors to the new recruit. Political leaders, from all parts of the world and of all ideological hues, came hurrying to bathe in the reflected glory of the South African 'miracle'. Furthermore, the miracle coincided with – and was in part explained by – the end of the Cold War. Initially expectations were high that East/West confrontation would be replaced by 'a new world order' in which peace and the rule of law would prevail. In this context the South African settlement was held up as a model for other strife-torn parts of the world. If it was possible, so the argument ran, to end apartheid by negotiation, it was possible to resolve other seemingly intractable situations by similar means. It was flattering for the new state to be held up as a model for others, and also to be seen as the best hope for an economic and political revival in Africa, but such hopes imposed a heavy burden of expectation on Mandela's government. It was a new, inexperienced administration, struggling with the problems of a society undergoing profound change, while finding its way in an international setting, which itself was disordered and uncertain. The international attention was welcome, the hope for the future was genuine, but could a new government, faced by major domestic problems, satisfy such expectations?

The government did not lack international ambition. It was eager to play an active role and project its values abroad. Before taking office the ANC published a set of principles as the basis of its foreign policy, including a commitment to help in the development of Africa. It was a bold and ambitious agenda, based on the ANC's aspirations. Yet, asked a returning exile:

Setting the Scene

> How much do ordinary South Africans black and white, understand what is happening around them? Are they able to understand the dynamics transforming their own individual political lives in the context of the global revolution – a revolution that has seen the end of 'the cold war', and the mythologies of 'deterrence', 'balance of power', 'total onslaught' and 'total strategy'? (Vale 1992: 98).

Aims of this Study – Change and Continuity

This study seeks to describe and analyse the international aspect of South Africa's development during the 1990s. During those years, Nelson Mandela stamped his personality on both the South African and international stages. This study is not about him as an individual, but, that having been said, it is impossible to ignore the impact he had, both at home and abroad. As a person, as the ANC leader and the new South Africa's first President, he played a major part in shaping the internal settlement, in creating the new government's foreign relations, and in establishing himself as a leading international figure. From a South African perspective it truly was 'Mandela's World'.

Although the focus of attention is on international affairs, domestic factors cannot be ignored. A state's domestic strengths, weaknesses and values shape its international role, establish the resources available for the pursuit of its aims, and the attitude of other international actors towards it. The question in analysing foreign policy/external relations is not whether domestic matters should be examined, but rather to what extent and which factors should gain most attention. Indeed, no better example exists of the interaction between domestic and external affairs than South Africa during the apartheid years, when the government's overriding aim was the preservation of a white-controlled state. All policy, including foreign policy was geared to that end.

When the new government came into power that changed, transforming both the domestic and foreign scenes, but domestic factors continued to influence external activities and values. The GNU faced similar tasks to those that confront all governments, as it sought to balance domestic and external interests and values, and to pursue a foreign policy to further its domestic aims. At the same time – in the two-way flow of ideas – domestic policies, including management of the economy, were strongly influenced by global developments. However, at first there was a distinctive situation in South Africa, in that most of the ANC leadership had been cut off from the domestic scene. They were of course South Africans, but many of them had been isolated from their own society, as political prisoners or by working in exile (as troops in the liberation army, or ANC diplomats, or students). From the time of their release or return, their hands were more than full, as they readjusted to living again at home, to building an effective political party when, because of the ban, none existed, and to conducting negotiations with the government.

The changes that took place inside South Africa were remarkable. As Deon Geldenhuys wrote: 'The abolition of apartheid represented more than a mere change of domestic policy, or even of government … It constituted a thorough-going regime change, in that political values, norms and authority structures were all affected' (Geldenhuys 1992: 35). In short it was a political revolution. To describe it as anything less would be to undervalue what had taken place. South Africa had been changed; irredeemably changed. However, such a revolution cannot be confined to a fixed point in time; rather it is a process that stretches over a period, with its triumphs and its tragedies; its achievements and its failures. The 1990s were part of the process, as the country absorbed the political changes, and, somewhat hesitatingly, set out to reshape its social and economic relations.

The domestic revolution transformed foreign relations. The emergence of the new government marked a change both in South Africa's self-perception, and in the way it was seen by others. From the end of World War II to 1990 South Africa had increasingly been treated as a pariah state – subjected to a range of sanctions, excluded from most international organisations, its government despised and rejected. In contrast, the new South Africa was held up as a model for others to follow. The old white regime had seen itself as a bastion of the West in Africa – an enclave standing firm against a tide of communism sweeping across the continent. It failed, however, to persuade the international community (including the Western powers) to accept this image. Instead it was damned as a racist society, hanging on to white minority rule. When Mandela's government came to power it rejected the old image, and presented itself as a Third World state of Africa, linked to the Non Aligned Movement, and with a commitment to promote human rights, democracy and respect for international law, and to eliminate racism.

At the same time the new government had to react to a changing external environment. The hopes of peace and stability that had ushered in the 'new world order' were soon shattered. Instead parts of the world – not least in Africa – were consumed by conflict and instability. The international scene was further characterised by increasing globalisation – especially of the economy, in which Western states were dominant. Within that context the new government inherited an economy that was a mixture of 'the developed North' and 'the developing South'*. With the great majority of its people (including the bulk of ANC supporters) living in Third World conditions, the government chose to associate itself with the developing South, rather that the developed North. Yet, the situation was far from straightforward. Although the ANC had been suspicious of Western capitalism, and had been backed by the Soviet Union in its armed struggle, and although it now identified itself with the poorer, developing states, it found it had little choice but to rely on the dominant West for trade, aid and investment. Furthermore many of the principles adopted by the ANC, both in the new constitution and in its approach to foreign policy, reflected 'liberal' values usually associated with the West. On occasion that led to suspicion among other poorer states, and particularly in Africa where South Africa's

* Various labels are used to categorise groups of states based on their development and ideological orientation – including 'West', 'North' and 'First World' for the 'developed' economies, and 'South' and 'Third World' for the 'developing'. I have used them interchangeably according to the context in which they appear.

strength was most marked and memories of white South Africa's aggression clearest (Taylor 2001).

Within the changing world order Mandela's government faced a variety of challenges in establishing its international roles. It had to identify policy priorities; to balance Western and Third World values; to revise internal processes; to bring in black officials and representatives; to allocate resources; to expand its representation abroad; to find its place in international organisations; to rethink security needs; and to recognise its limitations while responding to the expectations of others. All these factors played a part in an ongoing debate – inside and outside the government – about the country's international aims and the means of achieving them. The debate, which continued throughout Mandela's presidency, sought to balance the principles endorsed by the ANC, against clashing interests and principles both at home and abroad. The government soon discovered that foreign policy is often reactive – less a matter of taking initiatives than responding to unforeseen and sometimes unpalatable developments. Although Mandela and his colleagues came to power proclaiming their own values and aims they had to operate in an international context that was largely shaped by the values and interests of others. For instance, as noted earlier, a balance had to be struck between its self-identification as a member of the South, and the pursuit of its own interests in a Northern-dominated economic setting.

A particular dilemma for the new government was its role in Africa, and especially Southern Africa. While in global terms South Africa is a small/medium power, in Africa it is a giant – having the continent's largest and most vibrant economy, its most advanced infrastructure, an advanced (if uneven) educational system and substantial military forces. In the apartheid days these strengths had been employed against its continental neighbours. The new government was eager to right past wrongs, but that was no easy task. South Africa's size and strength, which gave it the capacity to help, also bred fears among its smaller neighbours that it would exercise a new form of hegemony. Despite Pretoria's protests that it had no such ambitions, the suspicions persisted, and its efforts were not always welcomed in a continent that continued to be plagued by strife, poverty and corruption. Frequently it found itself in the uncomfortable position of being 'damned if it did, and damned if it did not' take action. Added to that was a further burden of expectation, inside and outside Africa – based on hopes that Pretoria would bring political stability to the troubled continent and become its economic dynamo. Although never fully endorsing such expectations the new government committed itself to work in harmony and equality with its neighbours.

While change was a major theme for the new South Africa, a note of caution must be added. As Frederick Northedge wrote:

> Foreign policy constitutes an endless dialogue between the powers of continuity and the powers of change … We should not hope, or fear, that changes of government or ideology, or even domestic revolutions, will change the way in which a country conducts its foreign relations; or if it transforms its manner of diplomacy; it will do the same to its real substance … As in a game of cards, the government in foreign policy is dealt a hand of cards by circumstances. There is no freedom to play a card not in hand (Northedge 1968: 11).

That was the case in South Africa during the 1990s. The scene was shifting rapidly and dramatically, but not all was change. Although Mandela's government had a much stronger hand than its predecessors – not least because it held the high moral ground – many of the cards were the same as those held by the apartheid regime. Mandela's government had new aims and values, and enjoyed international approval, but its resources and many of its domestic constraints and problems remained the same. The country's political system had been revolutionised, but not its social and economic fabric. Also there was no altering the map, to remove from its borders unstable and poor neighbours. Northedge's message may seem too stark for the new South Africa, but it is a reminder that the government inherited constraints as well as opportunities, and its policies had elements of continuity as well as change.

The Structure of the Study

The years between 1990 and 1999 fall into two distinct periods. The first opened with de Klerk's speech in February 1990. Four years of tough negotiations and political violence followed before a settlement was achieved. The second period began in May 1994, when the GNU was installed, with members drawn from the three strongest parties – the ANC, the NP and the IFP. However, from the beginning the ANC was the dominant partner.

In this study, while much attention is given to the government – its foreign policy aims and achievements, and its role within the international community – the focus is wider, especially in the years before 1994. Until the new democratic South Africa was established the legitimacy of the National Party (NP) government – the 'apartheid regime' as it was known to its opponents – was persistently challenged, not only by the liberation movements (ANC and PAC) but by many states and international organisations. During those years the government and the liberation movements (backed by foreign states and anti-apartheid groups) competed in the international arena to be accepted as the legitimate representatives of South Africa's people. Neither succeeded completely.

Following the GNU accession to power in 1994, attention mainly concentrates on the government's foreign policy and particularly the activities of the executive – its aims, interests and resources; how it employs the resources; the pressures it faces at home and abroad; who makes decisions and how they are made; and the reaction of other members of the international community. However, my main concern is not with the processes that take place inside the government (although inevitably some attention is given to them) but with the following:

- The stated aims of the government and other South African groups;
- How these aims were shaped and reshaped by the country's past and its current domestic, regional and international settings;
- The debates that developed in South Africa over principles and interests related to international affairs;

- The patterns of events as they unfolded, and how they influenced policy and activities;
- The reactions of other international actors to developments in South Africa.
- The government's and other groups' success/failure in achieving their aims.

In writing about these matters I have from time to time introduced some theoretical approaches to International Relations, such as 'neo-realism' and the concept of a 'middle power'. The intention in using them is not to confuse the reader, but rather to contribute towards the understanding of South Africa's situation, while incidentally throwing further light on the approaches themselves.

⋆

Following this introduction the book is divided into four parts. The first – 'Prelude to Transformation' – briefly sketches the interaction between South Africa's domestic and international affairs from World War II to the end of the 1980s, with especial attention to developments in the 1980s. This provides a background that helps to explain developments in the 1990s, and a comparison between the 'old' and the 'new' South Africa. The second part – 'Negotiations and Competition for International Support' – focuses on activities during the period of negotiations (1990–94), when the ANC and the NP government were rivals seeking to strengthen their negotiating positions by gaining external support. The third part – 'The New South Africa: Seeking an Identity' – starts by examining contrasting views about the foundations for the new South Africa's foreign policy. Should it be based a set of ethical principles and values as pronounced by the ANC; or would it largely be determined by the opportunities and constraints of the external setting in which it has to operate? That dichotomy is examined against the experiences of the new government. The final part – 'South Africa Gains an International Identity: Its International Roles' – investigates four broad roles the new government had established by the end of Mandela's presidency. Two of these roles are related to the new state's position within the broader international community – 'The Middle Power' and 'The Bridge Builder and Accommodation' – while the other two are linked to its place in Africa – 'The African Power' and 'The Regional Giant'.

This book therefore examines the international relations of a society undergoing fundamental transformation at home, while, at the same time, its government seeks to establish itself and promote its values and interests in an international system that itself is undergoing profound change.

I
Prelude to Transformation

2
Pariahs & Exiles

De Klerk's speech, Mandela's release and the negotiations that followed, were part of a process that had earlier roots. These roots were found not only inside South Africa, but in the Southern African region and the broader international community. To understand the 1990s, therefore, it is important to know something of these earlier years.

South Africa had captured hostile international attention as early as 1946, when the Indian government brought a complaint to the United Nations (UN), arguing that discrimination practised against Indians living in South Africa was a source of friction between two UN member states. That was soon followed by pressure on Pretoria to place South West Africa (the future Namibia) under a UN trusteeship agreement. South West Africa, which had been a German colony, had come under Pretoria's control after the World War I as a League of Nations mandated territory. Following World War II South Africa attempted to absorb it as its sixth province, but ran into sustained opposition at the UN. There it was argued that South West Africa, like other former mandated territories, should fall under the trusteeship of the UN. Thus, although Pretoria continued to administer the territory, its claim to sovereignty was rejected by the international community. While that dispute and the clash with India were specific issues they were soon absorbed into a general attack on South Africa's racial policies. Pretoria vehemently protested that these policies were within its domestic jurisdiction and therefore outside the UN's competence, but most states and international bodies rejected that view.

In 1948 international criticism intensified following the electoral victory of the National Party (NP), with its rigid, doctrinaire racial policy of 'apartheid'. Although Pretoria stood firm, the tide of condemnation increased, reaching a new peak in the early 1960s, as independent African states emerged from the old colonial empires, and black protests inside South Africa erupted – first in 1960, leading to the Sharpeville massacre, and later in the Soweto rising of 1976. Faced by widespread hostility Pretoria tried to deflect criticism by its 'homelands' (Bantustan) policy – the core idea being to grant formal independence to the country's African/tribal 'nations'. This was to be achieved by carving out, from within the existing state's boundaries, separate territories for the African 'nations' (based on the old Native Reserves). Dr Hendrik Verwoerd, as Prime Minister between 1958 and his assassination in 1966, was the dominant prophet of apartheid. He admitted that the Bantustan policy,

> is not what we would have liked to see. In the light of pressures being exerted on South Africa, there is, however, no doubt that eventually this will have to be done, thereby buying for the white man his freedom and the right to retain domination in his own country (HA 10.4.61: 4191).

However, the Bantustan policy was opposed by most blacks at home, and failed to gain international acceptance. Elsewhere in Africa there was a sense of unfinished business; a conviction that until the blacks of South Africa were free the continent was not free.

'Apartheid' became a universal symbol of racism and unjust discrimination, and the struggle against it grew into a major international cause. The South African government was increasingly treated as an international pariah and subjected to a variety of sanctions. With the exception of other pariah states – such as Israel and Taiwan – most of Pretoria's diplomatic initiatives were frustrated. Meanwhile the campaign against apartheid became enmeshed in the internal structures and values of international organisations – such as the UN, the OAU, the Commonwealth and the Non Aligned Movement (NAM) – where conferences, special committees and bureaucracies were dedicated to the anti-apartheid cause.

The International Setting

While an important issue in its own right, the situation in South Africa was also caught in the broader Cold War conflict between East and West. The communist bloc came out unambiguously in support of the liberation movements' struggle against apartheid, whereas the major Western governments vacillated but retained links with Pretoria. Yet, although the Western states were sometimes condemned as a single unit, there were differences between them – based on self-interests, levels of involvement and political conviction. Those Western states with considerable financial and trading stakes in South Africa – like Britain and West Germany – were reluctant to impose economic sanctions, arguing that they would only harden white resolve and that the main impact would fall on blacks. Other Western states – usually those with few economic interests, or who might benefit from further limitations on Pretoria – favoured sanctions, claiming that this was the only peaceful way to make the whites abandon apartheid. Even when sanctions were agreed, they were unevenly imposed, because of the range of people and organisations involved in their implementation – departments of government, international bodies, business companies, banks, churches, civic authorities – each with their own interests to pursue.

Of Western states Britain was the most exposed, with its strong economic, strategic and cultural links with South Africa (itself a Commonwealth member until 1961), and with its imperial responsibilities in Southern Africa. Those responsibilities included the three small territories of Basutoland (later Lesotho), Bechuanaland (later Botswana) and Swaziland, which were heavily dependent on South Africa, and continued to be after they had gained their independence between 1966 and 1968. In Britain, and those Western states with strong interests, South Africa was a subject of public concern and dispute. There were clashes between and within political parties, while anti-apartheid groups organised rallies and mounted demonstrations, urging Western governments, banks, private companies, local authorities and universities to impose further sanctions on the apartheid regime.

However, the traffic was not all one-way. There were always some sympathisers in the West, and Pretoria tried to gain more by presenting itself as a general bulwark against communism. It also stressed the importance of the Cape sea route (especially for oil supplies); the country's vast mineral resources, and the mutual benefits of economic ties. In the case of France, where the anti-apartheid movement was weak, the South Africans even had success in military and nuclear co-operation and in using Paris as a route into Francophone Africa. Eschel Rhoodie, who led a covert attempt by the Information Department to break the isolation through contact with African states, wrote: 'The place to start was with the French speaking states, which did not suffer from the anti-White hysteria of the old English colonies' (Pfister 2002: 47). The attempt to penetrate Francophone Africa was one of the efforts – variously known as 'the Outward Movement', 'Dialogue' and 'Détente'- to counteract international isolation by building contacts in Africa. For a time in the 1970s Pretoria appeared to be making real progress. Malawi, under the eccentric leadership of Dr Hastings Banda, together with some former French colonies – with President Houphouët-Boigny of the Ivory Coast prominent among them – made contact. Yet, at best it was only a partial and temporary success, which eventually ran into the sand, as the African governments that started dialogue came under intense pressure from their fellow Africans to break the contacts. In any case it became clear to them that while they saw contact as a means of persuading Pretoria to change, or at least modify its policies, the South Africans saw it as a means of explaining apartheid and gaining endorsement for it.

While Western states retained diplomatic and trading links, it was an uneasy relationship. Many in the West thought that Pretoria's acute fears of a 'red menace' threatening Africa were exaggerated, and indeed that apartheid acted as a recruiting sergeant for the communists. The unease intensified when early in 1960 Harold Macmillan, the British Prime Minister, warned white South Africans that a 'wind of change' was blowing across the continent. 'The great issue', he told the South African parliament, was whether 'the uncommitted peoples of Africa will swing to the East or the West. The struggle is joined and it is a struggle for the minds of men' (Mansergh 1963: 347). Shortly after Macmillan's visit came the Sharpeville massacre, the banning of the liberation movements and their decision to take up the armed struggle (see below).

In the years that followed, although Western governments continued to criticise apartheid, their criticism was often drowned out by accusations of their hypocrisy. Opponents accused the West of protecting Pretoria by retaining economic links; by refusing to back the armed struggle; and by opposing comprehensive sanctions. In 1976 when Oliver Tambo, the leader of the ANC in exile, became the first black South African to address the UN General

Assembly, he attacked both the West and Pretoria. After denouncing South Africa's membership of the UN as 'an evil tribute to the arrogant power of international imperialism', he called for a mandatory arms ban, claiming that Western weapons were being used to oppress the mass of the people. The apartheid regime, he argued, only existed 'because of the economic and political support it receives from the West'. He went on to link the black people of South Africa with Western colonialism – we are, he said, 'a colonised people' (*ANC Speaks*: 198–211).

Britain's problems in Southern Africa intensified when in 1965 the minority white government in Rhodesia (a British colony which had internal self-government) made a Unilateral Declaration of Independence (UDI). This created an international crisis, involving the UN and the Commonwealth, and deepened disagreements between London and Pretoria. Previously they had disagreed about apartheid, decolonisation and how to counter the spread of communism; now Rhodesia was added to the list. Yet Britain retained the greatest external stake in South Africa, including a large number of British citizens who lived there, and well-established private companies. As successive British governments came under international pressure they tried to steer a course between continued contact and criticism by keeping Pretoria at diplomatic arm's length while protecting their economic interests. It was a compromise that failed to satisfy either side in a polarised struggle.

Changes in Western governments were also reflected in policy shifts towards South Africa. In Paris, whenever socialist governments were in power they reduced their links with Pretoria. In the US the 'realpolitik' of the Nixon/Kissinger era was replaced in 1977 by Jimmy Carter's emphasis on human rights. 'Because we are free,' said Carter with reference to South Africa, 'we can never be indifferent to the fate of freedom elsewhere' (Coker 1986: 135). In turn, Carter was followed by Ronald Reagan, who, viewing the world through Cold War eyes, saw South Africa as a potential, if embarrassing partner in countering the 'evil empire'. Reagan asked: 'Can we abandon a country [South Africa] that has stood behind us in every war that we have fought, a country that strategically is essential to the free world in its production of minerals we all must have?' (Shubin 1999: 234). It was in this spirit that in the early 1980s the US co-operated with South Africa in computer and civil nuclear industries. However, when the International Monetary Fund (IMF) agreed to a credit loan of $1bn for South Africa, the US State Department published a statement claiming that the loan did not 'in any way mean support for apartheid or the use of force in the region' (Coker 1986: 213).

The variety of Western responses extended to the ANC. While the Swedish Government gave it funds for organisational, educational and humanitarian purposes, Margaret Thatcher, the British Prime Minister, branded it as a terrorist organisation. While 'liberal' and 'left wing' British politicians, like Bob Hughes of the Labour Party (chairman of the Anti Apartheid Movement) and in the US Harold Wolpe, chairman of the House Africa subcommittee, were active in anti-apartheid causes, 'right wingers', like US Senator Jesse Helm supported Pretoria as a bulwark against communism, and dismissed ANC members as 'fellow travellers'. Yet, despite the diversity of views, Western governments, under pressure at international bodies and from anti-apartheid groups at home, slowly but steadily turned the sanctions screw. The sanctions were one of the factors that led to a steady deterioration in the South African economy, and made it more difficult for Pretoria to weather other hazards – such as droughts, volatile mineral prices, oil crises and global recession. In the 1960s the South African GDP growth rate had been an impressive 6 per cent, but by the mid-1970s it had fallen to less than 4 per cent, and by the 1980s it had dropped to 1 per cent. With a population growth of more than 3 per cent that meant that the economy was going backwards (McGowan 1993).

In the communist states there was little public awareness of South Africa, but the governments equated the struggle against apartheid with the fight against colonialism and capitalism. Western states were branded as supporters of apartheid and as capitalists who put profit before people and principles. At international gatherings the Soviet bloc mounted a sustained barrage against Pretoria and its Western allies. At the same time it gave material support to the liberation movements. From the early 1960s this was made manifest in aid to the ANC, particularly in training and equipping the ANC's armed wing, Umkhonto we Sizwe (MK). China played a similar if smaller and less consistent role in supporting the PAC.

The ANC in Exile and the Armed Struggle

At Sharpeville, in March 1960, the police shot dead 79 Africans who were protesting against the pass laws. To many, at home and abroad, Sharpeville was seen as the start of an insurrection that would sweep away the apartheid government, as colonialism had been swept away elsewhere. Crisis gripped the country. However, led by the granite-like Verwoerd, the government reacted fiercely by banning the ANC, the PAC and the SACP, and imprisoning their leaders. In response the banned organisations set about reorganising themselves in exile. It was not easy. As exiles they were suppliants, subject to the vagaries of their hosts, and they suffered the characteristic problems of internal bickering and loss of morale. Further, they soon came to realise that they could not anticipate an early return home, or gain much support from inside the country, where the government imposed an iron grip. Yet, even in adversity the ANC and PAC remained bitter rivals and efforts to reconcile them failed.

Nor were the exiles always safe abroad. Pretoria waged a 'secret war' against them. Government agents, working directly from embassies or under cover as journalists, businessmen and students, collected intelligence about the liberation movements and tried to undermine their activities. In 1971 *The Observer* newspaper reported that 10 of the 34 officials in the London Embassy were trained intelligence officers, and 12 more were attached to other organisations. These officials set out (through bribery, blackmail, flattery and alcohol) to induce exiles to report on their colleagues. For example, in 1962 an agent claimed to have obtained a list of PAC members who were active in South Africa, from the PAC leader (P.K. Leballo). Mass arrests followed, wrecking what remained of the movement's internal wing. Intelligence was also collected by theft. In London in 1982 a professional burglar confessed to having been employed by Pretoria to steal files, maps, photographs, letters and documents from the ANC and PAC offices. Some agents even penetrated anti-apartheid organisations. Among them was the notorious Craig Williamson, who gained a post in the Geneva-based International University Exchange Fund, which secretly channelled funds to the liberation movements (Barber 1983).

On occasion anti-apartheid groups enjoyed success in the 'secret war', as in 1975, when activists stole papers from the South African Embassy in West Germany, which revealed nuclear collaboration between Bonn and Pretoria. However, the main flow of information was to Pretoria, where it led to arrests, imprisonment torture and even death of its opponents. Outside South Africa government agents were involved in bomb attacks (for example, in March 1982, when the ANC's London office was damaged) and political assassinations (as in August 1982, when Ruth First, a leading SACP/ANC member, was killed in Maputo by a letter bomb, and in December 1988 when the ANC representative in France, Dulcie September, was shot dead in the street).

Yet, despite these difficulties the liberation movements learned to live in exile. The ANC, which formed an alliance with the SACP, proved to be better organised and in the long term more effective than the PAC. Yet for some African states the PAC's message of black exclusivity was more appealing than the ANC's non-racial approach. Added to which, the ANC's strong links with communists led not only to adverse reactions in Washington and London but to suspicion in Africa of the prominent part played by whites. Mandela later noted that although the PAC acted mainly as a 'spoiler' and 'divider', its simple anti-white rhetoric appealed to some African leaders more than the ANC's non-racist message (Mandela 1994: 215). Only in the 1980s did the ANC become firmly established as *the* liberation movement (Pfister 2003: 55).

At first the ANC based itself in London, where it gained support from a number of groups, including the British Anti Apartheid Movement (AAM), whose aims were 'to inform the public about the effects of apartheid, to campaign against apartheid, and to work with others who shared those ends' (Israel 1999:165). Then, as independent black states emerged, the ANC moved many of its activities to Africa, in 1970 making its headquarters at Lusaka in Zambia. From there Oliver Tarnbo, who became ANC President, said his aim was to 'bring under the ANC's revolutionary umbrella all actual and potential allies, inspire, activate, conduct, direct and lead them in a united offensive against the enemy', (Sampson 2000: 330). As well as its armed wing the ANC sought to gain its ends by diplomacy. A Department of International Affairs was established, which in its early years was led by Josiah Jele (1978–82), and Johnston Makatini (1983–88). They were followed by Thabo Mbeki, a bright young star, and a protégé of Tambo, who, after gaining a Master's degree at Sussex University in England, went on to study at the Lenin School in Moscow, and then represented the ANC in Zambia, Botswana, Swaziland and Nigeria, before taking over the department (Pfister 2003: 62). By then the ANC had built up a network of contacts – with 43 missions in foreign countries, of which three – India, Cuba and the USSR – enjoyed full diplomatic status; observer status at the UN; and accredited representatives at the OAU and the Non Aligned Movement (NAM).

Alongside their political and diplomatic activities, stood the liberation movements' armed wings. In the case of the ANC/SACP alliance it was MK; and in the PAC's case the Azanian People's Liberation Army (APLA). While APLA was prepared to attack whites, the stated aims of MK were to penetrate into South Africa, attacking official property and personnel, challenging the government's forces, promoting mass uprisings, and eventually overthrowing the apartheid regime. In seeking support they found they could expect little or nothing from the West. At first the ANC turned to African states. When in 1962 Mandela secretly left South Africa to attend the Pan African Freedom Movement for East and Central Africa (Pafmeca) he spent four months abroad, taking the opportunity to visit 13 African states, including some military training in Ethiopia. However, it soon became clear that the African states could not provide the financial and military support that was needed. As a result members of the SACP (Arthur Goldreich, Moses Kotane and Yusuf Dadoo) approached the Soviet Union. The response was positive. From a combination of ideology, Cold War 'realpolitik' Moscow was eager to support what it saw as a challenge to the West.

From the early 1960s the Soviet bloc backed the ANC/SACP alliance as the vanguard liberation movement, giving it material support in the form of academic scholarships, clothes and food as well as military training and equipment. In terms of equipment, Shubin has estimated that between 1963 and 1990, the USSR supplied several thousand AK-47 rifles; 3,000 SKS carbines; over 6,000 pistols; 275 grenade launchers; 90 missile launchers; 40 anti-aircraft missile launchers; 20 anti-aircraft launchers; and 60 mortars (Shubin 1996: 15). For MK the support was vital. For Moscow it was a small price to pay for an opportunity to attack capitalism and imperialism.

The ANC's strategy to overthrow the apartheid regime was, therefore, based on a combination of international pressure, the armed struggle, and the mobilisation of the masses at home. However, it faced a strong, determined government, and in the early 1960s suffered major blows. In August 1962 Nelson Mandela (the Black Pimpernel) was caught in a police road trap. Worse followed. In July 1963 a group of leading ANC/SACP figures – including Walter Sisulu, Govan Mbeki, Ahmed Kathrada and Denis Goldberg – were arrested in a hideout at Rivonia. The police also seized documents which incriminated Mandela as well as those arrested. Trial, conviction and life prison sentences followed for Mandela and his seven colleagues.

In the years that followed, MK, although trained and armed, had difficulty penetrating into South Africa in any strength, because of the vigilance of the government forces and because it had to operate from distant camps. In an early attempt to overcome these problems the ANC collaborated with the Zimbabwe African Peoples Union (ZAPU), led by Joshua Nkomo. In 1967 a combined ZAPU/MK force crossed into Rhodesia, with MK hoping to establish infiltration routes to South Africa. Disaster followed. In set-piece battles the liberation forces were heavily defeated. Although, by focusing its propaganda on the courage of its troops, the ANC salvaged something from the setback, it was a costly lesson in the problems of the struggle.

Prelude to Transformation

The late 1960s and early 1970s were years of frustration for the ANC: Pretoria was strong, the international attention from Sharpeville drained away, little help came from Africa, and the armed struggle was in the doldrums. In 1969, in an attempt to revive morale, Tambo called an ANC conference at Morogoro in Tanzania. There, despite strongly voiced discontent, he succeeded in holding the movement together. The conference confirmed the primacy of the political leadership, but added that the armed struggle was an essential ingredient in the struggle. 'When we talk of revolutionary armed struggle', stated the final communiqué, 'we are talking of a political struggle by means which include the use of military force.' This national effort, it continued, was taking place in an international context, which was witnessing a 'transition to the Socialist system, and the breakdown of the colonialism as a result of national liberation and socialist revolutions'. The men of Morogoro went away with the reassuring belief that history was on their side, that the balance of forces was moving against capitalism, and in favour of the socialist states and the associated liberation movements (*ANC Speaks*: 16–24).

An internal ANC debate persisted over the balance between military and political action. In 1978, when an ANC/SACP delegation visited Vietnam to learn from its revolutionary experience, their hosts, to the surprise of the South Africans, stressed the primacy of political action – that military activity should flow from the political. Following the visit the ANC's National Executive Committee meeting in Luanda, Angola, elected a small Politico-Military Strategic Commission – chaired by Tambo, and with Thabo Mbeki, Joe Gqabi, Moses Mabhida, Joe Modise and Joe Slovo as members. Although weighted in favour of MK the commission endorsed the primacy of a political approach. It identified the movement's four major tasks: first, to mobilise the masses inside the country; second, to form a united front with other activists; third, to foster underground activity; and finally, to develop military operations from political activity (Hadland and Rantao 1999: 49).

The Regional Scene

The situation inside South Africa interacted with developments across Southern Africa. During the 1960s and 1970s a group of white-controlled territories – comprising Rhodesia, the two Portuguese colonies of Mozambique and Angola, and South Africa – set out to defy the 'wind of change'. In 1965 international attention became focused on Ian Smith's white regime in Rhodesia, when it announced UDI from Britain. With Britain unable or unwilling to bring the rebellion to an end, the UN imposed mandatory sanctions against the erring colony. Inside Rhodesia a bloody civil war developed between the white regime and the armed wings of two black nationalist movements operating from neighbouring territories – Robert Mugabe's Zimbabwe African National Union (ZANU) and Joshua Nkomo's ZAPU.

The 1970s also saw dramatic developments in the Portuguese colonies. Following a coup in Lisbon in 1974 the Portuguese hastily withdrew, leaving

Mozambique and Angola as new but unstable states under socialist governments. Both territories, which had endured long anti-colonial wars of great ferocity and cruelty, now faced civil wars as rival factions fought for control of the new states. In Mozambique the white Rhodesians supported Renamo, a dissident movement, which challenged the Frelimo government of President Samora Machel. When the white Rhodesian regime fell in 1980 Pretoria took over support of Renamo as a means of destabilising the new Mozambique government and pressuring it into compliance.

In Angola following its independence an even fiercer conflict developed. It was fought at three levels, with Pretoria involved in all three. First, it was a struggle for control of Angola itself, between the Marxist MPLA government of President Jose dos Santos, and the Unita movement, led by Jonas Savimbi and supported by Pretoria. Second, it was a regional conflict, which drew in South African forces. Initially they acted in defence of South West Africa against the guerrilla forces of the South West African Peoples Organisation (Swapo) operating from bases in Angola. Later MK camps were established in Angola. Finally, South Africa became involved at the third level, in which Angola became a cockpit for the Cold War. At that level the MPLA government was backed by the Soviet Union and Cuba, which committed up to 50,000 troops; while Unita gained overt and covert support from the US and South Africa, who both saw Angola as part of a global struggle against communism.

Independence for Angola and Mozambique changed the scene for the ANC, giving it renewed hope. That hope gained a further boost in 1976, when in South Africa itself the youth of Soweto rose against the authorities. Incensed by racial discrimination, and inspired by Steve Biko's Black Consciousness message and the collapse of Portuguese colonialism, they started by protesting against the government's attempt to impose the use of more Afrikaans in schools. It did not end there. The youth of Soweto ignited a flame that spread like a bush fire across the country. The ANC played no direct part in it, but benefited from the revival of internal black political activity, from renewed international attention, and by gaining several hundred radical new recruits as youths fled the country and turned to the ANC to continue the fight from exile. The stimulus of the Soweto rising to the struggle was intensified when the police killed Steve Biko in September 1977. The international reaction to that brutal death was such that even some of those who had shown sympathy to Pretoria were appalled. Addressing the South Africa Club dinner in London, Lord Carrington (soon to be Foreign Secretary under Thatcher) said that the Republic's friends were 'saddened, bewildered and horrified by Pretoria's latest spate of repression' (*The Guardian* 26.10.77). In New York the UN Security Council imposed a mandatory arms ban on South Africa. Even France, which between 1962 and 1975 had delivered 230 aircraft, 150 missiles, 800 armoured vehicles and three warships to Pretoria, respected the ban.

3
The Total Onslaught & Botha's Reforms

In September 1978, P.W. Botha, a tough, authoritarian figure, became South Africa's Prime Minister. His aim was to maintain white control of the state by parallel policies of reform and security. To achieve that he drew on his experience as Minister of Defence. First, he set out to improve the efficiency of the central government, by concentrating control in his own hands, rationalising departmental structures, and enhancing the power of the State Security Council (SSC). That body, the SSC – composed of senior ministers and top security personnel – made its impact felt across government by integrating foreign and domestic policies into a single strategy to defend the white state. It was the age of the 'securocrats' (Grundy 1983, 1986; Frankel 1984).

Botha's time at Defence had also shaped his mindset. He was convinced that South Africa faced a Moscow-directed 'total onslaught', which could only be countered by adopting a 'total national strategy'. 'The ultimate aim of the Soviet Union and its allies', said Botha, 'is to overthrow the present body politic in the Republic of South Africa, and to replace it with a Marxist-orientated form of government to further the objectives of the USSR' (Spence 1988: 18). General Magnus Malan, the Chief of the Defence Staff and Botha's confidant, claimed that the struggle was not confined to soldiers; it involved everyone. The aim of the aggressor was, he claimed, 'total, not only in terms of ideology, but also as regards the political, economic and technological areas'. South Africa, said Malan, was a special prize because of its strategic position, its mineral wealth, its strong economy, and because it stood as a barrier to communist domination of the whole African continent. Moscow, he continued, realising that a direct military assault on South Africa was too difficult, employed indirect tactics – strikes, protests, black unrest, international boycotts, psychological warfare and support for guerrilla armies – and it used not only the ANC, PAC and the SACP, but neighbouring black states, international organisations, Western 'liberals' and anti-apartheid groups (Grundy 1986: 11).

In response Botha's government adopted a 'total national strategy'. This was applicable at all levels of state activities and policies. Military leaders openly stated that 80 per cent of the threat was political/social and only 20 per cent military, and that the danger came both at home and abroad. International opposition to apartheid was dismissed as appeasement. If defence of the white state meant standing alone and enduring criticism, so be it. Western states, said Malan, 'make themselves available as handymen of the communists and they are indirectly contributing to the destruction of capitalism and the establishment of world communism' (Grundy 1986: 51). While in one sense, therefore, 'the total onslaught' was a direct threat to the white population, in another it offered consolation – by giving an explanation for the hostility directed at them; by interpreting criticism as communist propaganda; and by providing, through 'the total strategy', a means of counteracting the threat.

South West Africa/Namibia and Regional Conflict

The day after Botha became Prime Minister the UN Security Council adopted resolution 435, concerning the future of South West Africa/Namibia. The resolution was based on proposals from the major Western powers setting out terms for Namibia's independence. Despite threats of increased economic sanctions, Pretoria ignored the resolution, and followed its own political agenda, by giving greater responsibility to a compliant local government in the territory.

Botha also introduced broader proposals for the whole region – a Constellation of Southern African States (Consas), to be grounded in 'respect for each other's cultures, traditions and ideals'. It was another attempt to gain international acceptance by establishing links in Africa. In its most ambitious form the constellation was to embrace the neighbouring black states of Botswana, Lesotho and Swaziland; together with South West Africa and Rhodesia (the future Zimbabwe); and the 'independent' tribal homelands inside South Africa. Pik Botha, the Foreign Minister, speculated that, as well as expanding economic links, member countries could also develop 'a common approach in the security field ... and even in the political field' (Geldenhuys 1981: 2). In the event the constellation proposal led nowhere. Any hopes it may have had foundered in 1980 with the emergence of an independent Zimbabwe under Robert Mugabe and his ZANU(PF) party.

Instead of welcoming Pretoria's approaches, the neighbours organised themselves into the Southern African Development Co-ordination Conference (SADCC), with the explicit aim of reducing their dependence on South Africa. In terms of security they saw themselves manning a front line against racism, and formed a loose alliance of Front Line States (FLS). Mugabe's victory and the formation of the FLS reinforced the hand of those in Pretoria who advocated military measures, rather than diplomacy. As a result Botha's regional policy increasingly relied on force. 'We are better able to defend South Africa militarily more than ever before,' he declared, and warned potential enemies: 'If they want to test us, our strength, we will hit back' (Geldenhuys1981: 62). Pretoria revealed its strength in a variety of ways – by direct military action (from small raids to major campaigns), by the use of proxy forces (e.g. Renamo in Mozambique), and by economic pressures (such as delaying rail supplies). The policy, which became known as 'destabilisation', was designed to punish and weaken those neighbours who were aiding the liberation movements, to deter others from doing so, to drive MK and APLA away from the borders, and generally to demonstrate Pretoria's power. With increasing military action on the borders and an escalating war in Angola, the vision of a peaceful region gave way to a regional battlefield.

On the other side of the battlefield MK had, by the early 1980s, established camps in Mozambique, and Angola, where Cuban instructors joined those from the USSR. Raids into South Africa increased. Between 1980 and 1983 they included spectacular attacks on the Sasol (oil from coal) plant; the Koeberg nuclear power station; a rocket assault on the army camp at Voortrekkerhoogte; and a bomb placed outside the Air Force headquarters in Pretoria, which killed 19 people and injured 217. Spectacular as these were, they only involved relatively few MK members. They were more important as 'armed propaganda', at keeping the name of the ANC alive and enhancing its morale, than offering a serious military threat to Pretoria.

Furthermore organising a guerrilla campaign over many years was a difficult and frustrating experience, especially as the troops were often living under harsh conditions in desolate camps far from the homeland. Among the strains the MK leaders faced were fears of penetration by spies, which were sometimes justified, but on other occasions led to savage witch hunts against innocent people. Added to such internal tensions were the nagging problems of dependence on the good will of other countries to accommodate and help to supply and train the liberation forces. There was chronic uncertainty about the attitude of the host country, which, although sympathetic to the liberation cause, naturally saw the situation in terms of its own interests. Those interests did not always coincide with those of the liberation movements. On occasion the MK and APLA were obliged to move camps sometimes to another country. During the 1980s the frustrations and tensions increased. Later internal ANC investigations revealed the harsh conditions and the brutal discipline in some camps, especially in Angola. Stephen Ellis wrote of conditions which 'provoked expressions of dissatisfaction which the ANC met with harsh and often arbitrary punishment particularly at the punishment camp known as Quatro'. Ellis went on to speak of 'corruption, authoritarian administration and other abuses including arbitrary detention, torture and murder'. The dissatisfaction of the troops became concentrated on leaders such as Joe Modise, the Army Commander and Jacob Zuma, the Intelligence Chief (Ellis 1994: 283/297).

To an extent Botha's regional policy succeeded. Despite their increasing resentment the neighbours could neither prevent the aggression nor break their economic reliance on Pretoria. Some eventually concluded that it was in their interests to toe Pretoria's line. In 1982 Swaziland made a secret non-aggression pact. Two years later, in March 1984, came Pretoria's principal success, when Mozambique signed the Nkomati Accord. Under this the two governments undertook to respect each other's sovereignty and to remove groups who were planning attacks against the other state. The Mozambique authorities followed up by closing ANC camps, seizing its arms, cutting off supplies, and restricting it to ten representatives in Maputo.

At the time the ANC's national executive 'regarded these developments as the most serious blow to the movement since its banning in 1960' (Shubin 1999: 254). Frustration again pervaded the movement – frustration at the situation inside South Africa, where the government had regained its grip; frustration at a lack of progress in the armed struggle, and frustration at the forced withdrawal from Mozambique. The discontent led to mutiny among some Unkhonto troops in Angola, when they were sent to fight against Unita. Why, they asked, were they not marching on Pretoria instead of dying in Angola? With discontent in the air, Oliver Tambo called another ANC conference at Kabwe in Zambia for June 1985.

Botha's Domestic Reforms, and International Reaction

Meanwhile in South Africa Botha bluntly told his followers to 'adapt or die'. He introduced policies designed to maintain white rule by combining security measures with internal social reforms, which were intended to reduce the causes of discontent. Apartheid was not abandoned but was recast in response to changing circumstances. One aim was to build a more prosperous and compliant black urban middle class, by modifying restrictive labour, residential and property laws and by reducing 'petty' apartheid. A further step was the introduction of a new constitution in 1984. This enhanced Botha's own powers by translating him from Prime Minister to State President – to be both the executive and symbolic head of state. The constitution also sought to recruit the support of the Coloured and Indian communities by a system of 'power sharing'. For the first time they would be represented in parliament – but their representatives sat in separate chambers and were in a minority position, while executive power remained firmly in white hands.

The new constitution immediately created political storms. Among the white electorate Botha managed to retain enough support to win a referendum and to push through the necessary legislation, but at the cost of splitting the NP apart. Led by Dr Andries Treurnicht, who described power sharing as 'a sickness', the right-wing dissidents left to form the Conservative Party (CP). At the other end of the white political spectrum, the liberal Progressive Federal Party also opposed the new constitution, but on the grounds that it entrenched ethnic divisions, excluded black Africans and gave too much power to the State President. Even Coloureds and Indians, who were supposed to gain most from the new dispensation, were divided and gave only limited support. In the elections that followed only 29.6 per cent of Coloured and 20.3 per cent of Indians cast their votes. However, the strongest reaction came from black Africans, who had been completely ignored.

Constructive Engagement

Botha hoped that his reforms would improve South Africa's international standing. He particularly wanted Western states to lift sanctions, in part or whole, thereby boosting the economy and enhancing the government's prestige. In the early 1980s he had grounds for optimism as conservative leaders, who saw the world in Cold War terms, came to power in major Western states – Helmut Kohl in West Germany, Ronald Reagan in the US, and Margaret Thatcher in the UK. Reagan, in denouncing Soviet imperialism at the UN in October 1985, specifically included Southern Africa. The trouble, he declared, was a 'consequence of a Marxist-Leninist ideology imposed from without', and he offered US help to those who were opposing it (Campbell 1986: 12). Reagan and his colleagues were, therefore, reluctant to isolate South Africa or to impose additional sanctions. Yet, while Pretoria welcomed the advent of the conservative leaders, the relationship was never intimate or relaxed. In Pretoria's eyes even the conservative leaders were too cavalier in their approach to the Soviet threat in Africa, and too sanctimonious and intrusive in South African affairs.

That view persisted in Pretoria as the Western allies – led by Dr Chester Crocker, the US Assistant Secretary of State for Africa under Reagan – pursued a policy of 'constructive engagement' in Southern Africa. Crocker, who was criticised from both the 'right' and the 'left' in the US, rejected Pretoria's claims to be of vital economic and strategic importance, and declared that the days of 'business as usual' were over – whereby the West directed rhetoric against apartheid but co-operated with Pretoria. Crocker urged the West to exert greater influence across the whole region. In South Africa itself, he claimed that the US had been ineffective because it had failed to appreciate the determination of the white Afrikaner government. 'Since', he stated, 'the power to coerce Pretoria is not in American hands, the limited influence available should be husbanded for specific application to concrete issues of change.' That, he reasoned, could not be achieved by hand wringing and looking the other way, but by direct contact and by giving support for orderly change. For Crocker the way forward was via constructive engagement, which combined encouragement and criticism (Crocker 1980: 323–51).

The ANC dismissed 'constructive engagement' as a cover for Western self-interest and support for the apartheid regime. Increasingly it attacked capitalism as an exploitative system. In January 1983 the ANCs National Executive claimed that: 'Every crime that the Pretoria regime commits, be it in South Africa, Namibia or elsewhere, bears Washington's stamp of approval' (McKinley 1997: 57). The ANC wanted confrontation, not contact.

1984: The Watershed Year

In August 1984, in his last public address before becoming State President, Botha confidently predicted that 1984 would be seen as 'a watershed year' for South Africa. He referred to regional 'developments of great significance' by which 'the diplomatic and political scene ... had acquired a new image, a new vitality', and whereby relationships were based 'on a new recognition of realities'. South Africa, he said, was emerging 'as a regional power willing to play a positive role in the normalisation of relations'. Finally, he referred to the domestic reforms, which he said had reinforced his confidence in the future (Botha 1984).

For a time Botha's optimism appeared to have substance. At home he had pushed through the reforms; the black townships were relatively quiet, and Pretoria's tough regional policy had driven MK from the borders and forced neighbours into compliance. In the broader international field the Western powers gave guarded approval to the reform programme. Crocker said of the new constitution that 'a clear majority of white South African voters had decided to take a step which opens the way to constructively evolutionary change' (Coker 1986: 172). In June 1984 Botha undertook a tour of Western Europe – visiting Portugal, Britain, West Germany, France and Italy. His reception was mixed. In Portugal he was received with the pomp of an official state visitor, whereas in Britain his visit set off mass demonstrations against apartheid. Even his meeting with Thatcher was tough, as she pressed him to continue the reforms, to grant independence to South West Africa/Namibia, and to release Mandela (Renwick 1997: 110). However, for Botha the nature of the reception was less significant than the fact that that he had been invited at all. There were even reports that he would soon be welcomed in Washington. Botha saw himself leading South Africa in from the cold.

4
The People's Rising: Domestic & International Reactions

Botha's hopes were soon dashed. The main flaw in his calculations lay in South Africa itself', where his reforms foundered on the rocks of a black 'People's Rising' – the greatest outburst of public protest ever seen in the country. To call it 'the People's Rising' is not to imply that everybody, or even all blacks participated, but rather to recognise the scale of the rising, and the part it played in moulding future political hopes and fears. For the ANC it was a major step in 'the struggle'; for most whites it was a frightening outbreak of 'black unrest'.

Behind the rising was deep, indelible resentment of Africans at their continued poverty and deprivation, and at the government's racial and discriminatory policies. Despite the reforms massive discrimination persisted as the government continued to implement some of the harshest aspects of apartheid. This included the forced removal of Africans from their homes – designated as 'black spots' in 'white areas' – to be resettled, sometimes on remote, inhospitable sites. Between 1981 and 1986 more than 200,000 Africans were moved (SAIRR 1986: xxiii). In the following year the Minister of Constitutional Development, Chris Heunis, confirmed that forced removals were still part of government policy and that 46,617 peple had been moved in that year alone, although he claimed that it was to improve their living conditions. He went on to explain that over the next eight years the government planned to move a further 248,000 people from sixty communities at a cost of R450m (SAIRR 1988/89: 170). Nor did the social reforms achieve their aims. For instance, the decision to revoke the Mixed Marriages and Immorality Acts was seen by many whites as a major and dangerous step, whereas it left many Africans cold. Mandela described it as a 'pinprick', saying that he had no desire to marry a white woman or swim in a white pool. He wanted full and effective political participation (Mandela 1994: 508).

The main resentment concerned the new constitution. For Africans it was not a vehicle for sharing power, but confirmation of their continued exclusion from government. They rejected Pretoria's insistence that their political future still lay in the poor, often overcrowded tribal homelands (the Bantustans). Their demand was for nothing less than full majority rule. Reform short of that was inadequate. Resentment boiled over in the People's Rising. Its scale and the associated suffering can be gauged from the government's own figures of casualties, which erred on the side of caution. While, in 1984, 175 people were reported to have been killed in political violence, in the three following years the figures were 879, 1,298, and 661 respectively. The rising was led by the United Democratic Front (UDF) – an umbrella movement formed in 1983 –

comprising a variety of organisations, including support from some Coloureds, Indians and whites. Initially the ANC leadership in exile had doubts about the prospects for an internal rising, but they were misplaced. It was under leaders with strong ANC associations that the UDF set out to challenge the government – stalwarts like Archie Gumede, Terror Lekota, Popo Molefe and Albertina Sisulu. Alongside them new leaders emerged: including Bishop Desmond Tutu, Cyril Ramaphosa of the mineworkers' union, and a Coloured clergyman, Rev. Allan Boesak. Support also came from the Congress of South African Trade Unions (Cosatu) formed in 1985. It too had strong ANC links, and with the ANC and the SACP was later to form 'the triple alliance'. Boesak voiced the demands of them all when he declared: 'We want all our rights; we want them here; and we want them now' (Sampson 1999: 331).

The government responded ferociously. The country lived under emergency regulations, with police and armed forces camped in the black townships. They swept the townships in armoured vehicles, made mass arrests (detaining 25,000 people in six months), issued banning orders, and used imprisonment, torture and death squads against their opponents. Society was brutalised by the behaviour of government agents, but the brutality was not confined to them. The black protesters backed up their action – of strikes, boycotts, attacks on government property and refusal to pay taxes – by intimidation. Young 'comrades' created people's courts, which handed out arbitrary justice; they assaulted local officials, policemen, 'collaborators' and their families, and sometimes indulged in murder and 'necklacing'. Not until late in 1987 did the conflict subside. Even then, although the government largely regained its security grip, tension persisted. The police spoke of a continuing revolutionary climate. More bloody civil strife seemed inevitable.

ANC Hopes Revived

Between 1984, when Oliver Tambo summoned the Kabwe conference, and June 1985, when it assembled, the People's Rising had transformed the scene. Within the ANC resentment turned to joy, gloom to hope. Now, alongside the armed struggle, the Kabwe delegates expressed their faith in the ability of 'the struggling masses' to wage 'a people's war', and use their economic muscle to make the country ungovernable. Speaking on Radio Freedom, Thabo Mbeki urged attacks on all fronts. We will, he declared, 'reply to reactionary violence with revolutionary violence'. He called on people to make the country 'ungovernable' (Kane Berman 1993: 41). So confident were the Kabwe delegates that they rejected the idea of a negotiated settlement, other than to arrange a transfer of power from the white regime. It recommitted itself to the revolutionary struggle. 'Let us go to war' was the Kabwe battle cry.

Away from the euphoria of the conference, however, Tambo recognised the ANC's limitations. He knew that despite the brave words MK could not force a military victory. Equally, although in his 1985 New Year message he repeated the call to 'render South Africa ungovernable', privately he admitted that he had 'no wish to celebrate liberation day surrounded by a desolate landscape of destroyed buildings, and machines reduced to scrap metal' (SAIRR 1985: 10). Those doubts grew as the government steadily regained control. The commitment to the struggle remained, but increasingly it was again hedged around by the recognition of limitations and difficulties. Joe Modise, a leading MK figure, spoke of changing circumstances leading to a 'new kind of struggle', whereby the ANC might negotiate to achieve its ends.

Western Reactions

Among the changing international circumstances were the ANC's relations with the West. Ironically, the militant anti-Western atmosphere of Kabwe gave way to a period of improved contacts. This followed increased Western public awareness, as vivid television pictures of the People's Rising brought the conflict into homes – stimulating sympathy for the protesters and anger at Pretoria's repressive measures. As public concern increased so the exiled ANC and anti-apartheid groups increased their pressure on Western governments and businesses to act against Pretoria. In Britain the AAM set up a permanent vigil outside the South African Embassy in Trafalgar Square. In the US TransAfrica, led by Randall Robinson, organised daily demonstrations outside the embassy in Washington. It attracted so much support that by March 1985 more than 2,000 protestors (including many prominent figures) had been arrested, often in the full glare of television cameras.

The media attention and the demonstrations marked a change in American awareness. Previously there had been relatively little public concern with South Africa. The US had few historic ties; its economic links (although important for South Africa) were small for the US. Interest in Africa had been confined to a political elite. In 1979 an opinion poll found that only 19 per cent of Americans had heard of apartheid. That changed in the 1980s, as awareness increased and as the struggle against apartheid was perceived to have similarities with the civil rights movement in the US itself.

The heightened awareness in the West led to an adverse reaction to Botha's address to the Natal Branch of the National Party in August 1985. Had it been a routine party meeting probably nothing would have been heard of it outside South Africa. But it was not. It was widely trailed abroad as an epoch-making initiative in which the State President would trace a radically new political course. Botha himself described the speech as 'a manifesto for the future of our country', and outside it was trailed as Botha 'crossing the Rubicon', with no way back. The speech, therefore, gained wide international attention, with live television coverage. In the event it was a disaster. It was not only what Botha said, but the way he said it. It was the declaration of an angry, resentful man. 'Don't push me too far,' he told his international audience. He was not prepared to 'lead white South Africans and other minority groups on the road to abdication and suicide'. He branded Mandela as a communist, and repeated that separate political arrangements would remain for Africans. 'I know for a fact', he asserted, 'that most black leaders, and most reasonable South Africans, will not accept the principle of one man one vote in a unitary state. That would lead to domination ... and to chaos. Consequently I reject it as a solution' (*Business Day* 16.8.85).

The impact of the speech was immediate. Internally it intensified African anger, it undermined white support for Botha, and it convinced many business leaders that the government was incapable of taking the required steps to revive the economy. In the West it met disappointment and resentment – reinforcing the hand of those who urged further punitive measures. Most important was the economic impact. Immediately the Rand plunged in value, and Western banks, led by the Chase Manhattan Bank of New York, refused to roll over short-term loans. The decision of the banks left Pretoria exposed and vulnerable, for during the 1970s and 1980s it had become increasingly dependent on international loan capital to finance its security and reform policies. Between 1972 and 1980 it borrowed US$7,000m, with British banks in the lead (Nerys 2000). In response the British AAM waged a campaign against banks with strong South African links. Barclays in particular – with its vulnerable high street branches – bore the bulk of the demonstrations, which led to a loss of business especially among students. Eventually, in November 1986, the bank announced that it was selling its stake in South Africa. As the foreign banks withdrew or refused new loans the country became a net exporter of capital.

Similar condemnation followed Botha's treatment of the Eminent Persons Group (EPG). The EPG was the brain-child of the Commonwealth conference at Nassau in October 1995. That meeting had followed a familiar pattern, with Britain resisting majority demands for further sanctions against Pretoria. Eventually an agreement was reached, which included the appointment of a group of senior figures (the EPG) 'to encourage through all practicable ways the evolution of political dialogue', the dismantling of apartheid and the erection of democratic structures (Commonwealth EPG 1986: 142–3). Botha, under pressure from Margaret Thatcher, reluctantly agreed that the group could visit South Africa.

At first the EPG's efforts appeared to flourish. It met a wide range of people – including Mandela, who was brought from prison. In March 1986 the EPG presented a 'negotiating concept'. This called on the government to abandon apartheid and lift restrictions on all political parties; and on the ANC to renounce violence and commit itself to negotiation. The ANC cautiously responded that the proposals were a basis for further discussion. Once again hopes for progress were raised, and once again they were dashed. On 19 May 1986, just before the EPG was scheduled to meet the cabinet's constitutional committee to discuss 'the concept', Botha, without consulting the full cabinet, ordered military raids against three neighbouring Commonwealth states – Botswana, Zimbabwe and Zambia. At home he imposed a state of emergency. An official statement said that the raids were directed against ANC and PAC bases, which would be attacked wherever they were found. Botha added that 'South Africa has the capacity and will to break the ANC' (Meredith 1997: 365).

Under public pressure at home, and despairing of fundamental reform from

Pretoria, the West reacted in two ways. First, sanctions were extended and tightened. In the US, despite Reagan's opposition, Congress passed the Comprehensive Anti Apartheid Act (CAAA) of 1986. Outside the government, US banks, some private companies, local authorities, churches and universities applied their own measures – acting from a combination of conviction, internal pressures and fear that their interests might be jeopardised if they failed to act. Second, Western governments made contact with the ANC. As doors opened that previously had been closed, Tambo seized the opportunity. 'It boils down', he stated 'to the question of how to win, how to compel the support of the United States, Great Britain and the Federal Republic of Germany for the cause of the victims of apartheid' (Thomas 1996: 204).

Previously the British Government had refused the ANC contact at ministerial level. Now Thatcher decided that because of Britain's extensive interests, 'we needed to try to play a more active role' in the Southern African region (Renwick 1997: 109). As a result, in September 1986 Tambo was invited to meet Geoffrey Howe, the British Foreign Secretary. That was followed by the appointment of Robin Renwick as Ambassador to Pretoria. Renwick, who had already played a leading part in the Zimbabwe settlement, was encouraged to be pro-active in South Africa. He did this with flair and distinction, gaining the trust of all sides. Meanwhile, in January 1987, Tambo had what he described as a 'very useful exchange' with George Schultz, the US Secretary of State. During their meeting they agreed on the 'objectives of our struggle and what we want to put in place of apartheid' (SAIRR 1997/8: 704).

The ANC continued to spread its wings, with visits by Tambo to Australia, New Zealand, Canada and Japan. These trips became so common that Ben Turok, an SACP member, commented that the ANC leaders 'were permanently in the air' and could never be found at their headquarters in Lusaka (McKinley 1997: 86). However, their efforts bore fruit. When George Bush replaced Ronald Reagan as US President he gave responsibility for African affairs to Herman Cohen, who was committed to seeking equal political rights for all, and described apartheid as 'an outrageous human rights catastrophe'. Bush sent a message of congratulations to Walter Sisulu, when the veteran ANC leader was released from jail; he met a delegation led by Archbishop Tutu; and sought advice on human rights issues from Mrs Albertina Sisulu.

Yet, differences remained between the West and the ANC. A conservative amendment to the US Anti Apartheid Act focused on the ANC's communist links, and stated that if it was unwilling to stop violence and commit itself to peaceful processes the US would support negotiations *without* the ANC (Thomas 1996: 205). More to the taste of some Western leaders was Chief Mangosuthu Buthelezi, leader of the predominantly Zulu Inkatha movement. Buthelezi – who favoured a market economy, and opposed both the armed struggle and the imposition of economic sanctions – met Reagan and Thatcher, who praised him as a 'stalwart opponent of violent uprising'. However, inside South Africa Inkatha and the ANC became bitter rivals. In ANC eyes suspicions of Buthelezi were reinforced by his contacts with conservative leaders; none more so than Thatcher. Although she pressed Botha to release Mandela, Tambo said: 'It's very difficult to excuse Mrs Thatcher for branding the ANC as terrorists, because we are victims. She's totally blind: she can only see the violence of the ANC. It was Britain which landed us with this racism' (Sampson 1999: 387). Nor did the new contacts remove the alliance's hostility to capitalism. In July 1989 a Cosatu paper warned against replacing apartheid with 'a reformed capitalist system'. The aim, it said, should be to use negotiations to divide 'the ruling class rather than have the issue divide us ... The imperialists want a modified, reformed capitalist society to replace the current apartheid regime. This is quite different from what we have been fighting for (Thomas 1996: 214). Mandela himself came out of prison saying that: 'The nationalisation of the mines, banks and monopoly industry is the policy of the ANC and a change or modification of our views in this regard is inconceivable' (Ward 1998: 46).

Soviet Policy: The New Thinking

In the early 1980s Soviet support for the ANC was as strong as ever. At Tambo's request Soviet military advisers were sent to MK camps in Angola, and in August 1981, after South African troops had again penetrated into Angola, Moscow publicly reaffirmed the Soviet-Angolan treaty, which included military support against invasion. In the same year, following a South African raid into Mozambique, Soviet naval ships were sent to Maputo. In December 1983, when Pretoria again threatened to attack Angola Moscow openly warned against it. Yet change was on the way.

In March 1985 Mikhail Gorbachev was elected General Secretary of the Soviet Union. From then – slowly at first but with gathering momentum – Soviet policy moved in a new direction. This led to profound changes in the global scene, and had a direct impact in Southern Africa. The alteration in policy was rooted in problems that beset the Soviet Union on all sides. At home there were major economic weaknesses and political stagnation; abroad the invasion of Afghanistan, which had started in December 1979, was bogged down in a bloody stalemate; and discontent simmered ominously across Eastern Europe. Responding to the deteriorating situation Gorbachev introduced policies based on 'glasnost' (openness) and 'perestroika' (restructuring), in the belief that recovery depended on internal reform, co-operation with the West, and the end of Third World adventures. In 1987 he told Western visitors that 'our international policy is more than ever determined by our domestic policy, by constructive endeavours to improve our country. That is why we need peace, predictability and constructiveness in international relations' (Campbell 1986; 3).

In the Third World the aggressive policies of the past gave way to the 'new thinking', with the emphasis on pragmatism not ideology. Gorbachev explained that his government had 'taken the steps necessary to rid our [foreign] policy of ideological prejudices'. The result was seen in revised estimates of Soviet economic capacity, its strategic interests and the limited potential for socialism in the developing world (Spence 1988: 25). In the context of the new thinking Third World involvement was to be abandoned, as it was said to achieve little at a heavy cost, and to carry the danger of a clash with the West. However, it took time for the change to penetrate. As a result from the mid-1980s Soviet policy in Southern Africa ran on twin tracks. One of these – the old track – was pursued by 'the old guard' in the military and bureaucracy who favoured continued support for the armed struggle. The other track reflected the views of the new thinkers – notably Gorbachev himself, and Eduard Shevardnadze, the Foreign Minister. They argued for an end to military involvement in Africa, and the need to halt economic and environmental deterioration by peaceful negotiations. Nobody, they said, would gain from inheriting a waste land.

Gorbachev and his supporters stressed that they still opposed apartheid and would continue to impose sanctions against Pretoria. They claimed that their aims had not changed, but fresh means were needed to gain them.

> The collapse of apartheid [said Gorbachev] is inevitable. But we do not support the theory that the worse it becomes, the better. There is no doubt that an elimination of the racist system by way of a political settlement would be in the interests of all South Africans – both black and white. One should look for and find the path for such a settlement ... New ideas, a fresh approach, and collective efforts are needed (Kuhne 1988).

In May 1986, Gorbachev, when entertaining President Dos Santos of Angola, reiterated that Soviet regional aims remained threefold: to eliminate aggression against African states, including Angola; to gain Namibia's independence; and to end apartheid in South Africa. But, he added: 'There exists a reasonable and realistic alternative to bloodshed, tension and confrontation' (Shubin: 1995; 11). The same message was given to Oliver Tambo and Thabo Mbeki in December 1986, when for the first and last time, they met Gorbachev in Moscow.

Despite protests that their aims were the same, more than a change of method was involved in the new thinking. There were even signs of sympathy for the whites. Within Moscow's more open debate, Gleb Starushenko of the Soviet Academy of Science, spoke of the need for the ANC to 'work out comprehensive guarantees for the white population which would be implemented after the elimination of apartheid'. He favoured a two-chamber assembly, with one of them – composed of equal representation from the separate communities – enjoying a right of veto. Although Gorbachev did not endorse Starushenko's views, he stressed that the Soviet Union would not try to dictate the structure of a post-apartheid society.

Among the critics of the new thinking – even if not always stated directly – were senior members of the ANC/SACP alliance. At a meeting in Moscow in 1987, to celebrate the 70th anniversary of the October revolution, Joe Slovo stated that the prospect of a settlement in South Africa had not reached the stage for peaceful diplomatic action. Instead he advocated extending the armed struggle.

> There are [Slovo said] certain regional conflicts (and our struggle is one of them) when the prospects of political settlement or real negotiation does not depend on diplomatic manoeuvre, but rather on the building up of the strength of the liberation forces and escalating blows against the Apartheid regime (Shubin 1995: 11).

At the same meeting, Tambo attacked Western imperialists, claiming that they opposed fundamental change in South Africa because it would remove the country from the grip of the capitalist system.

The ANC's hopes rested on the 'old guard' of Soviet officials who continued to provide military backing throughout the 1980s. The momentum of guerrilla attacks even increased, although, according to Ellis and Sechaba, the operational life of a guerrilla inside South Africa was 'a few months at most before death or capture'. Even so they kept coming. In 1984 the government reported 50 raids, by 1986 that had risen to 230 (Ellis and Sechaba 1992: 171). As late as 1990 Mac Maharaj and Siphiwe Nyanda had Soviet help when they were smuggled into South Africa to organise 'Operation Vula' – a secret, underground ANC operation.

However, the main Soviet military commitment in the region was not in South Africa, but in Angola. There, the bloody war dragged on, with support for the MPLA government from the Soviet Union and Cuba. In the mid-1980s Moscow agreed to supply Luanda with a range of sophisticated weapons, including Mig-23 fighter aircraft, MI-25D attack helicopters, Sam-9 anti aircraft missiles, and an advanced air defence system. By 1987 there were more than 1,000 Soviet military advisers in Angola; and Soviet technicians helped to build a line of air bases and radar stations across southern Angola – thereby restricting South Africa's military activities (Ellis and Sechaba 1992: 183).

In October 1987 the Angolan government, backed by strong Cuban forces, Swapo and MK units, renewed its offensive against the combined Unita/South African forces. In Pretoria, the Defence Minister, Magnus Malan, claimed that South African troops were there to prevent the whole of southern Africa being subjected to Russian domination. The fighting culminated in 1988 at the battle of Cuito Cuanavale, which Willie Breytenbach has described as the last of the region's Cold War proxy battles. Although in military terms it was a stalemate, and although the MPLA and its allies suffered heavy losses – including more than 100 MK fighters killed – in strategic and propaganda terms it was a triumph for the ANC. It helped to change the political stakes in Angola and Namibia, and from them into South Africa (Breytenbach 1997). The ANC and Swapo hammered home the message that the apartheid forces had not only been defeated, but now lacked the advanced equipment to match their opponents.

Pretoria itself recognised the problems. The immediate cost in terms of men and material had an adverse impact on white morale at home. Added to that was a recognition that because of the UN arms ban it had fallen behind in sophisticated weapons, especially in air power – a weakness that could not easily be remedied. Within the government the balance began to shift from those who favoured the battlefield to those who preferred the negotiating table; from those supporting war to those seeking a political settlement.

The situation also created an opening which the peace seekers in the two superpowers exploited. Senior US and USSR officials – Chester Crocker and Anatoly Adamishin – agreed that they should operate together to facilitate a settlement under the UN's umbrella. Even Pretoria accepted the Soviet Union 'as a key external player in the region, because it could deliver the Angolans and the ANC to the negotiating table' (Thomas 1996: 200). In the negotiations –

which started in London in May 1988 – it was decided to link together an end to the Angolan conflict with the implementation of UN resolution 435 of 1978, whereby Pretoria would abandon its claims to Namibia. In December 1988 a protocol was signed to facilitate the end of fighting in Angola and the withdrawal of foreign troops. In a separate accord agreement was reached on steps leading to a democratic and independent Namibia. For Pretoria there was a 'quid pro quo'. As a bargaining chip for its compliance it was further agreed that all MK bases would be removed from Angola. The Soviet and Angolan governments accepted the price, and obliged a reluctant MK to relocate in Tanzania, Ethiopia and Uganda. To rub salt in the wound, it was agreed that the independent Namibia would prohibit guerrilla bases on its territory. The overall result was that MK forces were further away from South Africa than ever.

The Angolan/Namibia peace accord was implemented but not without its rough moments. They included a last-minute crisis in April 1989, when Swapo forces invaded Namibia in defiance of the UN agreement. By chance Mrs Thatcher was visiting the territory, and she persuaded Perez de Cuellar, the UN Secretary General, to authorise the use of South African troops to counter the infiltration. To many the world seemed to have turned upside down, as South African troops acted for the UN against a liberation movement. But it worked. The peace settlement went forward. In November 1989, as the final 1,500 South African troops withdrew, the first democratic elections were held in Namibia. On 21 March 1990 Namibia became an independent state. It was the clearest indication yet of the changed international situation in Southern Africa.

Towards Negotiations

Although the military option had become less attractive for both the ANC and Pretoria it was not abandoned. Many in the two camps continued to believe that force was the best way to achieve their objectives. Even when the negotiations started some continued to tread the path of violence. However, in Pretoria the securocrats had lost ground to the diplomats of the DFA; and while the government had regained its internal security grip, it was tenuous and costly. Who knew when another black rising would erupt? On the other side of the fence 'the doves' in the ANC also became more prominent, as the military option became even less viable, when the Soviet bloc began its collapse from late in 1989, thereby removing MK's last hope of major external support. The ANC's Secretary General, Alfred Nzo, admitted that the movement did not have the capacity 'to intensify the armed struggle in any meaningful way' (*Independent* 19.1.90).

During the late 1980s the thrust of events was reshaping South Africa's international scene – the steady impact of sanctions on the economy; the shift in Soviet policy leading to super-power co-operation; the Namibian and Angolan settlements; the increasing dominance of the West; the disintegration of the Soviet bloc; the reduced role of force; the revival of diplomacy in Pretoria; and the continued interlocking of domestic and external factors. Already in October 1986 Gorbachev and Reagan, meeting in Iceland, had made specific mention of

Angola when they agreed to seek an end to military involvement in the Third World. In South Africa enthusiasm for negotiations emerged from various sources, including private individuals, groups and business leaders. Following Botha's Rubicon speech, a group of white South African businessmen (mainly English speaking), despairing of the government's intransigence, had flown to Lusaka for discussions with the ANC. One of them, Zach de Beer, explained: 'We all understand how the years of apartheid have caused many blacks to reject the economic as well as the political system. But we dare not allow the baby of free enterprise to be thrown out with the bath water of apartheid' (McKinley 1997: 92). Gavin Relly, the leader of the delegation, stated that nobody wanted to see the economy 'destroyed either by a sort of Marxist approach to wealth creation, or by a violent revolution'. He said that they were less concerned with who governs, black or white, than that South Africa 'will be a viable country and not destroyed by violence and strife' (Meredith 1997: 85, 361).

The Lusaka meeting marked out a path for others to follow. In August 1997 Frederick van Zyl Slabbert led a group of Afrikaners – politicians, businessmen, academics, clergy and journalists – to Dakar in Senegal to meet an ANC delegation, led by Thabo Mbeki. Following the meeting a joint communiqué was issued supporting negotiations, calling for the release of political prisoners and the unbanning of the ANC, and stating that the source of violence in South Africa was racial discrimination. To the fury of Botha, these meetings gained prominence inside South Africa, further enhancing the ANC's prestige. Yet, the ANC's leadership was cautious. Following the Lusaka meeting, Tambo said that while capitalists wanted to reform apartheid it was 'in such a way that the end result is a system that secures their business', but 'falls short of the stipulations of the Freedom Charter ... We do not think such a system is different' (McKinley 1997: 85).

Despite such doubts, further initiatives were launched. One came from a British businessman, Michael Young of Consolidated Goldfields. He arranged a series of meetings (from November 1987 to May 1990) at Mells Park in Somerset, between the ANC and leading Afrikaners. Although no government representatives were present, the meetings gained special significance because they became a channel between the government and the ANC. Professor Willie Esterhuyse, a leading Afrikaner academic, was asked by Niel Barnard, the head of the National Intelligence Service, to report to him about the discussions. Esterhuyse only agreed to do so if the ANC knew what he was doing. When Thabo Mbeki agreed to the arrangement a tenuous link was created between Pretoria and the ANC.

A further extraordinary channel was established through secret discussions between government ministers and the imprisoned Mandela. Working on the principle of 'out of sight, out of mind', the government had hoped that in time Mandela would be forgotten. He was not. Regular 'Release Mandela' campaigns were organised around the world. A spectacular demonstration of this came in July 1988, when the BBC celebrated Mandela's 70th birthday by televising a rock concert in Wembley Stadium, with such stars as Harry Belafonte, Whitney Houston, Roberta Flack and Stevie Wonder. Some 70,000 people attended and an estimated 200 million saw it on television. Such international attention bred increasing concern in Pretoria that if Mandela died in prison he would become a martyr to his cause. Six times in ten years Mandela was offered release but always under strict conditions. Each time he refused. When the People's Rising was in full swing, Botha tried again, offering Mandela release provided he rejected the use of violence. Replying publicly through his daughter Zindzi, Mandela asked: what 'freedom' was being offered while the ANC was banned, while if he left prison he could still be arrested for a pass law offence, and while he was not even regarded as a South African citizen? 'Only free men can negotiate,' he declared. 'Prisoners cannot enter into contracts' (Mandela 1994: 509–11).

For its part the ANC, although vigorously campaigning for Mandela's release, was not prepared to abandon the armed struggle to achieve it. 'There is no question', said Tambo, 'of his release being conditional on renouncing the armed struggle' (Sampson 1999: 371). In 1989 the government, hoping to create a rift between Mandela and the exiled ANC, yet again offered him release on three conditions – that he condemn violence, break with the communists, and reject the principle of majority rule. Inevitably he refused. He said he could not abandon violence while the government practised it, nor would he turn his back on those who – like the communists – had supported the ANC through thick and thin, or abandon the goal of majority rule, which was the only way to peace.

Although Mandela was not prepared to enter into contracts, that did not prevent him from conducting a personal dialogue with the government. Through Kobie Coetsee, the Minister of Justice, he held informal talks with ministers and officials to explore future options. In July 1989 he even had a brief meeting with Botha, although they discussed little of substance. In all these meetings Mandela made clear that he acted as an individual, not for the ANC. He tried to keep the ANC informed as best he could, but there was concern in Lusaka. Was Mandela making deals that were out of line with ANC policy? Was he setting himself apart from the movement? Was he weakening with age and the long years in prison? Even Tambo was sufficiently worried to smuggle a message to him expressing his worries; while an ANC working group asked him to operate in consultation with the leadership. Despite such concerns Mandela continued the discussions, stressing that the alternative was civil war. 'In any country', he stated, 'even if there is war, there is time for negotiations' (Sampson 1999: 397).

Under pressure from their African hosts the exiled ANC leaders, although sustaining the armed struggle, gave increased attention to the possibility of negotiation. Tambo travelled extensively around the continent to put the ANC's viewpoint. His fear was that the ANC might be dragged into negotiations by Pretoria or the Western powers without proper preparation. He confessed that he had a nightmare 'that we are going to get a message from P.W. Botha one of these days saying he is ready to negotiate, and we won't understand it because we don't know how they think' (Sparks 1995: 76). To avoid that, and to avoid having to work to an agenda devised by outsiders – as in the case of the British in the Zimbabwe settlement, and the super powers (in the guise of the UN) for Namibia – the ANC produced its own. In October 1987 it published 'Possible

Responses to Negotiations Initiative'; this was followed in July 1988 by 'Constitutional Guidelines', which set out to translate the 1955 Freedom Charter into a set of constitutional options. Finally, in 1989 came the Harare Declaration, which envisaged a negotiated outcome based on the ANC's Constitutional Guidelines. The declaration was endorsed by the OAU, and welcomed by the international community.

Yet the ANC remained cautious. In January 1987 the NEC laid down its preconditions for negotiations – including the release of political prisoners, lifting the state of emergency and repealing all repressive legislation. It added that it would only enter negotiations on the understanding that the aim was to achieve a united and non-racial democracy. There were further doubts within the ANC/SACP/Cosatu triple alliance. Late in 1989 the SACP, although endorsing the NEC's stand, placed negotiations in a subordinate position. 'All-round mass action', it stated, 'merging with organised armed activity, led by a well organised underground and international pressures, are the keys to the build up for the seizure of power' (McKinley 1997: 99). On its part Cosatu voiced doubts about the malign influence of Western capitalism and imperialism. A paper approved by its 1989 conference stated that: 'The imperialists want a modified, reformed capitalist society to replace the current apartheid regime. This is quite different from what we have been fighting for ... we have to dictate the terms of change. Nothing should start that we are opposed to' (Thomas 1996: 214). Attempts to reconcile these diverse views in the alliance were dealt a blow late in 1989 when Tambo was incapacitated by a stroke.

Although the doubts and divisions persisted, contact with the government continued and became direct, if still secret. In September 1989 Thabo Mbeki and Jacob Zuma of the ANC met two members of the National Intelligence Service in Lucerne, Switzerland. Such was the tension and anxiety that Mbeki confessed to Zuma that 'sitting here with the enemy I feel my stomach moving' (Waldmeir 1997: 145). Despite those worries the scene was being set for de Klerk's speech and Mandela's release.

II

Negotiations & Competition for International Support

5
Negotiations, Visions of the Future & the Economic Debate

In January 1989 P.W. Botha suffered a stroke, which temporarily incapacitated him. A month later, without consulting the cabinet or his party, he wrote from his sick bed to say that the two offices he held – party leader and State President – should be separated. He would remain President, as a 'special force for cohesion in our country', while the NP should elect a new leader. Despite disquiet among party members about the constitutional propriety of the arrangement the NP caucus went ahead and narrowly voted in F.W. de Klerk as its new leader. De Klerk, although a party stalwart, had never been close to Botha, and soon the rival poles of power – State President and party leader – led to tension and dispute. Eventually, after intense pressure from his cabinet colleagues, an angry Botha resigned from office in August 1989. De Klerk immediately succeeded him as State President.

In style and temperament de Klerk was much less aggressive than Botha, more a consensus seeker, but by reputation he was a conservative who had opposed some of Botha's reforms. Although a long established minister – at Minerals and Energy, Home Affairs, and Education – de Klerk had little experience in foreign policy. From Lusaka Tambo commented that he was a typical National Party politician, strongly opposed to majority rule. However, Tambo also recognised that, unlike Botha, 'he relies on argument and reason instead of wagging a finger and silencing debate', and that gave some hope for the future (Sampson 1999: 389). The overall view of the new State President was of a cautious man who would play safe and move slowly.

De Klerk quickly disproved that view. Within the administration he enhanced the role of the cabinet at the expense of the State Security Council, and restored the position of the Department of Foreign Affairs (DFA) under its able new Director General, Neil van Heerden. He gave his support to the 'New Diplomacy', which van Heerden and Rae Killen (head of the Africa Division) had initiated in a renewed effort to establish links with Black Africa. Although de Klerk's role in the final rites of the South West Africa/Namibia settlement was formal (the spade work having been done in Botha's time) he took the opportunity to make contact with African leaders. However, the earliest signs of change came at home, where he started to ease Botha's iron security grip in relation to political opposition. De Klerk allowed marches by anti-apartheid groups; in October 1989 he released a number of political prisoners, including two major ANC figures – Walter Sisulu and Ahmed Kathrada – and in December he met

Mandela himself. From the beginning the two men did not warm to each other but they recognised that they could do business together.

Seizing the Tide at the Flood

In retrospect it is easy to recognise that de Klerk's early moves as State President were the culmination of a process that had started in the 1980s, and that they, together with the changes in the international situation, laid the foundation for the political revolution. However, that was far from clear in 1990. It is one thing to discuss fundamental change; it is another to achieve it. F.W. de Klerk and Nelson Mandela did so by seizing the tide at the flood and guiding their parties to a negotiated settlement. Together they led the way in creating a new South Africa, although, as it transpired, it reflected more of Mandela's vision than de Klerk's.

De Klerk, although a man of strong religious convictions, grasped the initiative less from a moral conversion than from a pragmatic recognition of policy failure. As a life-long member of the NP, he continued to claim that the apartheid policy had been introduced in good faith. Now, however, he accepted that it had failed in practice, and therefore as a moral cause. Later he confessed that apartheid 'had dismally failed to bring justice to all South Africans ... It just resulted in racial discrimination and minority domination. It was a matter of conscience to say we were wrong' (Waldmeir 1997: 115).

Three factors determined the timing of de Klerk's actions. First, although the government had regained internal order it was fragile. The threat of a major new rising, backed by MK units, was ever present. The alternative to a settlement, said de Klerk, was 'growing violence, tension and conflict' (De Klerk 1991: 44). If that was to be avoided negotiations would have to be with the representatives of the black majority, and, unpalatable as that might be for the government, that meant the ANC. As Chris Heunis, the Minister of Constitutional Development, admitted, 'The more one spoke to black people the more one realised that they were afraid to enter into negotiations without the ANC.' Second, the economy was at best stagnant and could only be revived by the lifting of international sanctions. De Klerk spoke of the economy 'teetering on the edge of the abyss'(Sampson 1999: 402). To avoid falling into that abyss meant gaining the confidence of Western governments, banks and companies, and that could only be achieved through a negotiated settlement. Leaders like Mrs Thatcher had assured de Klerk that sanctions would be lifted if he initiated negotiations and released Mandela. The third factor that influenced de Klerk's timing was the changing global scene (Guelke 1999).

The collapse of the Soviet bloc had removed fears of a total onslaught, and weakened the ANC by removing its main backer of the armed struggle. De Klerk saw an opportunity to negotiate a new political dispensation while the government was in a relatively strong position, and its opponents were confused and uncertain. 'We have not waited,' he said, 'until the position of power turned against us ... . The risk that the ANC was being used as a Trojan horse by a superpower has drastically diminished.' He spoke of the collapse of the Soviet bloc 'as if God had taken a hand – a new turn in world history'; and told parliament that an unstoppable tide was sweeping away socialism. It was, said de Klerk, a lesson for those in Africa who had pinned their hopes on a socialist future, for now they would have to revise their views totally. He saw an historic opportunity for all the region's governments to work together. 'The season of violence is over,' he declared. 'The time for reconstruction and reconciliation has arrived' (De Klerk 1991: 34–46).

De Klerk's hopes of reconciliation, and the DFA's 'New Diplomacy' in Africa were founded on stronger foundations than previous efforts, because of the prospects of political transformation at home. His domestic initiative even gained approval from the outgoing UN Secretary General, Peres de Cuellar, who previously had been an implacable opponent of Pretoria. 'The bold and courageous policy to which President de Klerk has committed his government', said de Cuellar, 'opens up distinct possibilities for the dismantling of the apartheid system.' At the same time he judiciously praised the black leaders for their 'commitment to a peaceful process for ending apartheid and building a non-racial and democratic society' (Geldenhuys 1998: 82).

Mandela and the majority of the ANC were also prepared to seek a negotiated settlement. Although in the early 1960s Mandela had been a leading figure in persuading his colleagues to take up arms, he had emphasised that he did so reluctantly and that in the end a settlement would have to come by negotiation. Without giving ground in terms of the final arrangements, this was the position he had adopted in his talks with the government and the EPG. Added to that was the realisation that MK's military effort had no prospect of a quick victory. It was in that light that the ANC reacted to de Klerk's speech. From Stockholm, where he was recovering from his stroke, Tambo stated that the speech went 'a long way towards creating a climate conducive to negotiations' (Sampson 1999: 403).

A New World Order

The movement towards negotiations was aided by the changed international climate. Following the end of the Cold War US President George Bush spoke of a 'new world order', in which co-operation would replace confrontation, and long-standing disputes would be resolved by negotiation. He envisaged a world free from threats, with states living in harmony under the rule of law, and free trade and a dynamic private sector leading the way in global economic expansion. It was to be 'a world of open borders, open trade, and most importantly, open minds' (Millar 1992). Within this context the UN enjoyed a new lease of life, no longer frustrated by superpower rivalry. The Secretary General, Boutros Boutros Ghali, published his 'Agenda for Peace', and, by the end of 1992 the UN, in unprecedented demand for peacemaking and peacekeeping, had 52,000 troops deployed on peace missions. While peace was their avowed aim the leaders of the new order were prepared to back their beliefs with armed force.

Negotiations and Competition for International Support

Thus in 1990/91 a UN force, led by the US, drove Iraq out of Kuwait. 'What is at stake', proclaimed Bush, 'is more than one small country; it is a big idea; a new world order ... Our cause is just. Our cause is moral. Our cause is right' (Keesings Jan. 1991).

As seen from Washington the 'just', 'moral' and 'right' elements of the new order reflected the West's triumph in the Cold War. It was a triumph of economic and political principles, practices and values, in which Bush had no doubts that America led the way. The

> new freedoms throughout the world [he stated] have received their boldest and clearest expression in our great country, the United States. Never before has the world looked more to the American example. Never before have so many millions drawn hope from the American idea. And the reason is simple: unlike other nations in the world ... we enjoy powerful and mysterious bonds of affection and idealism ... what makes us American is our allegiance to an idea – that all people everywhere must be free (Millar 1992).

Bush urged the IMF and the World Bank to build on those values by encouraging the Third World to reduce the dominant role of governments, by establishing dynamic private sector economies. He wanted the Uruguay Round of the General Agreement on Trade and Tariffs (Gatt) concluded 'so that farmers compete with farmers, rather than the deep pockets of government treasuries'. Bush's vision was one 'not only of shared interests but shared ideals'. Even when Bill Clinton came to office in 1993, and the problems of the post-Cold War world had become all too clear, he too proclaimed a similar role for the US. He spoke of leading the world in 'the alleviation of human suffering, the continued march of democracy and human rights and the growth of market economies' (Hartley 1993).

In those early days of optimism for the new order, hopes were high that persistent regional problems – the Middle East, the Balkans, Cyprus, Afghanistan, Northern Ireland, as well as Southern Africa – could be resolved peacefully by negotiation. Most of those hopes ran into the sand. The rigid divisions of the Cold War gave way to a confusing, unstable world in which past prejudices and present hatreds persisted, and even flourished with the removal of the Cold War framework. The UN soon became bogged down in labyrinthine disputes and civil wars. In Africa the US itself, when leading a UN operation, became ensnared and humiliated in Somalia, where American lives were lost in brutal killings. Douglas Hurd, the British Foreign Secretary, spoke of 'a new world disorder'.

Yet, in the midst of the disorder stood one shining success: South Africa. The new South Africa – conceived from the moral concerns of the past and renewed hopes for the future – was the child (sadly a single child) of the short-lived new world order. There, wrote Chester Crocker, was to be seen the 'victory of ideas, of alliances and of technology' (Crocker 1992: 467). In the Cold War days Crocker had claimed that the conflicts in Southern Africa 'carried inherent weight in the balance of world forces'; and he believed that 'our values, our principles and our global standing' had been on trial there. Now he saw the break-up of the Soviet bloc as a victory in regional as well as global terms. He claimed that Western values and principles were the foundations, which 'helped us to win the Cold War in the Third World', and in Southern Africa to set the stage for the end of apartheid and the introduction of democracy and political reconciliation (Crocker 1992: 17–28).

Negotiations

Although the major South African parties had in principle expressed their willingness to negotiate that was only a first step. Much else had to be achieved before serious business could start. Agreement had to be reached on an agenda, on the terms and methods of negotiation, on which parties would participate; and within each party a consensus was needed on its aims and sticking points. The negotiations fell into three phrases. First were 'talks about talks', which stretched over almost two years. In November 1991, the second phase started with formal talks at the Convention for a Democratic South Africa (Codesa). However, Codesa broke down following a massacre of ANC followers at Boipatong in June 1992, and it took a third phase, the Multiparty Negotiation Process (March to December 1993), to reach agreement. From the beginning the negotiations had an international dimension, but to succeed the South Africans would have to reach sufficient agreement among themselves.

Although the ANC and the NP were the principal participants, the initial aim was to be as inclusive as possible, by involving other parties and groups with their diverse interests and hopes. Among them were the Inkatha Freedom Party (IFP), the Pan Africanist Congress (PAC); the white Conservative (CP) and Afrikaner Freedom Front (FF); and the Democratic Party (DP). Yet, while at one level there was broad participation (for example, the 'liberal' DP was an important source of constitutional ideas) as the negotiations proceeded it became increasingly clear that a settlement rested on the approval of the ANC and NP. Indeed, in the final stages the process was pushed forward on the basis of 'sufficient consensus', which in practice meant an ANC and NP agreement. As a result there were periods when other parties – including the IFP, the CP and the PAC – boycotted the proceedings, protesting that they were being ignored and/or treated unfairly.

At first the government held the initiative and through the Groote Schuur Minute (May 1990) and the Pretoria Minute (August 1990) persuaded the ANC *to suspend* the armed struggle, although the ANC refused *to abandon* it as de Klerk constantly requested. Indeed, the negotiations often came perilously near to breaking point, often less from differences in the negotiating hall than from the political violence outside. De Klerk had hoped that his initiative would reduce violence. In the event the early 1990s saw more than ever. In 1989, the year before de Klerk's speech, 1,403 people were reported killed in political violence. In the following four years the figures were 3,699, 2,760, 3,347, and 3,706 respectively (SAIRR 1991/2: lxiii, and 1993/94: 27). On occasions it threatened to overwhelm the negotiators. As Rodney Davenport commented: 'It was a chicken-and-hen situation; the suppression of violence required strong government, but there could not be strong government until the parties agreed where legitimate authority was to be located' (Davenport 1998: 29).

The sources of the violence were many and complex. In part it was a continuation of the old conflict between the government and the liberation movements, with neither side trusting the other. In the government's forces were some who were so opposed to the negotiations that they were prepared, even eager, to employ terror not only to weaken the ANC, but to create an atmosphere of fear and instability that would undermine the whole process. They included secret groups and covert 'third forces', who used vicious methods to attack their opponents, and intimidate the public. They further helped to train and arm Inkatha against the ANC. On the ANC's side were those who were equally ready to seek their ends by violence. Some prepared for the worst by continuing to operate underground and to recruit more MK fighters. Nor were the men of violence confined to the government and the ANC. Also involved were militant members of Inkatha and the PAC; right-wing whites; black 'homeland' governments; and young 'comrades' who slogged it out with older 'vigilantes' for control of black townships. Within the black community the bloodiest conflicts were between the ANC and Inkatha (backed covertly by government forces), as they sought to stake out their political territory in KwaZulu and along the townships of the Rand. The situation was further complicated by thugs and criminals, who used the political turmoil as cover for their activities.

Although much of the violence was intended to undermine the negotiating process, often this was done through indirect efforts to create general instability and mutual distrust, such as the indiscriminate killing of travellers on commuter trains by the 'third force'. There was, however, a dramatic attempt in June 1993 by white extremists – members of the Afrikaner Weerstandsbeweging (AWB) – to bring matters to a head, by storming the negotiating hall, smashing down the main doors with an armoured vehicle and forcing the delegates to flee. The fear of even greater conflict arising from Afrikaner opposition was stemmed by the efforts of Constand Viljoen, a former general in the defence forces, who became leader of the Freedom Front (FF). Viljoen, who claimed that the FF could have called on 50,000 armed and trained men, succeeded in bringing home to his followers the enormous dangers of seeking their ends by force, and persuading them to take the political road in their search for a distinctive identity and 'volkstat' (*Sunday Independent*, 1.4.01).

The violence had an adverse impact on the negotiations, breeding distrust and suspicion among the party leaders. Their attitudes to and responsibility for the use of violence were matters of increasing dispute and bitterness. Did they encourage their followers to use violence? Did they know about it but turn a blind eye? Were they unable to control their wilder supporters despite their best efforts? In response to such questions they all publicly condemned the use of violence. However, even if they were genuine in their commitment to peaceful means, their opponents were often unwilling to give them the benefit of the doubt. Instead they traded accusations and counter accusations, as violence compounded the difficulties of reaching agreement.

Visions of the Future

The ANC, initially having been pushed on to the back foot by de Klerk's initiative, took time to prepare itself for negotiations. At the beginning of 1990 it was a diverse and scattered movement, with its leaders and many of its members in exile, or prison or in hiding. The diverse experiences of sections of the movement led to different reactions to ongoing issues. For example, while most of those who had remained in South Africa – whether or not in prison – favoured full and open investigations into the accusations of ill treatment in the MK camps abroad, many of the exiles, and especially the MK leaders, opposed the idea. In the event a number of enquiries were conducted between 1990 and 1993, both by the ANC and external bodies – such as Amnesty International (Ellis 1994: 282/3). Moreover it was a movement whose underlying ideological base had been left in confusion by the collapse of the Soviet Union and communist states in Eastern Europe. As the ANC's journal, *Mayibuye*, admitted: 'With developments in Eastern Europe the anti imperialist cause has been weakened' (1, 3 1990). Meanwhile the ANC's immediate concerns were the return of the exiles, the release of political prisoners and the retention of MK bases abroad (in case the negotiations failed). At the same time it had to revamp itself from an exiled liberation movement into an effective internal political party. That was no easy task. In July 1991 Alfred Nzo, as Secretary General, presented a report on party organisation, which 'painted a picture of a reactive ANC, riddled with complacency, confusion and lack of initiative, and confined by "populist rhetoric and clichés"' (McKinley 1997: 118).

At first Mandela himself was a largely unknown figure – more a powerful symbol than a live political leader. During his years in prison his photograph and reports about him had been forbidden. The only ANC members to see him were fellow prisoners, or the few visitors he received, like his wife, Winnie. Others had not seen or heard him, or even knew what he looked like. Nor was Mandela the movement's President. Oliver Tambo held that position; but Tambo was a sick man, so that Mandela quickly became 'de facto' leader. At the ANC's conference in July 1991- the first inside South Africa after its unbanning – the ailing Tambo resigned and Mandela was unanimously elected as his successor.

No such problems faced the NP. It quickly presented its constitutional ideas for the future. These envisaged a state built on 'power sharing' between 'groups'. Although not explicitly stated, the groups would in large measure be composed of the separate races. There was, stated de Klerk, no escaping the reality that while all South Africans shared a common destiny, the population was composed of different races and groups. He argued that it would be pointless to replace the domination of the white minority with that of the black majority. Dr Gerrit Viljoen, the Minister of Constitutional Development, claimed that the politics of 'winner takes all' was inappropriate for South Africa: power must be shared. He explained that while the government now accepted a single South African nation, irrespective of race or creed, there must be protection for minority groups. In particular he spoke of the needs of 'the white population group for security against dominance and for guarantees of a significant share in decision making'. There were certain matters, said Viljoen, which the government would not accept. These included a 'unitary system with a black majority', as that would render white and other minority groups politically impotent (HA 5.2.90). With those fears in mind the NP flirted with the idea of a federal state to restrict the power of an ANC-dominated central government.

Although the ANC was slower in outlining its negotiating position, its broad, if somewhat vague vision of the future was already contained in the 1955 Freedom Charter. The Harare Declaration of 1988 was an attempt to translate the Charter into constitutional proposals, with their emphasis on a democratic state, in which all shall enjoy equal rights, including one person one vote, and an economic system to promote the well-being of all. From the start the ANC leaders stressed that the foundation for the new state must be majority rule with a strong central government, elected on the principle of one person, one vote, one value. They proclaimed as their ideal a unitary, democratic, non-racial state in which sovereignty would lie with the people. They rejected the NP's 'group rights' approach, claiming that it was designed to qualify the impact of the popular will, by protecting white privileges. The NP's position, said the ANC, was less concerned to preserve minority rights (such as in language and culture) than to ensure continued white control of government, or at least to give them a veto on its activities (*Mayibuye* 1, 3 1990). Mandela told de Klerk:

> It gave the impression that he [de Klerk] wanted to modernise apartheid without abandoning it, and that was damaging for whites because it would do more to increase black fears than allay white ones ... The ANC had not struggled against apartheid for seventy five years only to yield to a disguised form of it (Mandela 1994: 536/544).

The views of the parties were shaped not only by principle, but also by their political strengths and prospects. NP members supported groups and power sharing not only because they thought they were right, but because they knew that their main support would come from minority 'groups' – mainly whites but also the Coloured and Indian communities. On its part the ANC was committed to 'one person, one vote' majority rule both in principle and because it was confident it could win an overall majority and so control the central government.

The same reasoning prevailed in other parties. The IFP, which had its greatest strength among the Zulu people, was both suspicious of the NP's group proposals and feared an ANC-controlled central government. Buthelezi accused the ANC of seeking to dominate the state, to suppress other parties and to undermine the Zulu nation. He told a traditional Zulu gathering that a campaign was being waged 'to smash the Zulu sense of identity'. Instead of a concentration of power at the centre he called for a federal state, with substantial powers devolved to the provinces, and KwaZulu in particular. Equally the CP, representing the 'white right' in parliament, argued that South Africa was not a single nation but was composed of separate nations each with its own destiny. Dr Andries Treurnicht, the party leader, stated that the CP was committed to 'the continued existence of our own people and our own fatherland ... [because] a free people is only free within its own living space, under its own government'. Therefore, for the future as in the past, the best course lay in separation (HA 5.2.90).

Divisions within Parties and the White Referendum

Alongside the divisions between parties were differences within them. With so much at stake a major task for the leaders was to hold their followers together. Both the ANC and the NP had their obdurate hawks and flexible doves. Added to that a gap developed between those who were directly involved in the negotiations (and so recognised the need for compromise to reach agreement) and those outside, who were more concerned about the views of party members than accommodating political opponents. Whenever the leaders met a large gathering of their followers they were under pressure not to give ground, to stand firm. At an ANC consultative conference in December 1990 the delegates criticised the leaders (including Mandela) for their failure to protect township members from violence, and their supine attitude towards the government in the negotiations. Even the ailing Tambo was heckled when he suggested reining back on sanctions. A resolution was passed extolling the role of the masses in the process of change and rededicating the ANC to 'our revolutionary strategy, believing that there has been no fundamental changes in the political situation' (McKinley 1997: 112). An ANC National Consultative Conference of December 1990 declared 1991 as 'The Year of Mass Action' in which the people themselves would achieve the transfer of power, and in which MK would play a leading role in defending the people (*Mayibuye* Feb. 1991). Nor could Mandela forget that he was the leader of a tripartite alliance in which the SACP and Cosatu tended to be more radical than the main body of the party. At its eighth Congress, early in 1992, the SACP resolved that despite the demise of the Soviet union, 'the need for socialist solutions to the socio-economic problems created by colonial capitalism' was as great as ever (*Mayibuye*, 3, 1 1992)

The NP also had its divisions, stretching up to cabinet level. De Klerk managed to hold the party together, but it was often a close-run thing. Early in 1992 a crisis arose, following a by-election victory for the CP at Potchefstroom in what had been a rock-solid NP seat. The result was widely interpreted as a vote against the negotiating process. De Klerk immediately fought back. He called a national referendum among whites in which he sought a mandate to continue negotiations. In the referendum campaign – in which de Klerk claimed that a negotiated settlement would boost the economy without leading to majority rule – he played the international card for all it was worth, especially in relation to the economy and sport. A 'No' vote, stated an NP poster, would result in even heavier economic sanctions. It would mean that: 'Nobody will buy our steel. Nobody will sell us oil. Our coal will lie in heaps. Our grapes and apples will rot in the packhouses. Our aeroplanes won't take off'. Another stated: 'A "No" simply means strikes, sanctions, no export markets, no production and no work'. In contrast a 'Yes' would mean a further lifting of sanctions, and readmission to international activities. By chance, at the time of the referendum, a South African cricket side was enjoying the early lifting of sports sanctions by playing in the World Cup in Australia. A 'No' vote, claimed the NP, would lead to an immediate expulsion from the competition, and the message was reinforced when the team let it be known that they were 'Yes' supporters to a man. When the votes were counted a large majority of whites – 69 per cent against 31 per cent – favoured continuing the negotiations (Geldenhuys 1992).

The Economic Debate: The International Setting

Running in parallel with the formal negotiations, with their concentration on political and constitutional issues, was a debate about the country's future economic structure and policies. This sought to reconcile the twin aims of development and democracy in a deeply divided society, by asking whether it was possible to build 'a new social contract founded on the principles of social reconstruction, development, democratisation and transformation, reconciliation and nation building' (Kotze 2000: 59– 72). Again the ANC and the NP were the main participants and the main rivals in this debate. Both formed study groups to examine the issues – the ANC's Macro-Economic Research Group, and the NP's Central Economic Advisory Service.

The debate was profoundly influenced by the changing international scene, following the end of the Cold War. On one side of the old divide, the disintegration of the Soviet bloc and the collapse of communist governments led to a loss of belief in the efficacy of centralised socialist economies. Whereas the West rejoiced in the conviction that liberal democracies, and their capitalist, free enterprise economies, had proved themselves superior to other social forms. None rejoiced more than the American scholar, Francis Fukuyama, who triumphantly proclaimed the 'end of history', not in the sense of an end to events and activities, but rather history 'understood as a single, coherent evolutionary process'. For Fukuyama the end of the Cold War was more than the end of a power struggle, it was the victory of an ideology and a socio-economic system over its opponents. He pointed to the relationship between political and economic progress, and claimed that liberal democracies, built on capitalism and the free market, had outperformed all other systems, because they offered their citizens greater freedom, security and prosperity. Modern economies need speed of response, flexibility and ingenuity, which are fostered by giving people choice to operate within the discipline provided by the market. He concluded: 'The twin crises of authoritarianism and central planning, have left only one competitor standing in the ring as an ideology of potential universal validation: liberal democracy' (Fukuyama 1992: xii/42).

Others reached similar, if less strident conclusions. Strobe Talbot, who advised President Bill Clinton, claimed that an unprecedented international consensus had emerged on 'how we should organise ourselves ... As a general proposition democracy helps to bring prosperity to its peoples and peace to its neighbours' (Talbot 1995). In South Africa, David Welsh wrote that it was not necessary to accept Fukuyama's entire thesis to recognise that liberal democracies now had no serious ideological rivals. Welsh envisaged a situation in which political debates would henceforth not be concerned with principles, but would be 'second order ones, over the forms that institutional embodiments of liberal democratic principles should take ... and what constraints should be placed on market forces, how comprehensive welfare systems should be, and so on' (Welsh 1994).

Not everybody rejoiced, even in the West. Ian Taylor wrote of a new hegemonic world order based on three characteristics – ideas, material capabilities and institutions (Taylor 2001: 17). Hein Marais pointed to the danger of believing that there was no alternative. In South Africa he feared that the political settlement would be used as a platform for capitalist accumulation. (Marais 1998: 2). Yet, although they might resent it critics could not ignore the major change in global relations. In 1997 an ANC group, after stating its commitment to 'anti-imperialism, anti colonialism, and anti neo-colonialism', nevertheless accepted that the collapse of the Soviet bloc had 'altered both the global balance of forces and the content of international relations', leaving 'a world that is dominated by the capitalist system'. That, the group concluded, was dangerous for the developing world. No longer was there 'an alternative pole around which developing countries like ours could construct their trade, aid and strategic relations'. Now the West was free to pursue its objective 'of consolidating capitalism on a world scale', aided by the forces of neo-colonialism. The result would be an increasing gap between rich and poor, as the rich used the new situation to their advantage (ANC 1997).

During the Cold War African states had been wooed by the rival blocs, often irrespective of their domestic policies. Now the West laid down its terms. Working through institutions like the World Bank and the IMF, its economic message 'consistently took a "liberal" or market-orientated approach to economic management, which rested on the assumption that economic "rationality" was a constant across all societies, which applied regardless of the level of development reached by any particular economy' (Clapham 1996: 169). Based on these assumptions the IMF introduced its Structural Adjustment Programmes (SAP), which aimed at reducing state control of the economy, encouraging private enterprise, achieving 'realistic' currency exchange rates, the removal of controlled pricing structures and balancing the budget by the reduction of government expenditure. That was the international backdrop to South Africa's domestic economic debate.

The Domestic Economic Debate

Over generations the South African economy had been structured into two parts. One, which was dominated by whites, belonged to the advanced First World; the other, which contained the majority of blacks, was part of the underdeveloped Third World. (In practice, of course, the two parts of the economy were interlocked, for example, in the provision of labour from the Third to the First World element). The First World part had itself been developed in two segments. One was privately owned, and included large conglomerate companies, banks and financial institutions. Traditionally these had been in the hands of English-speaking whites, but during the 1970s and 1980s Afrikaners had made substantial inroads into this segment. The other segment was controlled by the government. It was characterised by protectionist policies, in which the state had sought to defend the economy against international sanctions and pressures, while at the same time promoting white interests, through education, health, social and employment policies.

Within this setting a central issue of the 1990s economic debate was the relationship between 'growth' and the 'redistribution' of income and wealth. The debate was not confined to South Africa, and was central to the global concern about ' underdevelopment'. A report from the IMF admitted that:

> Although poverty reduction and economic growth are correlated, the causal relationship between poverty or income inequality and growth is unclear ... In some cases policies that promote growth may not promote immediate poverty reduction ... In any case, the short run negative impact, if any, of necessary adjustment measures is typically modest compared with the long-run gains to the poor from additional growth (IMF 2000: 115).

Despite that uncertainty both the IMF and the World Bank backed the 'Washington Consensus', which broadly supported policies of growth though free trade, as favoured by the West.

In South Africa all parties were agreed that both growth and redistribution were desirable. There was also a consensus that the state had to provide major social services, such as health and education. After that, however, there was a divide, which reflected international positions. In broad terms, those who put their main emphasis on growth were sympathetic to a Western-style market economy. Those who gave priority to redistribution were more committed to a socialist approach with strong state involvement in the management of a demand-driven economy. The supporters of growth argued for rapid expansion. That, they said, would strengthen the country's international position, while generating prosperity at home for the mass of people, via 'the trickle-down factor'. Within this view the government's main role was not to manage the economy, but rather to create conditions favourable for private enterprise – by ensuring order, the protection of property, the provision of basic services, and by encouraging foreign investment.

In contrast those who gave primacy to redistribution favoured a 'hands-on government', that would be directly involved in managing the economy, and be prepared to nationalise its commanding heights. They argued that this would lead to a more equitable distribution of economic rewards and an extension of social services, while also helping to redress the injustices of apartheid. Unemployment would be reduced by job-creation schemes and by extending education and training so that the mass of the people could be gainfully employed. The result would be a larger workforce, which would create a mass market thereby leading to growth.

The NP government, despite the prospect of abandoning its protectionist policies, favoured a Western market economy system. They argued that once sanctions were removed, the rationale for protectionism would be reduced, and, as Afrikaners had advanced in business and commerce, economic protection for 'the volk' had become less relevant. Moreover, whites, because of their relative affluence and education, had a clear advantage over blacks in competing in the job market. Added to that the NP government was opposed to the control of a command economy falling into the hands of the ANC, which it branded as 'socialist', in the old-fashioned, Moscow sense. It was also eager to reopen links with the IMF, which had been blocked since 1983, when the US had opposed support for the apartheid regime. In line with this approach Pretoria took steps towards a market economy. Already in December 1989, it had privatised Iscor, the state-owned steel corporation, for R2bn. The government went on to establish an Economic Advisory Council (EAC), chaired by Warren Clewlow of the Barlow Rand Company, to help to co-ordinate the public and private sectors of the economy. In a strategy report, published in July 1992, the EAC favoured the market approach, by recommending the removal of protective barriers and boosting exports. However, it also concluded that the economy could not be left solely to the marketplace, that some government steering was required. Reports then circulated of plans to sell off more state enterprises, but, as it transpired, these economic concerns were pushed into the background, as constitutional negotiations took precedence.

The ANC was in a more difficult position. During the years of exile it had increasingly embraced socialist thinking. That was partly for practical reasons (not least Soviet support for the armed struggle), partly from its long association with the SACP and the impact of communist members, partly from the recent emergence of Cosatu as the alliance's third leg, but also the genuine belief that only direct state control of the commanding heights of the economy could lead to a genuine redistribution of rewards. On leaving prison in 1990 Mandela had declared that: 'The nationalisation of the mines, banks and the monopoly industry is the policy of the ANC and a change or modification of our views in this regard is inconceivable' (Ward 1998: 46). Added to these, socialism offered a clear – if disputed – analysis of South Africa's own divided society. It explained the exploitation of the black masses through the theory of 'colonialism of a special kind'; and, looking to the future, it held out a vision of an end to racial oppression and the creation of an egalitarian society. As Ben Turok wrote, 'it had always been understood by the drafters of ANC policy that South Africa would need a "strong development state" to overcome the apartheid legacy of a highly skewed economy and grossly unequal provision of public services'. Its task would be to 'deliver what apartheid had denied the mass of the people' (Turok 1999: 55).

With this background, members of the ANC alliance were reluctant to absorb the full implications of the discrediting of communist rule, and the undermining of socialist beliefs. Joe Slovo – in a 1990 article, 'Has Socialism Failed?' – declared that in the Soviet bloc 'real socialism' had not failed, it simply had not been tried (Slovo 1990). In 1992 Alec Erwin (an SACP member, who became Minister of Trade and Industry under Mandela) argued that to play an effective part within the alliance the SACP must have a clear economic plan. He favoured a 'redistribution' policy, which would result both in growth and in people's 'access to economic power and skills ... in effect developing the socio-economic capacity of society across the widest front'. He warned that if the ANC gave primacy to growth it would perpetuate existing capitalist structures and social divisions, and lose the support of the masses. To prevent that he advocated a leading role for the state, with the nationalisation of major industries. Erwin accepted that the state must work to an extent with business; but he warned that it must persist with its own policies, because redistribution needed a continuous effort. He concluded by insisting that: 'a link between reconstruction and socialism can, and indeed, must be found' (Erwin 1992: 12/23).

In September 1991 an ANC report called for a 'fundamental restructuring of the economy', in which 'redistribution acts as a spur to growth in which the fruits of growth are redistributed to satisfy basic needs' (ANC 1991). Although the report accepted that the country needed a mixed economy, a leading businessman, Brian McCarthy, noted that while the report contained 60 references to 'redistribution', 'productivity improvement' was only mentioned twice. Similarly, a Cosatu document, published a few months later, supported redistribution with greater state intervention, including price fixing and the break-up of business conglomerates. It favoured retaining existing nationalised industries and bringing more under state control, including the mining houses. The redistribution of income and wealth would be achieved by progressive taxation, by reducing production of luxury goods while increasing basic commodities, and by concentrating on labour-intensive activities. On the international front Cosatu opposed accession to the General Agreement on Trade and Tariffs (Gatt) – as this would limit the government's ability to manage the economy – opposed capital outflows, and wanted all foreign companies to be subject to rigorous codes of conduct (*Record* 24.4.92).

Yet, although members of the alliance might regret international changes, they could not ignore them. Added to that the ANC was a broad church with a diversity of views about the management of the economy. While some members defended the old socialist beliefs an increasing number were prepared to accept – even if reluctantly – a Western framework of ideas and structures. The differences were aired openly. Signs of backtracking from past positions came in May 1992, when an ANC economic conference favoured 'a new and constructive relationship between people, the state, the private sector and the market', and placed emphasis on the need for flexibility, 'rather than acting according to a rigid ideological framework'. It too came out in support of a mixed economy, but in doing so it was even prepared to consider privatisation of some state assets. Overall the conference envisaged the state taking responsibility for major services, such as health and education, the supply of water and electricity, and introducing legislation to achieve greater redistribution; but, at the same time, encouraging 'a major and dynamic private sector' (*Report* 22.5.92). The increasing flexibility was further illustrated when Mandela, on a visit to Norway in that same month, spoke of 'commercialisation', which he saw as a halfway house, whereby the state became a major shareholder in enterprises run on private company lines.

The ANC's internal debate rumbled on. Although, in broad terms, it came out in favour of 'a mixed economy', differences persisted about the nature of the mixture, of the balance between central planning and a free market system. In October 1993 at a meeting in Durban to celebrate his 75th birthday, Mandela spoke of moving away from nationalisation, and he stressed that the private sector as well as the state was needed to meet black aspirations. Yet a couple of weeks later the party's Witwatersrand regional congress passed resolutions supporting an extensive programme of nationalisation, and government management of the economy. The differences were never fully reconciled. Before the ANC's 1997 conference, Peter Mokoba, once the radical leader of the ANC Youth League, claimed that the Freedom Charter had 'always aimed to build a capitalist South Africa'. He went on to criticise the role of the SACP in the alliance, saying that its members attended ANC meetings and then went around criticising their decisions (Lodge 1999: 10).

Economic Uncertainties

As with political leaders so with the business community the changing South Africa stimulated a wave of international interest. Business conferences and visits from trade missions – mainly from the West – became the order of the day. Yet, while for politicians there were obvious advantages to be gained in identifying themselves with 'the South African miracle', the picture was less obvious for business leaders. By the early 1990s it was clear that the South African economy was in recession. In 1990 and 1991 the Gross Domestic Product (GDP) had fallen by 0.5 per cent and 0.6 per cent respectively, and the predictions for 1992 were equally gloomy. Sanctions were only one of the problems. Others, such as the continuing drought and a world recession, were out of South Africans' hands, but some were of their own making, and bred caution in the international business community. Some foreign companies were prepared to renew or initiate contacts at once, but most hesitated. Caution prevailed. The ANC's internal debate – admirable as it might be in terms of transparency – led to chronic uncertainty about a future government's economic policies. Western businesses adopted a wait-and-see approach, as they asked: Would the negotiations succeed? Could the violence be controlled? Would the ANC make up its mind about future economic policy? Could the new government gain stability?

For all the warm political sentiment directed towards it South Africa was economically vulnerable. It was seeking support when there was strong competition for investment and business development elsewhere. The World Bank categorised South Africa as a small/medium economy alongside such states as Mexico, Brazil, Korea, Portugal and Greece. In this international setting South Africa had advantages, which, if properly exploited, could give it an edge over competitors. It had rich natural resources with great mineral wealth; relatively low debts; a good record of repayment; a strong infrastructure of banks, transport and communications; some areas of high technology (such as mining); a reasonable if uneven education system; an experienced business community with a Western business culture, operating in English (the international language); and a land of great beauty and diversity for a tourist industry. Both the ANC and the NP, despite their differences, were eager to underline these advantages for future development.

Yet in the early 1990s there were as many voices of doubt as of hope. In 1993, when Patrick McGowan examined future economic prospects, he too placed South Africa in a middle group of states, which he labelled 'semi-peripheral' – i.e. standing between the rich 'core' economies and the poor 'peripheral' ones – but he foresaw a danger of South Africa slipping into the periphery. He pointed out that between 1965 and 1990 the average GNP growth rate of the middle-group states had been 2.8 per cent per capita, whereas South Africa's had been only 1.3 per cent, and had continued to decline. He concluded: 'The performance of the South African economy since the 1970s has been terrible.' Growth rates had declined from 4 per cent in 1970– 75, to a negative situation, while the population had been increasing by almost 4 per cent per annum. McGowan gave a number of explanations for the decline: apartheid (which had frustrated human development, created large inefficient bureaucracies, and fostered corruption); high government expenditure (which between 1980 and 1990 had grown from 20.5 per cent to 33 per cent of GDP); trade barriers (created in part to counter sanctions); poor management (which had thrived on protection and the inefficient use of labour; and trade unions (which had gained wage increases without increased productivity). McGowan feared that South Africa would fail to retain a place in the middle group and become a larger Zimbabwe (McGowan 1993).

Similar fears were found outside South Africa. In Germany an article in the *Frankfurter Allgemeine Zeitung* of 27 October 1993 stated:

> Things are not looking good in South Africa. In particular the economy is going downhill. Very little is being invested. Domestic and foreign investors are waiting to see whether the change from white minority rule to black majority rule will succeed without shocks and to see which course the leaders will follow. Should it come to a division of power among the parties in a government of national unity ... so much the better. But the outlook is grim and in a period of uncertainty the economy will stagnate at best. Instead of new jobs being created existing ones will be cut ... Politicians from all parties must concentrate on ending the bad situation rapidly. If it continues much longer the economy will be weakened to such an extent that it will be impossible for the new constitution to give political order (Report 30.10.93).

Fortunately, all was not gloom and doom. As the negotiations moved towards a successful conclusion so aspects of the economic climate improved. Some sanctions were lifted, the IMF arranged support (part grant, part loan) of $850m for drought relief, and the global economic situation improved. An indication of greater optimism came in December 1993, when an American business mission led by Ron Brown, the US Secretary for Commerce, signed an investment agreement and formed a joint committee on commerce and trade. Brown claimed it would raise the 'comfort level and confidence level' for future deals. He went on to announce that since 1991 30 US companies had either returned to South Africa or invested in the country for the first time. He stressed the importance of those steps because of the American conviction it was the private sector that could fire the economy into action and growth. The sense of optimism was greatly reinforced when the ANC succeeded in reaching agreement on a broadly based economic policy – the Reconstruction and Development Programme (RDP), which is discussed in Chapter 7.

6

Mandela & de Klerk Compete for International Support

Now that the parties were prepared to negotiate there was a degree of co-operation between the government and the ANC. This included informal discussion of foreign policy issues between the Department of Foreign Affairs (DFA) and the ANC's International Department. Yet, while there was some co-operation, all sides were fully aware that they were involved in a struggle for future power. 'The point which must be clearly understood', said Mandela, 'is that the struggle is not over; negotiations themselves are a theatre of struggle, subject to advances and reverses as any other from of struggle' (Mandela 1994: 584). It was in this light that the ANC and the NP sought international support.

Shortly after Mandela's release he and de Klerk became world travellers, both spending substantial time and effort competing for international backing. In Mandela's case he made 16 overseas trips between 1990 and mid-1992, visiting 49 countries, of which 20 were in Africa (Pfister 2003: 65). His first long-distance destination was Sweden, and while en route he visited some African states, included Zimbabwe, where he set out to improve relations with President Robert Mugabe and his ZANU(PF) party – the ANC having previously been in alliance with Joshua Nkomo's ZAPU. In May Mandela made another African trip, visiting Zambia, Angola and Nigeria, and in the next two month he spent no less than six weeks abroad, visiting 14 countries in three continents – Europe, Asia and the Americas. At the same time de Klerk was pursuing his global circuit. Between May 1990 and June 1992 he visited 32 countries including 16 in Europe, and some, like Britain and France, he visited more than once. He became the first South African head of government since Jan Smuts after World War II to be received officially in the US, and he made determined efforts to visit African states on the assumption that the road back to international acceptance lay through the continent.

Why did the two leaders spend so much time on these punishing rounds of foreign visits while they faced so many challenges at home? The answer lies partly in the past. So much attention had been paid to South Africa that its leaders had been drawn into international politics – whether they were from the ANC seeking support against the apartheid state, or the government trying to throw off the shackles of its pariah status. Mandela and de Klerk now set out to harness the momentum of the past to achieve their future goals. Both saw the international setting as a platform from which they could project themselves and their causes. They aimed to improve their negotiating positions; to reassure their domestic bases; to gain additional resources; to enhance their personal prestige and to help achieve their preferred constitutional outcome.

In seeking support both Mandela and de Klerk spoke of 'normalising' South Africa's international relations, but by that they meant different things. On Mandela's part normalisation could come only when South Africa was a fully democratic state, accepted and respected by the whole international community. Normalisation, he argued, should not be used as a prop for the existing regime, or a reward for progress so far, for then it would be employed to retain apartheid in a new guise. In December 1991 Mandela told the UN General Assembly that: 'The new South Africa will seek to normalise its relations with the rest of the world and gain full integration into the community of nations,' but he went on to underline that the day had not yet arrived. Meanwhile he asked for sustained pressure on the present government, including the retention of international sanctions by all states and organisations.

In contrast, for de Klerk normalisation meant bringing South Africa in from the cold and doing so now. He argued that although much had already been achieved in dismantling apartheid and moving towards a new political settlement, the government needed external support to reinforce and further the process. He wanted immediate rewards for the steps that had already been taken, thereby demonstrating to all South Africans the benefits of peaceful negotiations. Without those rewards, he argued that the economy would continue to flounder, while the opponents of negotiation and the men of violence would flourish. In May 1990 he told Margaret Thatcher that he wanted 'the widest possible international support for what he was doing, leading to a fundamental revision of attitudes towards South Africa'. In response she promised to help in the lifting of sanctions, provided negotiations continued (Thomas 1996: 220).

Mandela: The International Star

In seeking international support both Mandela and de Klerk concentrated much of their effort on the dominant West. Yet initially neither could be sure of their reception. Was de Klerk to be seen as the leader of a government that had brutally imposed apartheid; or as the man who had set South Africa on the road to democracy? Should Mandela be greeted as the hero of the liberation struggle against racism and oppression; or a terrorist leader and an ally of the communists? In the event both were treated sympathetically and proved to be skilled advocates of their causes.

On his release Mandela was an unknown quantity, but he soon became an international superstar. Feted as the world's most famous political prisoner, he revealed himself to be a man of dignity, humanity, charm and humour. Furthermore he held the moral high ground and used it to full advantage in winning over diverse audiences and leaders. Because of his personality and the cause he represented, almost every door was open to him. In Rome he met the Pope; in Paris President Mitterrand gave him a state reception; in Bonn he was received by Chancellor Kohl and Foreign Minister Genscher and in London he had a long (if delayed) meeting with Thatcher. In June 1990 New York welcomed him with a massive ticker-tape reception along Broadway, and that evening the Empire State building was lit with the colours of the ANC. In Washington he had the rare privilege of addressing Congress.

On these visits Mandela continued to emphasise that the ANC was involved in a struggle for democratic rights. He told Congress: 'We are engaged in a struggle to ensure that the rights of every individual are guaranteed and protected through a democratic constitution, the rule of law, and an entrenched bill of rights.' On that same visit he told a predominantly black rally in Harlem, that 'all of us, descendants of Africa, know only too well that racism demeans the victims and dehumanises its perpetuators'. He spoke of living in a country still enslaved by apartheid, in which 'the vote, the land, the economic wealth and power remain a monopoly of the white minority'; while blacks endured poverty, slum dwellings and police brutality.

Mandela did not hesitate to voice his distrust of de Klerk and his government. He rejected the claim that it was irreversibly committed to end racism or to a fully democratic society. He told Congress that despite recent developments South Africa was still in the grip of racism. 'To destroy racism in the world,' he stated, 'we must expunge apartheid racism in South Africa.' The ANC was seeking a society free of discrimination by race, sex and creed, and in which all had political rights, whereas most South Africans did not enjoy such rights. They were still, he continued, victims of an apartheid regime backed up by powerful security forces. 'We have yet to arrive at the point when we can say that South Africa is set on an irreversible course leading to its transformation into a united, democratic and non racial country' (Clark 1993: 31/32/40).

Inevitably there were hiccups and differences of view between Mandela and Western leaders. In 1990 he refused President George Bush's request for the ANC to renounce the armed struggle. Instead he offered a 'cessation' of hostilities if talks continued to go well. Following that, Bush declined Mandela's request for US Federal financial aid, and added that Congress and not the ANC would decide when sanctions were to be lifted. According to a South African government publication, Bush was 'irritated' and said he had not had a good day (*Focus* August 1990). On another occasion Mandela faced adverse American public reaction when, in a TV interview, he stoutly defended the ANC's ties with the SACP, the USSR, East European states, Cuba, Libya and the Palestine Liberation Organisation (PLO). He declared that he was not going to desert those who had 'supported our struggle to the hilt' (Thomas 1996: 224, and 1994: 177). A Western ambassador claimed that: 'He wants to exorcise the idea that America is unchallengeable', knowing that most of the Third World was behind him (Sampson 1999: 561). There were also some resentment in Britain, when in May 1993 Mandela addressed members of Parliament. He accused Britain as the imperial power – through the 1910 South African Act of Union – of creating the situation whereby black South Africans had to seek freedom by force. 'Your right to determine your own destiny', he said, 'was used to deny us to determine our own.' History, he continued, demands that Britain should aid us now to achieve our freedom, by helping with the elections, promoting the new South Africa, and supporting the ANC (Clark 1993: 248).

However, such was Mandela's personality that these occasional spats did little or nothing to undermine his popularity or prestige in the West. His reputation remained undiminished despite his criticism, not only of past events, but of current Western policies (such as sanctions against Iraq), and his advocacy of what, in Western eyes, were 'rogue states'. He praised and visited states that had supported the liberation struggle. In Libya he described Colonel Gadaffi as a 'fellow in arms'. In Cuba – the US 'bogeyman' – after receiving that country's highest civil award, Mandela praised the government and its leader, Fidel Castro. He spoke of the Cuban revolution as 'a source of inspiration to all freedom loving people', and of his admiration for the Cuban people, who had retained their independence 'in the face of a vicious imperialist orchestrated campaign to destroy the impressive gains made in the Cuban revolution'. Mandela claimed that Cuba had given a lesson to other oppressed peoples: not to give ground in the struggle. He went on to make special mention of Cuba's international record, its contribution to Africa in general and in particular the defeat of the apartheid forces in Angola. 'It is unparalleled in African history', claimed Mandela, 'to have another people rise in defence of one of us' (Clark 1993: 121–4).

Mandela's international successes extended to fund-raising, which was a matter of central importance for the ANC, because of its dependence on external support. Adam and Moodley noted that ninety per cent of the ANC's 1990 budget of $27m came from foreign sources (Adam and Moodley 1993: 175). The search for funds was continuous. In July 1993, for instance, the ANC took out a full-page advertisement in *The Guardian* newspaper seeking financial help in Britain. On his travels Mandela openly, persistently and successfully sought financial backing. Again his personality came into play, for he was known to be a man of propriety and honesty, with a simple life style. As a result, almost everywhere he went – from Sweden to Taiwan – he succeeded in raising funds for the ANC. He told the European Parliament that to rebuild itself internally and to negotiate with the NP on equal terms the ANC needed 'buckets full of money' (Thomas 1994: 174). And buckets he filled. On his first US visit he raised more than $10m at private functions, and Congress voted $4m for the ANC. In Indonesia President Suharto personally presented Mandela with a cheque for US$10m, and he received US$5m from President Mahathir in Malaysia. One of Mandela's few failures was in Japan. There, to his annoyance, his request to the Japanese Parliament for US$25m was turned down on the grounds that the government never gave financial support to foreign political parties. Mandela's request, which Ambassador Ohta described as 'extremely embarrassing and shocking', offended the Japanese sense of propriety (Custy and Van Wyk 1994: 64– 70). Despite that particular setback, by April 1994, when the first democratic elections were held, the ANC was said to have a larger election fund than the NP.

Mandela, the ANC and the West

Mandela's activities abroad were enthusiastically applauded by most ANC members, but criticism arose on two issues. First, there were complaints about the amount of time he was spending abroad while there was so much to do at home. Mandela responded to this by saying that he did so as a servant of the party and at its behest. The second criticism, which itself divided into two parts, concerned those with whom he made contact overseas. One was related to human rights concerns. For example, Mandela was criticised for accepting financial support from the Suharto military regime in Indonesia, whose hands were soiled by its oppression of the people of East Timor. The second complaint came from 'the left wing'. They criticised Mandela for his increasing contacts with the West, including friendly gestures to conservative leaders – to the extent of his describing Mrs Thatcher as 'an enemy of apartheid'. In the eyes of these critics, such contacts were compounded by his readiness to reassure Western capitalists that the ANC was not a socialist party, but rather a broad-based nationalist movement, without commitment to socialist policies.

Mandela defended his attitude towards the West on two counts. First, although the ANC had worked with the SACP the alliance had been built on opposition to apartheid, not on a common commitment to socialism. Also, he could point to the emphasis he had given during his early visits to the West to the central role of the state in managing the economy. It was inevitable, he told Congress in 1990, 'that the democratic government will intervene in the economy'. He went on to say that the ANC did not favour privatisation, nor, in its search for growth with equity, did it believe that the market economy could self-regulate itself to achieve those ends (Clark 1993: 38). The second reason was more pragmatic, and became increasingly significant. As the old Soviet bloc was no longer able or willing to support the ANC it had to look elsewhere. As a result Mandela paid increasing attention to the West and to private business. He toned down his criticism of capitalism, as he sought aid and investment. He did not abandon entirely the views he had expressed to Congress, but he modified them as he revealed more sympathy towards the West and the market economy. When, in October 1993, he spoke at 'Why Invest in South Africa?' conferences in the US and Britain, he assured companies and investors that their interests would be safe under an ANC government. 'We will guarantee the security of all investments against appropriation, and also ensure that companies are free to repatriate after-tax profits and any proceeds accruing to them' (*Report* 15.10.93). A year later, shortly after becoming President, he told an American television audience: 'Forget the past and come to South Africa to make money. All of you will, and should make your investment decisions based upon the real opportunities you seek and find in South Africa [which] provides an economic and social climate that will create opportunities for investors' (Mills 1995: 15).

Contact with the West by Mandela and other leading ANC figures, which started pragmatically, therefore, led over time to an adjustment in their assumptions and attitudes. At the same time the weakness of the Soviet bloc, combined with its withdrawal of support to liberation movements, undermined the influence of the hard liners in the triple alliance and allowed the moderates to seize the initiative, thereby contributing to an increasing convergence of views in negotiations with other parties. The change came gradually, perhaps unconsciously, as with increasing contact and the search for support the ANC absorbed more Western views and outlooks. The conversion was never absolute.

The ANC would never accept Fukuyama's world view, and it continued to stress its identity as a Third World state and to challenge specific Western policies. However, the shift was real enough. Mandela had left prison talking of further nationalisation; by the time he came to power he was speaking about privatisation.

He and his ANC cabinet colleagues came to support a mixed economy, and were prepared to follow policies similar to those proposed by the IMF for other African states. They explained their position in terms of the national interest, arguing that to flourish the new South Africa needed aid, trade and investment, and that the West was the only show on the road that could offer them, but such views continued to be challenged within the movement. The outcome was that the ANC continued to identify itself publicly with the Third World, while building a working relationship with the First, and consciously or unconsciously absorbing some of its values. There was, however, a price to be paid. From the West's viewpoint the ANC's continuing internal debate, its communist members, and its contacts with radical states, left doubts about future policy. In contrast, some African and Third World leaders accused the ANC of acting as the West's poodle; of becoming an agent of capitalism and neo-colonialism. For those who demanded clear-cut commitments the new South Africa was characterised by ambiguity.

De Klerk Seeks International Support

De Klerk led the government's drive in its attempts to gain external support. In doing so he was supported by senior officials and by the business community. The officials were active in promoting the image of a post-apartheid South Africa, and in seeking to normalise relations. They moved quickly and carried their message across Africa. For example, in January 1991 Rusty Evans visited the Sudan, focusing on military assistance, overfly rights for South African Airways, and economic contacts. This was followed in September by exchange visits from both sides, with a delegation from the Sudan led by the Minister of Energy and Natural Resources; while a South African group representing transport, minerals and technology visited the Sudan. Between 26 October and 2 November 1991 Derek Auret (Deputy Director General of the DFA) visited a number of West African states (including the Republic of Congo, the Ivory Coast and Senegal) in an attempt to enlist support for readmission to international organisations, like the Food and Agricultural Organisation. There were even hopes that the OAU would open its doors to South Africa. With that in mind the South Africans paid court to Uganda and Nigeria, which held the OAU Chair in the early 1990s. In July 1990 Niel Barnard – the Director of the National Intelligence Agency – visited both Nigeria and Uganda. In Kampala he had a two hour meeting with President Museveni. In Nigeria's case de Klerk himself became directly involved, and there he had business support. When he visited Abuja in April 1992 de Klerk was accompanied by a business delegation, including the Presidents of the Afrikaanse Handelsinstituut and the South African Chamber of Business, and the Chief Executive of the Foreign Trade

Organisation. At other times businessmen took the initiative themselves in seeking to gain advantage abroad from the political developments at home (Pfister 2003: 337–360).

Yet, although de Klerk can be seen as the leader of a team, as indeed can Mandela in relation to the ANC, their attempts to gain external support took on the air of a gladiatorial contest. Although Mandela held the moral high ground de Klerk was an effective exponent of the government's case, and he too was an energetic traveller.

As an individual de Klerk also had great charm and ability, and as the leader who had abandoned apartheid, he had a strong case on which to base his appeal. On his visit to the Netherlands in November 1990 *De Telegraaf* described him as having 'old fashioned French charm, Dutch level headedness and the unfailing British feeling for diplomacy' (*Focus* December 1990). De Klerk's task was easiest in the West, where most governments were eager to end sanctions, and restore trade and investment links. In urging de Klerk to push ahead with reform, Western governments used both the stick and the carrot. For example, following America's limited lifting of sanctions in 1991, Margaret Tutwiler, a senior official in the Department of State, enthusiastically praised de Klerk's efforts on one hand, but on the other, stressed that if there was backsliding the sanctions would quickly be reimposed. However, in the changing international circumstances, de Klerk's welcome was not confined to the traditional Western contacts, and he was eager to break new ground. In June 1992, for instance, he made official trips to Japan and Singapore. He was well received, and returned home optimistic about the chances of new investment, especially from Singapore, where he had talks with Prime Minister Goh Chok Tong and elder statesman Lee Kuan Yew. Shortly afterwards trade delegations from Singapore visited Johannesburg, and a Singapore computer company announced its intention to open a factory in South Africa.

Even some of apartheid's strongest past opponents were now ready to roll out the red carpet for de Klerk. To the chagrin of the ANC, members of the old Soviet bloc, having thrown off communism, were ready to explore links with South Africa. As early as January 1990 (even before de Klerk's speech) Hungary welcomed Pik Botha, the Foreign Minister, to discuss economic co-operation. The climax of these new contacts came in December 1991 when de Klerk visited Moscow. It was a remarkable reversal of form, which was further underlined by Mandela's failure to visit Moscow during the early 1990s – one of the few gaps in his global journeys.

De Klerk was also able to exploit a growing interest in the rest of Africa following the prospect of the end of apartheid. In part this came from the fascination of the previously forbidden land, in part from the hope of material rewards. Based on the view that the road to international acceptance ran through Africa, de Klerk set out to stress the benefits of co-operation, and to make what contacts he could. The Namibian independence celebrations enabled him to meet several African leaders for the first time, and where possible he followed up with exchange visits. His approach was captured in a letter he addressed to thirty African heads of state in May 1991. In this he reflected on the rapidly changing international scene, with the end of the Cold War, and the establishment of large trading blocs, which threatened to marginalise Africa. To counter that de Klerk urged co-operation in the common interest. 'The time for isolation and mistrust has passed', he argued, and, citing Namibia's independence and Pretoria's efforts to bring peace to Angola and Mozambique, he claimed that 'South Africa's record in recent times speaks for itself ... South Africa', he concluded, 'does not seek to overwhelm or dominate. We believe that it has become imperative that co-operation in all fields of development be established to safeguard and advance our common interests' (Pfister 2002: 61).

At first there was some hesitation among African leaders. In 1990 de Klerk had to be content with visits to Madagascar and Senegal, but in the years that followed came major break-throughs. They included exchanges with Kenya and Nigeria, which were seen as important states both in their own right and as continental leaders. During his visit to Kenya in June 1991 de Klerk discussed with President Arap Moi the potential for continental development in four blocs – North, East, West and South, led respectively by Egypt, Kenya, Nigeria and South Africa – the 'four locomotives', as Pik Botha described them. In June 1992 the government gained a further boost when President Moi visited South Africa on his way to the 'earth summit' in Brazil. The discussions centred on economic co-operation, but the content was less important than the fact of the meeting itself. It was the first visit from an African head of state for 21 years.

Nigeria was another target state, which de Klerk followed up after meeting President Babangida at Namibia's independence ceremonies. On its part the Nigerian government, as early as April 1990, arranged an internal seminar on relations with South Africa, which concluded that it would be wise to gain an early foothold before the formal end of apartheid. In July 1990 Olusegun Obasanjo, a Nigerian statesman (who had served on the Commonwealth's EPG) visited Pretoria 'to learn what Nigeria could do to help the process along, and to encourage the South African Government to sustain the good things being done' (Pfister 2002: 137). An invitation eventually followed for de Klerk to visit Nigeria in April 1992. He was delighted to accept, because as well as its own importance, Nigeria was currently holding the OAU presidency, and furthermore the invitation infuriated the ANC. When the ANC complained that it had not been consulted about the invitation, the Nigerians brushed it aside, saying that they did not seek approval from outsiders to conduct their business. 'We have our own policies and will not be dictated to by anyone's business but our own' (*Report* 10.4.92).

One measure of the extent both of de Klerk government's successes and limitations in extending external contacts came in the spread of diplomatic relations. At the beginning of 1990 Pretoria had formal links with only 39 countries; by 1993 that had increased to 63. The government hailed it as a success, but it was still less than half of the UN's members. De Klerk blamed the ANC for the limitations, not only for its socialist leanings, but for the continued violence inside the country. He accused the ANC – with its bloody rivalry with Inkatha, and its 'mass actions', and 'stayaway strikes' to back up its negotiating position – of undermining efforts to extend external relations and improve the economy by frightening away traders and investors. He asserted that ANC was the major source of the problem. The ANC hotly denied the accusation, and in turn, pointed its finger at the government as the real source of violence. Whatever the reasons, de Klerk's efforts to extend external relations had only limited success, whereas when Mandela took over power virtually all the world wanted to be represented in Pretoria. Even some of de Klerk's 'successes' may well be explained – as with Nigeria – by the eagerness of other states to establish links in anticipation of the advent of Mandela's government.

The Dispute over International Sanctions

The ANC and the government were in constant dispute over international sanctions. 'Sanctions' – a broad umbrella term for a range of actions and boycotts taken against the apartheid regime by the international community – had built up steadily over the years. They included restrictions on trade, finance, investment, arms sales, tourism and sport, and they were imposed (to a greater or lesser extent) by a diverse set of organisations – governments, local authorities, civic bodies, non-governmental organisations (NGOs), churches, trade unions, universities and individuals. The UN sanctions were universally applicable, but because South Africa's most important links were with the West it was over them that the main struggle was fought. For South Africa the impact of sanctions had increasingly been felt over a range of contacts, which had set it apart as a pariah state. Most whites resented sanctions, not only because of the material cost but the sense of isolation and rejection it fostered. Black opinion was more divided. The liberation movements and their followers strongly supported sanctions as a contribution to the struggle, but others, including Buthelezi and his Inkatha movement, opposed them because of their adverse impact on black employment and income.

By the time de Klerk became President the country was facing severe economic problems, in which sanctions played a part. De Klerk spoke of a sanctions net 'tightening around us', and of a 'financial crisis caused by the decisions of international banks to pull the financial plug'. Later he gave as one of the main reasons for abandoning white minority rule the need 'to end our economic isolation and to restore normal trade and financial relations with the rest of the world ... We desperately needed foreign investment and loans to get our economy going again after years of stagnation' (De Klerk 1998b: 37/41). Following de Klerk's initiative, the government argued that sanctions should be lifted – even if only step by step – as a reward for its efforts so far, as an encouragement to continue the reforms, and as a means of stimulating the economy for the benefit of all. As it was the economy was in grave difficulties – from the combined effects of drought, global oil crises, volatile mineral prices and world economic recession as well as sanctions. De Klerk argued that the removal of sanctions was an essential step on the road to recovery.

The ANC was equally adamant in advocating the retention of sanctions. In the past it had seen them as a touchstone of support. Now, added to that, they became an instrument in the continuing struggle – a lever, as they saw it, to maintain pressure on an untrustworthy, racist government. Mandela explained to the US Congress: 'Sanctions should remain in place because the purposes for which they were imposed have not yet been achieved' (Clark 1993: 40). Later, he bluntly told the European Parliament that the lifting of sanctions would be a 'stab in the back' (Thomas 1994: 174). Yet, the ANC was aware of the country's economic plight. In September 1992, following a breakdown in the negotiations, Derek Keys, the Minister of Finance, briefed Trevor Manuel of the ANC about the situation. When Manuel reported back, the gloomy economic prediction was a major factor in persuading Mandela that the negotiation deadlock must be broken, and broken quickly. Mandela confessed: 'I got frightened. Before Trevor finished I said to him, "now what does this mean as far as negotiations are concerned? Because it appears to me that if we allow the situation to continue ... the economy is going to be so destroyed that when a democratic government comes to power, it will not be able to solve it"' (Waldmeir 1997: 212/13).

Mandela was also concerned about a division that had emerged within the ANC. The leaders, conscious of the economic situation and the need for flexibility in the negotiations, were prepared to modify their stand by accepting a phased programme for lifting sanctions. But they failed to convince the bulk of their followers. Even Mandela was heckled on this issue. For most ANC members sanctions were weapons to be used against the apartheid regime, and should not be lifted until a democratic government was in power. Yet, without convincing their more militant followers, the leaders set out a graduated timetable, whereby selected sanctions would be lifted in return for specified steps by the government. Finally, all remaining sanctions would be lifted when a democratic constitution had been agreed and an election date confirmed. But this was gesture politics, for few if any, either inside or outside the country, followed the ANC's guidelines.

Abroad there was a mixed response, depending both on developments inside South Africa and the interests of the state or organisation imposing the sanctions. As expected Western states and companies with large stakes were among the first to lift sanctions. However, matters could quickly be reversed. For instance, following the Boipatong massacre in June 1992, some US sanctions were reimposed. But although neither the government nor the ANC emerged as undisputed winners in the sanctions battle, the general drift was in the government's favour. This came about because of economic interests, and because once the process of removing apartheid had genuinely started the principal aim of sanctions had been achieved. That aim was to end apartheid, not to favour one party against another. That was the finding of the British Parliament's Committee on Foreign Affairs, in its report of February 1991.

> It is clear to us [stated the committee] that President de Klerk is genuinely committed to the abandonment of apartheid and the creation of a multi racial democracy. Sanctions were imposed on South Africa not only because of its rejection of universal suffrage and its imposition of authoritarian rule but because apartheid imposed by law segregation and discrimination on the basis of race and colour. When the legal foundations of apartheid are uprooted, sanctions which were intended to achieve precisely that result will be no longer required, while South Africa badly needs new investment and greater trade links (HC 1991: 6.8).

A similar conclusion was reached in the US by President Bush and the Republican administration. When de Klerk visited the White House, as early as September 1990, Bush, who had never been enthusiastic about sanctions, confirmed that in his view the internal process was irreversible, and therefore sanctions should be lifted, even if step by step. In July of the following year he signed an executive order terminating many sanctions. Yet, although that went through with hardly a murmur, the broader American sanctions story was not yet over. A few Federal sanctions remained, but more important was the retention of sanctions by many states, local/city authorities, private companies and banks. As late as January 1993 in the US, 16 states, 23 cities and 43 universities were still applying sanctions. By the end of the year, however, when agreement had been reached on a date for the first democratic election, and a Transitional Executive Council (TEC) had been appointed, with the task of overseeing the demise of white government, President Bill Clinton announced that the remaining US Federal sanctions would be lifted, and he would support Pretoria's access to international financial institutions. It was the end of the sanctions saga.

Nuclear Weapons

In the search for international acceptance de Klerk gained further attention and support when, in March 1993, he announced that the government had developed nuclear weapons during the 1970s and 1980s. He went on to say that the weapons and the technology associated with them had now been destroyed. Although Pretoria's possession of 'the bomb' had long been suspected, de Klerk's was the first public admission of it. He explained that as South Africa became more isolated, and faced the 'total onslaught', the government had decided to go ahead with the development of the bomb. Following a research and development phase six bombs were manufactured. The bombs – which could be delivered by Buccaneer aircraft – were, de Klerk claimed, intended as a deterrent, based on a strategy of three stages of response. The first stage was one of ambiguity, when the government would neither confirm nor deny their existence, but would encourage others to suspect it. If the danger increased a second stage would have involved covert warnings to the major Western powers, who, it was assumed, would be prepared to involve themselves to prevent nuclear warfare. However, if that still failed to deter Pretoria's enemies, the final stage would be a public declaration of the existence of the weapons and the government's readiness to use them. Other than stage one, said de Klerk, these steps had been unnecessary. Commenting on de Klerk's statement, Marie Muller concluded that the weapons were 'never intended for actual military use', because the government realised that 'their use would have been akin to committing suicide'. Their aim was purely 'political', to bring the West to South Africa's aid against a major Soviet-inspired attack. However, in Muller's view the strategy was far too simplistic to be a real deterrent (Muller 1996: 34/35).

Returning to de Klerk's position in 1993, he hoped that the destruction of the weapons would improve South Africa's international standing. According to Waldo Stumpf, a member of the Atomic Energy Corporation, he and other leading figures had been called together by de Klerk who told them: 'In order to take South Africa back into the international community we need to do two things: dismantle the political system and dismantle the nuclear weapons programme'. De Klerk explained that the key mover with regard to nuclear weapons was the US, which had made clear that a new South African state would not be welcome if it still possessed nuclear weapons. 'It was', de Klerk told the assembled scientists, 'a matter of world politics' (Hadland 2000). Two years earlier with the same aims in mind de Klerk's government had signed the Nuclear Non Proliferation Treaty (NPT).

As striking as what de Klerk said in announcing the destruction of the weapons was what he left unsaid. He made no mention of the reports and rumours of substantial help that Pretoria had received along the nuclear road from Israel, Germany and France. Nor did he refer to speculation that the bombs and the technology associated with them had been destroyed in response to Western pressure, based on fears that a future ANC government might be prepared to co-operate in weapon development with rogue states like Cuba and Libya. Instead de Klerk stressed that the decision was taken in terms of preventing the proliferation of nuclear weapons, and 'was widely welcomed and further helped to strengthen our international credibility'. Pik Botha, the Foreign Minister, added that 'we want to be included in the [peaceful nuclear] club'. (De Villiers 1993: 108).

If there were fears that an ANC government would have become involved in nuclear proliferation, they appear to have been ill founded, at least in the short term. The ANC had made clear its opposition to nuclear weapons, with Mandela personally repudiating weapons of mass destruction, and the party announcing that it favoured making Africa a nuclear-free zone. Yet, despite those reactions, had an ANC government inherited nuclear weapons it would have faced the dilemma of what to do with them. It may, as the Americans feared, have decided to share the weapons or their technology with others. Even if it had decided against that, it may have been tempted at least to retain them – just in case, or for the diplomatic clout associated with them. There is no other example of a state abandoning its nuclear capability.

International Recognition and Rivalry

Both Mandela and de Klerk had their efforts recognised through the receipt of prestigious international awards. In 1993 they were jointly awarded the Nobel Peace Prize, and the US Philadelphia Peace Prize. Standing together before distinguished audiences to receive their honours, the two men – each resentful of the presence of the other – captured the paradox of the negotiating process. On one hand they were its main movers and shakers, who relied on each other to keep it on track. Yet, at the same time, they were the main rivals, who attacked each other with increasing bitterness. After the initial euphoria of his release, when Mandela had described de Klerk as 'a man of integrity', no love was lost between them. With their different aims and backgrounds it was perhaps inevitable that rivalry would develop, but it acquired a personal edge – a feud that fed on itself. De Klerk later wrote of a relationship that was characterised by 'vitriol and suspicion' (De Klerk 1998a: 300).

Nor was the vitriol and suspicion reduced by similar matrimonial crises each faced during the negotiation. In Mandela's case the rift with his wife Winnie Madikizela Mandela was exposed in a way that was humiliating for the dignified Mandela. Winnie – dubbed as 'the Mother of the Nation' – had been a fearless, outspoken opponent of apartheid, and a major political figure in her own right. However, by the time Mandela was released from prison her vitality had turned to ungovernable wildness – with heavy drinking, infidelity and a reign of terror that she imposed in Soweto through a band of thugs, known as 'Mandela United'. Although retaining a prominent position in the ANC – including President of the Women's League, and being given a junior ministerial post when Mandela formed the government – her behaviour did not improve. In March 1992 Mandela summoned a press conference to announce his separation from Winnie. However, she remained a loose cannon in the party and the government, and in March 1995 Mandela dismissed her from her ministerial position. A year later he divorced her. Fortunately for him there was a happy ending, when he met and married Graca Machel, the widow of the former Mozambique President, an able, strikingly attractive woman who shared Mandela's zest for life and his sense of fun.

De Klerk's matrimonial problems were less public, but no less agonising. Marike, his wife, was not a major public figure, but was reputed to be a woman of conservative views, and not in sympathy with her husband's radical reforms. It was not, however, political differences that ended their 39 years' marriage, but de Klerk's relationship with Elita Georgiadis, a married, wealthy, beautiful Greek woman he first met in London in 1989. After much agonising de Klerk left Marike in 1998 and eventually married Elita.

While they wrestled independently with their personal problems the chief source of friction between them came over responsibility for the continued violence. That led to a public spat at a plenary session of the negotiating forum Codesa. Speaking to the delegates and a world wide television audience de Klerk attacked the ANC for breaking promises by continuing to retain its armed wing – a 'private army', as he described MK. He questioned whether in the circumstances the ANC should even be allowed to attend the peaceful negotiations. Mandela was furious. He turned on de Klerk, accusing him of going back on his word, and claiming that he had specifically agreed not to raise the MK issue. 'Even', Mandela thundered, 'the head of an illegitimate, discredited minority regime, as his is, has certain moral standards to uphold. He has no excuse, just because he is head of such a discredited regime not to uphold moral standards' (Mandela 1994:588).

Writing later about this incident, de Klerk revealed the two sides of the negotiating coin – the rivalry and distrust on one side and the dependence on the other. 'Mandela's vicious and unwarranted attack', he wrote, 'created a rift between us that was never again fully healed. Nevertheless, we would both frequently have to rise above our personal antipathy to resolve deadlocks and keep the negotiations on course' (De Klerk 1998a: 224). The paradox was equally appreciated by Mandela. 'My worst nightmare', he stated, 'is to wake up one night and de Klerk is not there. I need him. Whether I like him or not is irrelevant' (Waldmeir 1997: 231). Fortunately the nightmare was not realised as they worked together to reach a settlement.

7

International Support, End of the Soviet Bloc & the Negotiated Settlement

Difficult and tension-ridden as the negotiations proved to be, South Africa continued to attract international attention and support. If it is valid to ask why the South African leaders gave so much attention to the international scene it is equally valid to ask why the international community retained its concern for South Africa. Why did it not breathe a collective sigh of relief and leave the South Africans to sort things out for themselves? Again the answer lies partly in the past. The struggle against apartheid had become so enmeshed in the values and structures of international organisations and the individual states that it had acquired its own momentum. As with the South Africans, the past was the foundation for the future. Nor could those outside South Africa be sure that the negotiations would succeed without help. They realised the high price that would have to be paid if the process broke down, not only in South Africa but internationally as racial antagonism intensified and the negotiating process was discredited. Added to this the South Africans themselves appealed for support, as witnessed by Mandela's and de Klerk's travels.

The NP government, with bitter memories of past treatment and claiming that it would compromise the country's sovereignty, was more reluctant than the ANC to accept direct international involvement in domestic affairs. As a result it rejected proposals for an international peacekeeping force to help curb the internal violence, but it accepted other types of support. The European Community (EC) was particularly active. It reorganised its Special Programme for the Victims of Apartheid, so that, as well as its conventional education and training schemes, it supported the promotion of democracy and good governance, through voter education and knowledge of the law. The UN also expanded its activities. It opened an office to facilitate the return of political refugees, so that of the 11,000 exiles who returned by May 1993, almost 7,000 were helped by the UN High Commissioner for Refugees. In 1992 the IMF, after excluding Pretoria for many years, agreed to lend US$850m to help with the ravages of drought. In return Pretoria undertook to shape its monetary policy along lines favoured by the IMF.

At the same time came an increase in development aid – R960m in 1992 and R1,046m in the following year. It came from a variety of sources – the UN's Development Programme, Western organisations and states – including EC members, US, Japan, Canada and Australia. George Soros, the American businessman/philanthropist, personally gave US$15m. While the NP remained in power most aid continued to be channelled through NGOs. In broad terms it was spent on education and training, community development, and work on human rights, legal aid and democratisation. Within that framework donors made specific contributions – the US included help for black empowerment, while the British focused on training civil servants, diplomats and the police (Geldenhuys 1998: 88–90).

The Disintegration of the Soviet Bloc

While the past helps to explain the continued international interest in South Africa, present concerns also came into play. As noted earlier developments were set in the context of a changing international system – the elusive 'new world order' – with its hopes of peace and co-operation. Although the early optimism soon vanished, the end of the Cold War and the disintegration of the Soviet Union profoundly changed the structure of international relations, and had a direct impact on South Africa.

Initially the ANC assumed that Moscow would continue to be its major external prop. On his first visit to Lusaka, Mandela told a Soviet delegation, led by Professor Vassily Solodovnikov, that: 'We in the ANC believe that the Soviet Union will support us at the present crucial stage of the struggle' (Shubin 1995: 31). At Namibia's independence celebrations, in March 1990, when Mandela and Mbeki met the Soviet Foreign Minister, Eduard Shevardnadze, they urged him to continue the struggle, and to ensure that the Soviet Union retained leadership of the anti-apartheid forces. Shevardnadze, a leading figure of 'the new thinking', responded ambiguously. He spoke of a continuation of policy, but also of establishing a diplomatic presence in Pretoria. For a short time the ambiguity and the dual policy persisted, as Moscow continued to offer military training for MK and to impose sanctions on Pretoria, while at the same time urging a negotiated settlement. When, therefore, in July 1990, Soviet delegates attended the ANC's National Conference Walter Sisulu, as chairman, still greeted them as the movement's 'natural ally'.

However, beneath the outward show of friendship, the ANC was concerned at the changes in the Soviet bloc. Already in February a Russian business delegation had visited Johannesburg, having been reassured by the Russian Minister of Trade that although the Soviet Government had agreed to continue imposing sanctions, Russia had not. The pace of change increased. In August 1990 Shevardnadze approved a visit to the USSR of a South African trade mission, led by Kent Durr, who spoke of opening the trade gates of Eastern Europe. In the same month Moscow announced that free military training for foreigners (including the ANC) was to end. In November Pik Botha, the Foreign Minister, visited Moscow, where he signed a protocol to restore consular relations. So it continued, as the Soviet Union and its Eastern European empire disintegrated. By the beginning of 1992 the old bloc had broken up, and Russia had established diplomatic relations with Pretoria, without consulting the ANC.

As Moscow's attention was increasingly consumed by domestic problems, no longer did it welcome foreign 'adventures'. If South Africa featured at all in the Kremlin's agenda, it had a low priority. No longer was it seen in the context of a struggle against capitalism; but rather as a long-shot trading partner. Paradoxically, therefore, as the West moved towards the ANC, Moscow showed signs of sympathy for the white government. Thus in May 1993 – with the ANC and the government still locked in negotiations – Grigory Karasin, the Head of the Africa Directorate in the Russian Foreign Ministry, stated: 'We are maintaining a balanced "equal distance" approach to development of our ties with all constructive forces, including the government and the African National Congress' (Shubin 1999: 409). However, it soon became clear to Moscow and Pretoria that they had little to offer each other in terms of trade, aid or investment. That, plus the revision in the Kremlin's policy priorities, contributed to the shift by the ANC leaders in playing down their socialist orientation, and wooing the West. It also helps to explain Mandela's failure to visit Moscow until the very end of his presidency. When eventually he did arrive, in April 1999, it was a swan-song trip. He responded to Boris Yeltsin's welcome by saying that he had come in recognition of the great help given to the ANC by the former Soviet Union. 'Russia', he stated, 'should have been the very first county I visited and I have come to pay that debt now.' But then, Mandela was always a gracious guest (Helmer 1999).

International Support for Negotiations

Whenever the negotiating process faltered the instinctive reaction of the international community was to prop it up. That was amply demonstrated in 1992. It started with the white referendum campaign, when international organisations and foreign governments strongly supported a 'Yes' vote. In America the State Department declared that a 'No' vote would be a devastating backwards step, leading 'towards international isolation and domestic discord'. The White House was even blunter, stating that if de Klerk lost the referendum, and the right wing took power, the US would 'hit South Africa like a bomb'. So overt was the external support that Treurnicht, the CP leader, accused de Klerk of using foreigners to blackmail voters into submission, so that the CP had to campaign not only against the NP but against 'interfering foreigners like US President George Bush and British Premier John Major' (Geldenhuys 1992).

External help was also at hand in June 1992 when 45 people were killed at Boipatong. Boipatong was a turning point in the negotiations. Before that the government had made most of the running, and on 6 June, on his return from an overseas trip, a buoyant de Klerk declared that: 'South Africa is back in the international community. This time I am more convinced of it than ever before' (Pfister 2003: 06). On the night of June 16/17 that changed at Boipatong. The ANC accused Inkatha of responsibility for the killings, and claimed that the government had given support and then arranged an elaborate cover-up. A furious Mandela stated: 'I can no longer explain to our people why we continue to talk to a regime that is murdering our people and conducting war against us' (Waldmeir 1998: 206). The massacre led to a breakdown of Codesa, as the ANC walked out, it introduced a stronger international element, and it shifted the balance of power in the negotiations in the ANC's favour, as it waged a campaign of direct action through strikes and mass action that brought the country close to chaos. By chance the OAU summit met at Dakar only days after Boipatong. Mandela, despite ill health, insisted on attending and urging OAU members to resist 'hastily re-establishing relations with Pretoria'. He further persuaded them to request intervention by the UN (Pfister 2002: 26).

The lack of trust between the major parties was such that if they were to return to dialogue they needed an intermediary to ease them back, without losing face. As Mandela proposed, that intermediary role was provided by the UN. The ANC had long favoured increased international involvement, recognising that it would generally be sympathetic to its cause; whereas the government, soured by its previous experience of international bodies, had resisted it. Following Boipatong, the government relented. After a joint appeal from the Secretary Generals of the UN (Boutros-Boutros Ghali), the OAU (Salim Ahmed Salim) and the Commonwealth (Chief Emeka Anyaoka), Pretoria agreed to accept external help.

The result was a special session of the UN Security Council in July 1992, at which representatives of the government, the ANC and Inkatha presented their cases, and, in doing so, exposed their divisions. For the ANC Mandela accused the government of 'criminal intent' in instigating violence and conducting a 'cold blooded strategy of state terror' as it tried to bully its way at the negotiations. He added that even if the violence were now brought under control the ANC would only resume negotiations if the government was prepared to accept the principle of majority rule. Speaking for the government, Pik Botha rejected the ANC's accusations, and attempted to turn the tables by accusing the 'ANC-Communist alliance' of promoting conflict and of smuggling arms into the country from Zimbabwe and Angola. He offered talks with the ANC on disputed issues – including the release of political prisoners and the repeal of oppressive legislation – and he called on the ANC and Inkatha to join with the government in a body to counter township violence. Finally, he rejected the accusation that whites wanted a veto in future constitutional arrangements (*Report* 24.7.92).

Having heard the protagonists, the Security Council, without allotting direct blame on any side, condemned the 'escalating violence', expressed concern at the 'break in the negotiating process', and called on all parties to combat conflict and return to the talks. Under resolution 765 the Council asked the Secretary General to appoint a special representative to seek an end to violence and encourage a renewal of negotiations. His choice fell on Cyrus Vance, the former US Secretary of State (Geldenhuys 1998: 84). Within days Vance and his small team were in South Africa. There he reaffirmed that the UN's aim was to help in achieving a peaceful transition to a non-racial democracy. Recognising the urgency of his task, he quickly reported to Boutros-Boutros Ghali. On the basis of the report the Secretary General made recommendations to the Security Council, which were incorporated in resolution 772 of August 1992, and that in turn was accepted by the government and the ANC. At the heart of the resolution was an appeal to all parties to reject violence and return to the negotiating table. The Council called for an investigation into the sources of violence, including the roles of the security forces and private armies, and agreed that the UN would help towards 'the resumption of the process of negotiations'. To that end the Secretary General was asked to send observers, and to encourage other international bodies to do the same, but the importance of gaining local support at every step was stressed.

The UN Observer Mission to South Africa (Unomsa) was headed by Angels King, a Jamaican diplomat. By the end of the year it had 50 members from 36 countries, all civilians, but, before it was in full operation, a further crisis blew up. In September a large body of ANC members, led by Ronnie Kasrils, tried to march on Bisho, the capital of the Ciskei Bantustan ('independent homeland'). They were hoping to topple the homeland authority by mass peaceful protest – the Leipzig method – and they planned to follow up with marches on the other Bantustans. General Gqozo, the Ciskei leader, sent a message banning the march and warned that if it went ahead it would be forcibly resisted. The marchers, rejecting the whole concept of Bantustans, insisted that it was their right to demonstrate in what they regarded as part of South Africa itself. However, as they penetrated into the Ciskei the homeland troops opened fire, killing 29 of the marchers and injuring many more. Again crisis gripped the country. The threat of civil war hung in the air. The Danish Ambassador bluntly stated that 'the process of negotiations could not sustain any more Bishos and Boipatongs'.

With such warnings ringing in their ears the leaders on all sides drew back. The ANC leaders urged caution on their followers and quietly cancelled marches in other Bantustans, while this time it was the government itself that appealed to Boutros-Boutros Ghali for help (Landsberg 1994: 286). The Secretary General immediately dispatched Virendra Dayal to mediate and try to prevent further violence. Dayal, after meeting the various parties involved, managed to defuse the situation. One of the results was that the further ANC marches to Ulundi in KwaZulu and Mmabatho in Boputhatswana were cancelled.

Unomsa was then able to continue its work, supported by observers from three other bodies – the EC, the Commonwealth and the OAU. Under the UN mandate, their tasks were to investigate and discourage political violence, and to encourage the negotiating process. Later the same international organisations, again co-ordinated by the UN, were asked to observe and check the arrangements for and the conduct of the election. In practice there were two observer groups from each international body – one concerned with violence ('peace observers'), the other with the elections. The peace observers, who spent many months in the country, numbered only 100, whereas the election observers, who spent a shorter time, consisted of almost 2,500 people (Anglin 1995: 525). The groups were drawn from people with relevant experience and qualifications. The EC peace team, for instance, included police officers, lawyers and economists, and was similar to a mission sent to Yugoslavia.

The tasks of the peace observers included checking on marches, mass meetings, the conduct of political parties, and the armed forces. In doing so they worked closely with the government-appointed Goldstone Commission, which was investigating the sources of political violence. The commission itself appointed further international experts to help with its own work. The observers were confident that their efforts helped to reduce violence and so further the negotiations. The Commonwealth mission concluded that the presence of observers 'has played a visible and widely acknowledged role in helping to calm the political atmosphere'. The UN reported that Unomas had 'helped restore confidence that violence could be brought under control and facilitated the resumption of talks between the Government and the other parties, particularly the ANC' (Geldenhuys 1998: 87). As noted above, alongside their efforts to resolve immediate problems the international bodies contributed towards long-term democratic development, such as electoral education and training.

Reactions of Foreign Governments

Although the main thrust of the external support was to enable the South Africans to help themselves, inevitably there were some attempts to shape the end result. For example, Hank Cohen, the US Under Secretary, supported the ANC in its criticism of the NP's proposals for group rights and minority group vetoes. However, in the dispute between the IFP and the ANC over federalism, sympathy was mainly with the IFP in favouring a federal solution, especially in states that themselves have federal constitutions. Hank Cohen stated that Washington believed it would suit South Africa, and the German and Australian governments arranged visits for party leaders to see their federal systems in operation. In the event, the constitutional balance came down against the IFP's federalism and in favour of the ANC's centralised model of government.

While supporting a negotiated settlement individual governments saw the situation through the prism of their own interests and values. For instance, while Japan's interests in South Africa were mainly economic – as a source of raw materials, a market for its products and a potential springboard for access to the rest of Africa – the government was cautious about lifting sanctions. The Kyodo News Agency explained this caution by pointing to Tokyo's anxiety to avoid offending African states, as it wanted their support in its bid for a seat on the UN Security Council (Custy and Van Wyk, 1994). While Japan hesitated, India, which had been among the severest critics of apartheid, was not only prepared to throw its weight behind the negotiations, but quickly reduced sanctions in the hope of new trading opportunities. The Indian authorities also lifted the sports boycott, and, reflecting the country's passion for cricket, gave an enthusiastic welcome to a visiting South African team. Foreign statesmen, who previously had studiously avoided contact with the old regime, now almost queued to visit the country. They came to show their support for the negotiations, to lay foundations for future business, to be associated with a success story, and to have a photo opportunity with Mandela. As John Major, the British Prime Minister, told the South African Parliament in 1994: 'We want to take part with you in the great and exciting enterprise to the furthest extent we are able, and in all ways that you think best' (Geldenhuys 1998: 1). South Africa, which had gained attention in the past because of its sins, now retained attention because of its new-found virtues.

In the case of the old Soviet bloc, Moscow's hopes of playing a major diplomatic role, similar to its contribution in Namibia, ran into the sand, as it struggled to restructure its domestic economy and resolve its political and social problems. The days of support for liberation movements were over. Moscow was now more concerned with improving economic relations than competing with the West, and that continued after the demise of Gorbachev and the rise of Boris Yeltsin. Yeltsin assured de Klerk that although Mandela would be welcome to visit Russia, the invitation would be as a human rights hero, not as ANC President. It was a similar picture in Eastern Europe, where, in February 1992, de Klerk visited Poland, Czechoslovakia and Hungary. The result was an exchange of trade missions. Some economic fruits were harvested from these contacts: a small, steady trade developed in clothing and foodstuffs; Hungary bought South African technical mining equipment; in Romania South African companies refurbished the public phone system; while South African Breweries made a substantial investment in Czechoslovakia. However, the overall results were disappointing. In the case of Russia, with a few exceptions – such as the marketing of diamonds through de Beers – it soon became clear that neither side had much to offer the other. A similar picture prevailed across Eastern Europe. The result, wrote Sara Pienaar, was that: 'Curiosity had given way to friendly indifference' (Pienaar 1997: 130).

The Reconstruction and Development Programme

While the main immediate concern of the ANC was to achieve a satisfactory constitutional settlement, it did not ignore the future. Running in parallel with the constitutional negotiations ANC working groups prepared policy guidelines for its anticipated future role in government. Among the groups was one examining the economy. The economic debate, which had lost none of its passion, persisted inside the tripartite alliance – ANC, SACP and Cosatu – throughout the 1990s. And it continued to be influenced by international developments. As Chris Liebenberg stated in introducing the 1996 Budget: 'In the global village in which we live there is no escape from the (sometimes) harsh discipline imposed on individual countries by the international community and international markets' (Ward 1998: 40). Yet, despite the internal differences, the ANC succeeded in hammering out a policy that was flexible and broad enough to gain general support. This was given flesh in the Reconstruction and Development Programme (RDP), which linked economic progress with social development. Although an ANC creation, the RDP was widely examined outside as well as inside the alliance. Mandela explained that among others he had discussed it with officials of the IMF and the World Bank, and with Harry Oppenheimer, the doyen of South Africa's capitalists. The RDP itself went through several drafts. The first read like a blueprint for a socialist society, but with each revision it moved away from that model, so that Mandela, with an eye on the prevailing international climate, could underline that the final version made no mention of nationalisation or contained a single Marxist slogan.

The RDP did not set out detailed policies; rather it offered a framework for socio-economic development. It did, however, identify a set of five-year targets – covering health, education and social welfare, with specific aims, such as the redistribution of 30 per cent of the land, the creation of 500,000 new jobs in the public and private sectors and the electrification of 2.5 million houses. To achieve these ends it recognised that the government and the private sector must work together, and it optimistically assumed that growth and redistribution would go hand in hand. 'Without growth', it stated, 'there could be no development', while 'economic growth without development would fail to bring about ... a more advanced economy and a more equitable and prosperous society'. When the party came to accept the RDP it claimed that the 'programme will both meet basic needs and open up previously suppressed economic and human potential in urban and rural areas. In turn that will lead to increased output (i.e. growth)' (Lodge 1999: 27). Similar sentiment was expressed in a White Paper which the new government published in September 1994. It started by declaring that 'society is in need of transformation ... following centuries of oppression and decades of formal apartheid', but, influenced by the prevailing mantra, it went on to state that policies to achieve that should be neither inflationary nor liable to create balance of payments problems (Deegan 1999: 127/8).

Mandela embraced the RDP with enthusiasm. He saw it as a contribution to a more just society, by combining the virtues of a centralised economy and a free market. It would, he believed, provide the foundation of the social and economic revolutions that must follow the political transformation. In his first speech to parliament as President, he underlined that the RDP must be backed by fiscal and monetary discipline, and by the combined efforts of the public and private sectors. He called for private and foreign investment. He then went on to set short-term targets to be achieved in a hundred days – including free medical attention for pregnant women and children under six, and the electrification of 350,000 homes – and he announced that the state was setting aside R2.5bn to 'kick start' the programme. When he formed his first cabinet Mandela appointed Jay Naidoo as a minister for the RDP. Naidoo explained that the RDP was not an 'add on' to the government's main programme, but rather its central plank. Yet Naidoo had no illusions about the size of the task he was undertaking. The political system had been revolutionised but not the socio-economic structure. To change that, said Naidoo, meant 'transforming the way people think, work and deliver ... transforming attitudes' (Turok 1999: 59).

Outside the ANC doubts were expressed about the costs and practicability of the programme. Was it possible, within five years, to build all those houses and extend the social services? Was an inexperienced government capable of implementing such ambitious plans? Was it possible to transform attitudes? There were further doubts about trying to satisfy divergent constituencies – with Cosatu and the SACP favouring increased state involvement, while business interests cherry-picked those parts of the programme that emphasised the market economy. Nevertheless, the RDP gained broad support. Michael Spicer, of the Anglo American Corporation, stated that he was impressed by the balance between people-centred aims, the requirements of economic growth and foreign investment. Similar confidence was expressed by Derek Keys, who was widely admired for his financial competence, and retained the post of Finance Minister in Mandela's government. When in 1994 Keys introduced the first Budget of the new government, he claimed that it was based on the RDP, by blending spending in new directions with traditional fiscal discipline, and combining social justice with aggressive growth. It offered, he said, 'the best of both worlds' (*Report* 24.6.94).

Yet, inevitably, acceptance of the RDP by business only intensified suspicion among radical members of the alliance. Charles Nqakula, the SACP's General

Secretary, told Cosatu's annual conference in September 1994, that the RDP must be 'people driven' to give practical application to the 'fundamentals' that had shaped the Freedom Charter. Crucially its central aim must be 'to ensure the redistribution and redirection of resources, wealth and opportunities'. It was not enough, he said, to draw up a programme. Its implementation would involve continued struggle to prevent opponents of the people hijacking it. He accused private companies of using the RDP as a public relations stunt to attract foreign capital. Such people, argued Nqakula, were not concerned with redistribution; their God was profit. Cosatu and the SACP could not sit back and leave matters to the government. 'Unless', he urged, 'we organise, struggle and assume responsibility for the RDP ourselves, we will not have an RDP.'

Nqakula was equally concerned to avoid complacency. 'How often', he asked, 'do we hear reassuring phrases like "South Africa can now take its place among the family of nations"? Comrades,' he warned, 'the world out there is not a family picnic.' He spoke of death, disease and the suffering found in the Third World and in First World slums. He accused the IMF, World Bank and the Gatt of imposing their agendas on the poor, and argued that South Africa must resist by relying on its own resources, looking to its own needs, rejecting export-led growth, which would leave it vulnerable to external masters. Nqakula urged the delegates to struggle for a socialist future, which was more relevant than ever. Socialism, he proclaimed, is 'not a foreign country ... not some utopian dream ... [it] is about building an economy on social needs, not private profits ... about rolling back the empire of market totalitarianism [which is based on] decades of racial oppression and capitalist exploitation'. 'Who said socialism is irrelevant?' asked Nqakula. 'Who said socialism is dead?' (Nqakula 1994: 7–13).

The Constitutional Settlement

Meanwhile, the constitutional negotiations continued, although still plagued by uncertainty. Almost on a daily basis the mood shifted from high hope to deep gloom, as the two principal parties (NP and ANC) jockeyed for advantage. The ANC, far from collapsing in confusion and division – as some critics had predicted – held together. Furthermore, it demonstrated its strength outside the conference hall by its ability to bring the country to its knees through mass action – including strikes, 'stayaways', marches, demonstrations and refusal to pay for services. Added to that, Mandela, for all his charm and benign appearance, was a tough negotiator. He demonstrated that once again following the Boipatong massacre. The immediate outcome was the breakdown of Codesa. When negotiations were resumed he succeeded in moving the balance decisively in favour of the ANC. He correctly saw that the government's options were poor, and played on that.

When de Klerk launched his initiative, he had hoped for a speedy economic revival. That had not come, as many international investors and traders were reluctant to commit themselves while the situation was so volatile. Breaking off negotiations would only have made matters worse for the government, as it would have faced mass action at home by the ANC and punishing sanctions from abroad. But more than the economy was at stake. The government appeared to have a choice:

either to resort to the repression of the past, or to resume negotiations, even from a weaker position. In reality there was no choice. De Klerk realised that by following the path of negotiation he truly had crossed the Rubicon. There was no going back. To try to do so would have been to prompt a brutal civil war with heavy loss of life and to devastate the country. He also realised that backsliding would bring down the full wrath of the international community on him and his government. He had no choice but to bite the bullet and return to the negotiating table, although, in doing so, he knew he would have to give ground to the ANC.

In its search for a settlement the government, therefore, dropped reference to 'groups' and 'minority vetoes'. Instead it spoke of unity in diversity, and of the protection of individuals and different cultures through a Bill of Rights. It also reluctantly accepted majority rule, based on one person, one vote, one value; and a centralised (not a federal) state – in which the Bantustans were reabsorbed into South Africa. For its part the ANC, although in a much stronger position, realised that it too had to make adjustments, both to gain an agreement and to strengthen the future running of government. Although it rightly assumed it could comfortably win an election, it was conscious of its lack of administrative experience, and the need to retain white skills and experience if the new government was to function effectively. 'To take power is easy', said Mandela, 'the most difficult thing is to retain that power.' As a result the ANC, appreciating that it could not afford to antagonise large sections of the white community, accepted a phased approach to majority rule. The first stage would be built on a five-year interim constitution, when the country would be led by a Government of National Unity (GNU) based on 'power sharing' between the major parties. In that interim period a final constitution would be agreed by the National Assembly (sitting as a constitutional assembly) based on principles drawn up during the current negotiations, and backed up by a Constitutional Court. Meanwhile a range of 'sunset clauses', proposed by Joe Slovo, were designed to ease the transition to majority rule, by gaining white confidence through such measures as offering a degree of job security to the existing civil service.

Having reached agreement on future arrangements, a further compromise was reached to cover the short period before the election. The ANC wanted the NP government to stand down, to be replaced by a transitional administration; while the NP was equally determined to stay in power. The compromise was to appoint a Transitional Executive Council (TEC), whereby the NP government remained in office, but its activities were overseen and checked by the TEC. The TEC, which was installed in December 1993, was given a broad, if ambiguous brief. It operated as a series of committees, shadowing existing departments of state. Judgements of its performance depended on the interpretation of its brief. For some it was too intrusive, for others it was too supine, but the overall result was effective in that it served as a device to allow the process to go forward. International influence continued into the final period, including support for the TEC and in setting a date for the election. In July 1993, before he awarded the Philadelphia Liberty Medal, President Clinton told Mandela and de Klerk that he would urge the ending of all US sanctions and introduce a generous American aid programme once an election date was agreed. Having a firm date was important, in that it committed the parties to a timetable to complete the negotiations.

Negotiations and Competition for International Support

Following the agreement both the ANC and the NP claimed success. The NP pointed to the constitutional checks and balances on the government, the sharing of power for the five-year interim period, and the constitutional principles (backed by a court), which, reassuringly for Afrikaners, included a recognition of diversity in language and culture. However, to his white critics de Klerk had failed. He had supervised a negotiated surrender. They pointed to earlier commitments, many of which had been abandoned in the face of ANC opposition. Even some of his colleagues despaired at the outcome. When de Klerk presented the final agreement to the cabinet an infuriated minister – Tertius Delport – shouted at him: 'What have you done? Why have you given South Africa away?' (Waldmeir 1997: 232). The ANC, on the other hand, although it had accepted compromises, had achieved most of its aims. Slovo had no doubts. He spoke of 'a famous victory' and concluded that 'we got pretty much what we wanted – including a central, not a federal system with the purse strings in the hands of the central government' (Waldmeir 1997: 242).

Delighted at the outcome of the negotiations and confident that it would win the election the ANC declared that it would create a government based on the principles agreed for the final constitution. These principles embraced a multiparty political system, universal suffrage, proportional representation, separation of the judiciary, the supremacy of the constitution and transparency in government activities. Another striking feature was the emphasis on individual rights and freedoms, which were entrenched in a Bill of Rights, and backed by a variety of commissions, covering such matters as elections, gender and human rights. The institutions with the task of implementing the new constitution included a bicameral parliament and a constitutional court with the final word on disputed issues. While the constitution had been agreed by South Africans themselves, it reflected the prevailing international values of the day. A striking feature of the new constitution was its embodiment of the principles and values of a liberal democracy. 'Liberalism', wrote Ali Mazrui, 'is that system of values which puts a special premium on the individual and his autonomy. To ensure the freedom and dignity of the individual, liberalism has sought to devise constraints on government. Liberalism has been distrustful of concentrated power' (Mazrui 1979: 21). Parliamentary democracy was seen as one of the instruments to achieve these ends. It was agreed that there would be two chambers. The leading chamber – the National Assembly – was elected on a proportional representative method, based on party support. The second chamber – the National Council of Provinces – was, as its names implies, to give the regions a voice at the centre of government.

Returning to Mazrui: although he was sympathetic to liberalism, he identified it with capitalism and colonialism. It was no surprise, therefore, when radical critics directed their ire at the constitutional agreement. Western liberalism led to accusations that Mandela and his fellow negotiators had failed to appreciate the inbuilt tension in the settlement. Critics pointed out that, as with its economic policies, the ANC had declared its identification with 'the South', but was building the new state on values derived from the capitalist West. Some critics claimed that the ANC had abandoned an 'African approach'. Among them was Fasil Nahum, who contrasted Western and African attitudes towards the individual and society. He argued that: 'African humanism does not alienate the individual by seeing him as an entity all by himself, having an existence more or less independent of society ... The individual does not stand in contradistinction to society but as part of it' (Nahum 1992). Olusola Ojo sounded a similar note, when he wrote: 'Africans assume harmony, not divergence of interest ... and are more inclined to think of their obligations to other members of society rather than their claims against them.' He concluded that as Africans have been exploited as a group they should concentrate on developing society rather than the individual; on the rights of the collective over the single unit (Ojo 1997).

The ANC, in responding to such criticism, stressed that government must be built on the foundation of majority rule, by which the rights of the individual and society are harmonised. In that it had the support of Mazrui, who had written: 'The system of values which permits elections ... on the principle of the choice of the majority, and which bases parliamentary procedures on similar majoritarian principles was bound to provide the critical missing link between liberal individualism and the national self determination' (Mazrui 1979: 25). As an illustration of this in practice the ANC could point to the experience of South Africa's first democratic election in 1994.

The 1994 Election

The election that heralded the new South Africa was held on 27 April 1994. It was a remarkable event – remarkable in the high turn-out of voters (87%); in their patience and commitment as they waited long hours to cast their votes; in the absence of violence; in the exhilarating experience for all who participated, and in the organisational confusion. It was also remarkable in producing a 'win-win' result for the three main parties – ANC, NP and IFP. Each emerged with a sense of achievement. Finally, it was remarkable in the degree of international involvement. According to Douglas Anglin, it had 'a strong claim to be the most monitored election ever' (Anglin 1995: 519).

The TEC invited the four international organisations that were already operating in the country (UN, EC, OAU and Commonwealth) to monitor the election, with the UN again acting as co-ordinator. Unomsa's mandate was extended to cover this new role, which included voter education, ensuring freedom of movement and electioneering, checking on balanced broadcast reporting, and observing the work of the Independent Electoral Authority (IEA), the body responsible for organising the elections. The IEA itself had a direct international presence, in that five of its 16 members were selected from outside South Africa – namely from Canada, Denmark, Eritrea, the US and Zimbabwe.

The country was awash with foreign observers. Never had an election been so closely scrutinised. 'South Africa's first non-racial democratic elections', wrote Deon Geldenhuys, 'set new standards for international involvement' (Geldenhuys 1998: 91). In all there were 2,513 from the four international bodies, with the bulk under the UN banner (Anglin 1995: 525). Alongside them were another 3,000-plus observers from 97 NGOs, including jurists, trade unionists, churchmen, anti-apartheid groups and members of US black organisations. When the election was held more than 6,000 foreign observers were in place. The groups varied in their interpretation of their tasks. Douglas Anglin distinguished between what he described as 'minimalists' – who believed that they should simply stand on the sidelines as spectators – and 'maximalists', who saw themselves as political actors, influencing the course of events, rather than as passive spectators (Anglin 1995: 534). The differences rested on individual predilections and the attitude of the originating body. Of the four main organisations the Commonwealth was the most politically active and the OAU the least. The more active observers sought to anticipate and resolve problems, such as biased media coverage, the threat of the losers rejecting the election results, and the activities of dissident groups in the armed forces. In the run-up to the election they also castigated the IEA over its inept organisation, and obliged it to reform itself.

A further dramatic example of international involvement came in the IFP's last-minute decision to participate in the election. The IFP had accused the ANC and NP of monopolising the negotiations and excluding other parties. On that basis Chief Buthelezi declared that the IFP would boycott the polls, thereby creating a real danger that the violence would escalate into civil war. Sustained efforts failed – including personal appeals by Mandela and de Klerk to Buthelezi. With only a fortnight to go, in a last despairing effort, two major international figures – Henry Kissinger and Lord Carrington – were invited to lead a team of mediators. Yet again hopes were dashed. The two men discovered that the internal parties had failed even to agree on terms of reference for them. Carrington and Kissinger, therefore, packed their bags and left. Astonishingly, an international saviour appeared in the person of Professor Washington Okumu from Kenya. Okumu, who knew Buthelezi from the past, had been billed to play a support role to Kissinger and Carrington. He stayed on when the others left, and with only days to go, he achieved the breakthrough, by persuading Buthelezi that it was his Christian duty and in the interest of all South Africans to participate.

While the international contribution in achieving the new democracy was real, in the end the settlement was made by South Africans themselves. As Chris Landsberg concluded, foreign governments and organisations were only able to exert influence when the major parties had concluded that a settlement was necessary. 'If world trends were themselves a key factor in bringing them to that conclusion, so too were important domestic factors' (Landsberg 1994: 295). Even the IEA, which on occasion appeared to be in utter confusion, succeeded in organising an election that all the international observers declared as 'free and fair'. Even Judge Johann Kriegler, who headed the IEA, marvelled at the outcome: 'If you don't believe in miracles, you haven't seen an election in South Africa' (Anglin 1995: 521).

When the election results were declared the major victor was the ANC, with 63 per cent of the vote and 252 seats in the National Assembly. The NP was also reasonably satisfied with 20 per cent of the national vote (giving it 82 seats in the Assembly) and a majority in the Western Cape Province; while Inkatha gained 10.5 per cent of the national vote (43 Assembly seats) and a majority in KwaZulu/Natal Province. When the new GNU was formed Mandela became President, with Thabo Mbeki and de Klerk as Deputy Presidents and Chief Buthelezi the Minister of Home Affairs. The 'political miracle' had been achieved. A new South Africa had been born.

III
The New South Africa: Seeking an Identity

8
Principles & Practice

'When I look around the world,' declared Warren Christopher, the US Secretary of State, 'I see very few countries with greater potential to shape the 21st century than the new South Africa' (Schoeman 2000). Christopher was expressing a widely held view that further gains could be anticipated from South Africa's political 'miracle' – that it would act both as an immediate example to others and as a future pillar of strength. If, it was reasoned, a problem as intractable as apartheid could be settled by negotiation, so could others – whether they were in the Middle East, the Balkans or Northern Ireland. Even in less acute situations South Africa's experience was seen as a benchmark for desirable reforms. Thus, for example, when Mandela visited Brazil he started a debate there about improving its own race relations. The 'pillar of strength' aspect was related mainly to Africa. The high hopes of the 1960s, which had followed the emergence of new, independent states from colonial control, had given way to a sense of despair, as economic failures, military dictatorships, corruption, famine, wars and poverty disfigured much of the continent.

The despair was compounded in the early 1990s by the failure of the flamboyantly named 'Operation Rekindle Hope', when a UN 'humanitarian force', led by the US, had gone into Somalia to resolve a famine situation by restoring peace and order. It finished in disaster, with fierce fighting, resulting in the killing of Pakistani and American troops, alongside Somali militiamen. The scars of that case led to reluctance in the international community and the major Western states to involve their troops directly in Africa again, and it helps to explain why they stood aside from the Rwanda bloodbath in 1994.

Within this gloomy continental scene the emergence of the new democratic South Africa came as a beacon of light. The hopes pinned on it in relation to Africa were fourfold. First, that its economy – by far the most powerful and advanced in the continent – would act as a dynamo for the rest. Second, that the end of apartheid (and Pretoria's border wars) would lead to peace and stability in Southern Africa. Third, that South Africa's presence would reinvigorate the continent's weak multilateral organisations (notably the OAU and SADC). Finally, that Pretoria would take the lead as a continental peacemaker and keeper, by using its diplomatic, economic resources and (if necessary) its armed forces to those ends. Outside the continent these roles were presented as a means of allowing Africans to settle their own affairs. To more cynical observers, it was a way of letting the international community, and especially the West, off the African hook. Whatever the explanation it was an attractive prospect for the richer states, for it would remove a burden that had grown heavier despite (or because of) their previous efforts – whether in terms of diplomacy, or aid, or military intervention. In short, the hope was that South Africa had transformed itself from major international problem into a major asset.

The Formation of the Government of National Unity (GNU)

In South Africa, following the election, the Government of National Unity (GNU) was formed, based on the power sharing formula agreed in the negotiations. This meant that while the ANC held the majority of the ministerial posts, others were filled by leading figures from the NP and IFP, with Mandela as President, Thabo Mbeki and de Klerk Deputy Presidents, and Buthelezi Minister of Home Affairs. Mandela fully appreciated the challenge that faced the government, and the ANC ministers in particular.

> We had [he explained later] no experience of elections, of parliamentary practice and of state administration … We were taken from the bush, or from the underground outside the country, or from prisons, to come and take charge. We were suddenly into this immense responsibility of running a highly developed country (Sampson 1999: 495).

In this situation Mandela and his ministerial colleagues recognised that power sharing, which they had accepted as a compromise, had advantages. It offered an effective way of steering the government through its infant days, although it meant working with the party of apartheid, and as it transpired, the experience of the NP ministers was valuable in the GNU's early days. Better, reasoned Mandela, to start by capturing the main beachheads, from which, over time, the ANC could spread itself out. Yet at the same time the ANC as a political party was in disorder, as its leading talents moved into government, leaving the party organisation in inexperienced hands.

Not all ANC members were reconciled to compromises, such as the GNU. Some fretted at the internal constitutional arrangements, at the sharing of power, at the continued influence of white civil servants, while, within the triple alliance, Cosatu complained that the government listened too eagerly to big business. Summarising such concerns, Tokyo Sexwale, the ANC Premier of Gauteng Province, asked: 'Are we in power, or merely in office?' The answer to that question, concluded Professor Tom Lodge, was at the same time both obvious and yet elusive. It was obvious in that the new government was predominantly in the hands of the tripartite alliance, in which the ANC was the major partner. The alliance appeared, therefore, to have the power to reshape political and economic policies and situations. However, the alliance was a broad social and ideological mix: from organised labour to the rural poor; from black entrepreneurs to a mixed racial intelligentsia; from youth groups to women's organisations. In practice it was further constrained by having to operate within the capacity of the civil service, and by the need to interact with powerful business interests and civil society organisations, as well as within the GNU and the triple alliance itself. Thus, Lodge concluded, in these circumstances 'power' was an elusive concept, as no one group 'holds undisputed power' (Lodge 1999: 11).

Mandela: the President

As President, Mandela had full rein to exhibit his extraordinary combination of personal dignity and strength, combined with public warmth, humour and the ability to respond to a diversity of people and circumstances. Even de Klerk acknowledged that Mandela 'had an exceptional ability to make everyone with whom he came into contact feel special – whether they were the gardeners at the Union Buildings, or the white policemen who continued to protect him, or schoolchildren of any race or colour' (De Klerk 1998a: 346). In office Mandela was loyal to those who had contributed to the struggle, and, with some justification, was accused of being too tolerant of ANC ministers who did not match up to their jobs. The parliamentary opposition also accused him of failing to distinguish between his position as head of state and as ANC leader, and in particular of continuing using his office to seek party funds. For a time Mandela refused to answer questions on this issue, but in April 1999, shortly before he retired, he disclosed that on some foreign visits and when meeting foreign leaders at home he had sought funds for the ANC. He revealed that – among others – in 1998 King Fahad of Saudi Arabia and Saikh bin Sultan al-Nahayan of the United Arab Emirates had each donated US$10m to the party (Mills 1999: 6). However, within the party he could show his teeth when he saw injustice, or deceit, or inefficiency. At the 1996 ANC conference he attacked party officials for their wastefulness and incompetence. He told them publicly that they must mend their ways, and warned that corruption would not be tolerated.

Mandela's style was that of the gracious patrician: a natural, instinctive leader. He was a competent, not a great public orator, but in his speeches he was able to convey his personal commitment, charm and humour. He did not take easily to the routine of government, and so left much of the day-to-day business to Mbeki, but he was difficult to tie down, and was prone to arbitrary interventions. Anthony Sampson noted that:

> The President could be aloof one moment and immerse himself in detail the next. He enjoyed the personal scope – but he never worked easily with bureaucracies, and disliked paperwork ... He made the most of his easy access to the media, sounding off with strong views, and sometimes forgetting he was part of a collective Cabinet. Some commentators became alarmed, and he was accused of being a 'reckless gambler' and 'shooting from the hip' (Sampson 1999: 506).

That included foreign policy, in which, Mandela, like all leaders of states, became directly involved in an age of summits and instant communication. In his case he became a giant on the world scene. Yet even his towering international status had its downside. While it meant, noted Abdul Minty, that the new South Africa gained prominence and support that was denied to others, and while Mandela could exert exceptional personal influence, the result was to create false expectations of Pretoria's capabilities, and to impose extra burdens on an already overstretched administration.

Yet Mandela was more than a political leader or even a head of government. In seeking to reconcile the deep divisions in his own society he came to encapsulate a spirit of tolerance and hope not only at home but across the globe. In October 1994 he told the UN General Assembly that the aim of his government would be to heal past wounds, and 'to ensure that colour, race and gender become only as God given gifts to each one of us, and not as an indelible mark that accords special status to any'. He stood as an embodiment of those virtues.

The Search for a Foreign Policy

Although the GNU was based on power sharing the dominant voice was that of the ANC. Nowhere was that clearer than in foreign policy/external relations, where the ANC became the international face of the new government. The principal posts in foreign relations were filled by party members – Mandela as President; Mbeki his Deputy; the ministers in the Department of Foreign Affairs (Alfred Nzo and Aziz Pahad); and those in the related departments of Defence (Joe Modise and Ronnie Kasrils), and Trade and Industry (Alec Erwin and J. Ngwane). De Klerk had hoped to continue to participate in foreign affairs and, from time to time, he accepted personal invitations to travel abroad. These, he wrote, gave him the opportunity of 'marketing the new South Africa to the international community', and of persuading foreigners to invest in its future. But, in doing so he was acting on a personal basis, not as a formal representative of his country. That hurt him, and he complained, 'I was never asked to represent the country at international meetings' (De Klerk 1998a: 347).

Before it took office the ANC had published a number of papers and articles about future foreign policy. They included an article by Mandela in the American journal *Foreign Affairs*. (Mandela 1993: 86–97), and papers from an ANC study group, including 'Foreign Policy Perspective in a Democratic South Africa' (ANC 1993 and 1994). Although the group's papers were more detailed than Mandela's their thrust was very similar, so that together they can be seen as 'the ANC's view' of foreign policy as it came to power. In contrast a different approach was contained in a paper written by L.H. (Rusty) Evans, the Director General of the DFA. Evans, who had served the old government, was retained by Mandela as the department's senior official. Although his paper was presented as a personal opinion it provides a 'departmental view' of future policy.

The ANC View

As it came into office the ANC's position was premised on a set of moral imperatives, with human rights as the centrepiece. In Mandela's words, 'South Africa's foreign policy will be based on our belief that human rights should be the core concern of foreign policy'. Alongside that was respect for international law, a commitment to seek peace and disarmament, and to promote policies and institutions that would 'make a world safe for democracy'. The ANC's 1994 document claimed that the first principle of foreign policy was a 'belief in and preoccupation with human rights', because just and lasting solutions to problems 'can only come through the promotion of democracy worldwide'. South Africa would put human rights and democracy at the top of its priorities, and would neither be selective nor afraid to raise human rights issues, even if it was 'with countries where our own or other interests would be negatively affected' (ANC 1994).

The ANC claimed that the political prerequisites for peace and stability were democracy, freedom and respect for human rights, and went on to argue that 'rights' should extend beyond politics, to embrace economic, social and environmental concerns. The first priority was to build a stable democratic society at home, in the belief that effective democratic government was the foundation for economic as well as political success. Although not explicitly stated this approach had, at least, strong echoes of a prevailing Western assumption that democracies do not fight each other. The ANC extended that further, to the point where it claimed that the use of force by one state against another was unacceptable, and it supported the UN's commitment to 'a general and complete disarmament under effective international control'.

Despite the influence of Western ideas, the ANC continued to associate itself with the South. 'As a country of the South,' stated the study group, 'it is in our interests to ensure that the position of the South is not prejudiced in the world economy.' There was particular concern that Africa was being marginalised by an unjust global economic system. The counter to that, argued the ANC, was co-operation, which must be fostered through bodies like the OAU and SADC. In identifying future problems, the accent was again on those of the underdeveloped South – slow growth, poverty, inequality and racism. Based on those concerns the ANC identified four key policy aims – first, greater global economic equality; second, support for international institutions; third, a commitment to disarmament; and fourth, fulfilment of an African destiny.

Mandela and his colleagues accepted that South Africa needed external investment, but he claimed it would not be gained by kow-towing to the rich. For example, while he sympathised with the broad principles of GATT he concluded that the applications might not be in South Africa's interests. 'We are not prepared', he stated, 'to place the demands of the global community ahead of the desires and needs of our people.' Yet, the ANC strongly supported international organisations. It envisaged the UN and its agencies playing a pivotal role in international affairs, by the peaceful resolution of disputes, extending the remit of international law, seeking greater economic equality and promoting human rights. To achieve these ends the ANC advocated a revision in the UN's structure, to make it more democratic and less dominated by the rich and powerful.

Further, the ANC assumed that international organisations should play a leading part in security matters, and that 'security' should not be confined to military concerns, but should embrace economic and social matters. Physical security would be gained 'through adherence to international law, the peaceful settlement of disputes, common security arrangements and region wide disarmament'. The only exception to the prohibition of the use of force should be in peacekeeping operations and self-defence against armed attack. As a result the ANC envisaged a substantial reduction in defence spending, thereby releasing funds for social needs. It undertook to examine the arms industry, created by the apartheid regime, in the light of responsible global citizenship, which would 'have priority over considerations of the arms industry'.

The ANC reasserted that the new South Africa's destiny lay in Africa, where South Africa's foreign policy would reach its full fruition. 'We dedicate our foreign policy', stated the study group, 'to helping to ensure that Africa's people are not forgotten or ignored by humankind.' Special attention would be given to Southern African neighbours, who had contributed so much to the liberation struggle. Mandela claimed that the colonial economy – by subordinating the neighbours to the status of labour reserves and client markets for capitalism – was responsible for South Africa's regional pre-eminence. The new government would, he claimed, avoid domination and 'resist any pressure or temptation to pursue its own interests at the expense of the rest of southern Africa'. Pretoria would shoulder its regional responsibility, 'not in a spirit of paternalism or dominance but with mutual tolerance and respect'. Hegemonic ambitions were dismissed. The ANC's watchwords were co-operation and equality.

Alongside the mainstream ANC views were those of the other alliance members. One example was an article published in *The African Communist* by Raymond Suttner. Suttner – a SACP member, who became an MP in 1994, and chaired the parliamentary Foreign Affairs Committee – was mainly concerned with the new world order. He did not like what he saw. He regretted the collapse of the Soviet bloc and the current dominance of the West. The US, 'the pre-eminent imperialist military power', and its capitalist followers were increasingly dominating international bodies. As a result, continued Suttner, they were able to employ their armed forces under the cloak of UN respectability, and 'to impose a universal conception of economic development and growth', through the IMF and World Bank. In response to this 'unfavourable international environment', he urged the government to stand firm against a global order 'which might aim to subvert South Africa's independence, reconstruction and internal liberty', and 'to throw its weight behind those forces committed to struggling against the injustices of the so called new world order'. Suttner went on to underline the tripartite nature of the alliance, noting that the SACP and Cosatu had 'a foreign policy potential, a potential that is crucial at this time of the decline of the left'. He feared that the mix of parties in the GNU would lead to compromise and policy obfuscation. He concluded, therefore, that the alliance, as distinct from the government, needed 'to conduct its own international relations'. In doing so it 'would be able to make essential interventions that may be too sensitive or unsuitable for the government'. Suttner's article could be seen as a warning – a radical shot across the government's bows.

A Departmental View

'Rusty' Evans – the senior DFA official – presented his paper to a seminar in Pretoria University. Like Suttner Evans's main concern (although from a very different viewpoint) was Pretoria's position within the post-Cold War world. Evans started his paper by noting the apartheid government's unhappy international experience, in which it had constantly been on the defensive. He recognised that the emergence of a new democratic government had changed that, while, at the same time, the collapse of the Soviet bloc had removed the communist threat to Africa. Evans saw both as major advances, but they were only part of the story. He warned that the new international order was unstable – characterised by uncertainty, confusion and contradiction. Yet, argued Evans, South Africa could not isolate itself from the uncertainty. It was 'only a medium to low priority partner', and, while it enjoyed some influence, it could not play a major role in shaping the international order, nor could it afford to be out of step with the dominant West on major issues. As a result it was obliged to operate within a set of parameters largely determined for it. Foreign policy, he stated, is 'not a one-sided affair, but a question of interaction with other countries and it is multi-dimensional'.

With such considerations in mind Evans believed that it was essential to have good relations with the US (the only superpower) and with the European Community (South Africa's main trading partner). Also, because foreign investment was needed, it was important to establish working relationship with the leading financial and banking institutions – including commercial bodies, the World Bank, the IMF and the African Development Bank. Yet, although Evans recognised the importance of the Western states and institutions, he had no illusions about them. He noted how they had formed powerful blocs, thereby obliging poorer states to 'compete with each other in providing the industrialised nations with primary products and resources, often at unreasonable prices, and in some cases to become the industrial dumping ground'.

Nor did he see an easy road ahead, especially for Africa. 'There should', he said, 'be no illusions about the marginalisation of Africa.' At international conferences the message was that 'there is no hope for Africa'. Although that was an unfair judgement, Evans concluded that South Africa could not escape from 'a reality, which creates a series of common interests, needs and problems'. If, for example, order collapsed in neighbouring states Pretoria would face major refugee problems. Evans's attitude to Africa was one of resignation and hard-headed calculation. Yet, as he saw South Africa as a major continental power, he advocated taking the bull by the horns and adopting a leadership role both in the continent and in international organisations that were relevant to Africa's needs – such as the Food and Agriculture Organisation and the World Health Organisation. Although he approached regional matters from a different angle, Evans, like the ANC, concluded that Pretoria had to dispel its neighbours' fears by promoting mutually beneficial economic and security arrangements and initiating constructive co-operative ventures.

Idealism and Realism: The Two Sides of the Foreign Policy Coin

It is easy to understand why – coming from such contrasting backgrounds and experiences – the ANC and Evans adopted different approaches. Mandela and his colleagues had sacrificed themselves for a moral cause and fought a prolonged liberation struggle for their beliefs. On his release from prison in 1990 Mandela had repeated the ringing declaration he made at his trial, when he spoke of 'the ideal of a democratic and free society in which all people live in harmony and with equal opportunities ... It is an ideal for which I am prepared to die' (Mandela 1978: 175). For Mandela and the great bulk of the ANC the driving force of politics had been a moral struggle to end racial oppression and build a new democratic society. Their cause had been based on universal principles of right and wrong, not the messy compromises and the give and take of day-to-day politics and government. It was with that driving force in mind that they laid out their ideas for future foreign policy.

Evans's background was very different. He had risen through the diplomatic ranks of a government facing persistent international condemnation, in which its foreign policy was a prolonged, frustrating effort to defend its status and security. In a hostile world, apartheid South Africa had constantly been on the defensive, its beliefs and values rejected. It had survived by making what deals it could, overt and covert, by rejecting the mainstream of international values, and by aggression against its neighbours (Barber and Barratt 1990).

The approach adopted by the ANC can broadly be classified as 'idealism'. Idealism concentrates on what 'ought to be', and in doing so seeks to change what 'is'. Graham Evans (no relation to Rusty) and Jeffrey Newham stated that idealism 'stresses the importance of moral values, legal norms, internationalism and harmony of interests as guides to foreign policy making, rather than the considerations of national interest and power'. Idealists, they continued, emphasise the need for peace and the peaceful settlement of disputes; they believe that peace is both achievable and indivisible; they have faith in reason and conscience as sources of international behaviour; and they are advocates of collective security. Further, they assume that the conditions within a state can be projected into international politics – that the values and principles of their own society can be replicated elsewhere (Evans and Newham 1992). In the ANC's case it reasoned that as it had achieved a settlement with the vile apartheid regime it could do business with anybody. In that spirit it declared itself ready to establish links with all members of the international community, through the policy of 'universality'. As explained to parliament's Foreign Affairs Committee, 'universality' was an attempt to de-ideologise foreign policy, so that relations could be established 'with all countries without implying support for their internal or external policies' (NA-FPC 1995).

In contrast Rusty Evans's 'departmental' views can be classified as 'neo-realist'. As the name implies 'neo-realism' is a development of the 'realist' approach to international relations, which was based on the assumptions that, within an anarchic international system, states are the main actors, and 'power' the central concept. Although other actors are involved, for realists states remain the dominant players, and although they vary greatly in size, strength and capacity all pursue their national interests in a constant search for security and prosperity.

Advocates of 'neo-realism' build on those premises, by moving the main focus of attention from individual states to that of the structure in which states operate. That structure provides the boundaries of the international system and shapes the behaviour of those inside it. The success or failure of a state to gain its ends depends on how it relates to the structure and to those within it. Those states that successfully fit in rise to the top; those that don't sink. 'The game one has to win', wrote Kenneth Waltz, 'is defined by the structures that determines the type of player that is likely to prosper.' The ability of states to achieve their ends is determined by their capacity and skill when acting in the context of the structure. Thus, although the neo-realists accept that the system is anarchic, the structure provides a dynamic setting for interaction, and explains change and relationships in a way that cannot be achieved by concentrating on individual states (Waltz 1979: 96).

Although the ANC and departmental approaches have been presented here separately, they are better understood as comprising the two sides of the foreign policy coin. One side reflects the state's interests and values, which the government seeks to translate in universal terms; the other side concerns the international setting in which a state pursues its interests and values. While idealists are eager to project values and principles, realists are more concerned with external constraints and opportunities, including the way the state is perceived by and subject to the reactions of other international actors. However, both approaches have their part in foreign policy making. Governments vary in the emphasis they put on one side rather than the other, but none can ignore both sides of the coin.

Policy Implementation: Charting a Course through a Troubled Sea

Initially, therefore, Mandela's government stressed its ethical principles. It came to power believing that it would be 'a symbol of democracy and human rights ... an even handed friend of all, as epitomised by the underlying spirit of "universality"' (Mills 2000: 252). Shortly after taking office Mandela asked the US Congress whether each state should not 'begin to define the national interest to include the happiness of others', and 'cease to treat tyranny, instability and poverty anywhere as being peripheral to our interests and our future?' (Olivier and Geldenhuys, 1997: 364). Admirable as such sentiments were the new government was soon wrestling with the constraints imposed on it by the external setting and so left itself open to accusations of inconsistency, failure to implement its claims and double standards. The implementation of policy – whether it is overtly based on ethical grounds or not – involves compromise, uncertainty and an element of inconsistency. An image of policy makers following a predetermined set of rules, whatever the circumstances, is misleading. Not only are ethical standards open to dispute in themselves, it is impossible for any government to apply the same standards in every situation. In policy and decision-making, a variety of motives are present, involving both principles and constraints. As Michael Howard wrote, international political activity 'takes place on a two dimensional field – a field which can be defined by the co-ordinates of ethics and power' (Howard 1977: 374).

This is not to suggest that Mandela's government should have abandoned its principles, but rather that in applying them it was obliged to operate within the limits of its domestic and external settings. Like all governments Mandela's had to decide in each case whether or not to act, and if it did act in what way and what resources to employ. And, as with other governments, alongside its ethical concerns, it pursued what it perceived to be its 'national interest'. Chris Brown has argued convincingly that in decision-making each case has to be judged on its merits, and the 'judgement will sometimes involve a tough minded acknowledgement that there are wrongs that cannot be righted'. Brown wrote that a 'decision whether to act in a particular case rests on a judgement of the circumstances in the case, and those circumstances necessarily include interests – there is no reason to think that there is anything inherently immoral about this'. He concluded that 'there is no viable universal moral rule that can tell statespersons what is the right thing to do in response to particular circumstances; they must exercise their judgement as best they can' (Brown 2001: 16–19).

While struggling to handle the situation the ANC's dominance in foreign policy making did not always lead to a uniformity of approach or effective co-ordination. There were too many fingers in the policy making pie to avoid at least a degree of confusion – Mandela, Mbeki, ministers and officials from the DFA, the DTI and Defence – and there were regular complaints (in the media, at conferences, and even inside the ANC) of contradictions, confusion and bureaucratic rivalries. The complaints were both about policy content (or lack of it) and implementation. Writing in 1997, Greg Mills, the Director of the South African Institute of International Affairs, stated that the government had no clear orientation or strategic purpose. He wrote of the danger of it 'developing a self image as a benign fairy godmother', full of good intentions, wanting to be the friends of all, but without the wherewithal to achieve these ends. He recognised that the ANC had fought a great moral cause, but claimed that in government it had lost its ability to discriminate by trying to treat all comers equally. It was, he argued, trying to be all things to all men. 'Unless', Mills concluded, 'South Africa is to end up with an insolvent foreign policy, it will have to define and prioritise its objectives and take cognisance both of its own limits and the nature of the world outside' (Mills 1997: 4).

Conrad Strauss, the Chairman of Standard Bank, expressed similar doubts. He spoke of the government's foreign policy aims and its attempts to implement them, with the clear implication that it had failed on both counts. He argued that the government should develop a coherent world picture, which would enable it to identify and pursue its aims and interests, based on a realistic assessment of its strengths and weaknesses, its opportunities and constraints. With regard to policy implementation, Strauss criticised Pretoria's confused chain of decision making, its refusal to take the lead in the Southern African region, and its failure 'to enhance investment and trading opportunities' (Strauss 1997).

Denis Venter, from the Africa Institute, added his voice to the critics, by stating that the heart of the problem was a 'lack of a clear "conception of the self"'. For Venter, the ambiguity lay in the image of national identity, which Archbishop Tutu had captured in his catchphrase 'the rainbow nation'. Although, argued Venter, this may have helped to create an internal sense of identity, it was no guide for foreign policy making, because the government could not afford a 'rainbow' foreign policy – 'it cannot be everything to everyone' (Venter 1997: 78).

Complaints were also heard about the internal workings of the government, and the DFA in particular. The criticism was directed at the top down. Alfred Nzo, the Foreign Minister, was accused of lacking drive and initiative, so that the department's views were ignored at cabinet level. As a result, the President, Deputy President and more forceful ministers and departments filled the vacuum in policy making. The size and distribution of DFA staff also became caught in controversy. The department was partly reorganised and restaffed to reflect both the new political dispensation, and the new range of responsibilities, as diplomatic contacts multiplied. Alongside the new Ambassadors and High Commissioners the DFA absorbed 140 ANC members who had gained diplomatic experience abroad. It also inherited 415 diplomats from the Bantustans, some of whom gained a reputation for idleness and inefficiency. One DFA official claimed that the only thing heard from their desks 'is the rustling of newspapers'. When, in March 1996 the department announced 188 redundancies, 138 were from the former homelands (Mills 1996). Yet, while staff changes took place, initially they were not dramatic. Under the terms of the interim constitution, many of the existing 1,900 DFA staff were retained, and for a time most senior posts remained in white hands. For the first two years of the new government they included the reappointment of Rusty Evans as Director General – from 114 applicants for the post (Muller 1997: 64).

The staffing situation was criticised from both sides – from those who thought that the changes had gone too far, and those who believed they had not gone far enough. Gerrit Olivier, who had worked in the DFA, claimed that because of restructuring and affirmative action the government had 'lost the cream of its experienced career diplomats' while 'it was expanding at an unprecedented scale'. Olivier was concerned at the replacement of experienced white officials by less experienced blacks, and complained that in the DFA 'personnel policy enjoyed precedence over foreign policy' (Olivier and Geldenhuys 1997: 35). In contrast, others complained at the continuing influence of white officials. For example, Barbara Masekela, the Ambassador to France, criticised the slowness of the integration of ANC diplomats into the service. She said that she was 'fighting for changes in the way the things are done', and was trying to engender 'a culture of democracy in a system run on hierarchies and turf' (Muller 1997:

69). Criticism was also directed at Rusty Evans, who, as part of the discredited old white guard, was accused of failing to respond to the political change by transforming the department's personnel, attitudes and working practices. Evans, in his turn, had to deal with white officials concerned about their future, and black officials complaining that whites were filling most of the senior posts. On a different tack the Parliamentary Foreign Affairs Committee complained that the DFA spent a disproportionate amount of its resources on representation in the advanced West, while much less was spent in Africa, despite the government's claims that the continent was its first priority.

When put together this litany of complaints sounds formidable. However, although there was some justification for the criticisms the overall picture was not so bleak. To start with, the ANC – as noted above – did set out broad principles on which to base its foreign policy. They may have been idealistic, but they were a genuine attempt to establish guidelines. Apart from that, however, all governments, and not just the fledgling South Africa, were having difficulty in making their way in the post-Cold War world. Uncertainty reigned as established signposts shifted or disappeared. It was, therefore, an especially difficult time for the new government to orientate itself. First, there was fundamental change at home, as new ministers, parliamentarians and officials introduced new policies and values. Second, the country's international position underwent a fundamental shift as it moved from pariah to paragon within the new, uncertain world order. Whether they had served the old apartheid regime or been part of the liberation struggle, officials found themselves having to operate in new political environments at home and abroad. Nzo, who was more astute than his sleepy cartoon image suggested, told a meeting in Copenhagen in March 1995:

> The end of the Cold War has created a new global situation in which our young democracy must find its feet. The new world order, if it exists at all, is fraught with uncertainties and insecurities. Ideological conflict has to a large extent been replaced by economic competition, the rules for which have not yet been fully agreed upon. The ground beneath our feet is not firm: it is volatile and unpredictable (DFA 1996).

As Robert Schrire and Daniel Silke wrote: 'In historical terms, it is very rare for the basic inter-state relations to change dramatically. It is only somewhat less unusual for the domestic arrangements within a state to change fundamentally' (Schrire and Silke 1997:13). Yet, in South Africa's case, with the end of the Cold War and the demise of apartheid, both happened simultaneously. It was an extraordinary and demanding situation, calling for ingenuity, flexibility and resilience. While overall the government scored reasonably well in meeting these challenges, inevitably there was an element of confusion, some loss of efficiency, and ministers and officials who failed to live up to the challenges.

Even in calmer times, the vagaries and uncertainties of international affairs make it impossible for a government to lay down a precise foreign policy in advance. James Mayall concluded: 'Most countries make up their foreign policy as they go along, mainly because though their interests may remain constant, the circumstances to which they must react are not' (Mayall 2000: 80). Frequently a government will find itself responding to unforeseen events and developments, and having to modify its original intentions and/or give priority to others. Abraham Lincoln confessed: 'I have never dictated events. Events have dictated me' (Morris 1999: 115).

Another area of uncertainty concerns the resources available to the government, and whether it is prepared and able to employ them specific circumstances. Depending on its interests it has to decide on what resources it will commit, and how they will be committed. It may be constrained by the inappropriateness of the resources available, or it may simply choose not to commit them, either in part or in whole. For example, while Mandela's government retained powerful armed forces it was not prepared to use them in the same way as its white predecessor. A further consideration is that a state cannot create its own external status and image. They are dependent on the judgement of others – on the views, values and interests of other states, organisations and the media – both in general terms and in response to individual events. In the case of Mandela's government it gained widespread sympathy and support, but even so differences arose. These became clear when interests clashed, as in the trade negotiations with the European Union. At the same time the delight elsewhere in Southern Africa at the overthrow of apartheid was interleaved with concern among the neighbours that Pretoria would still dominate the scene, even if in a different way from the white regime.

Finally, an obvious point is that foreign policy is shaped by the domestic as well as the international setting, and acts as a link between the two. Domestic considerations shape the values, principles and interests that are pursued, and provide the resources that are available in pursuit of policy aims. Taking account of the factors noted above, foreign policy can often be understood most clearly in retrospect. Frequently it comes about through the accumulation of day-to-day decisions and actions, which may seem to be separate in themselves, but over time create a pattern and direction. As a result a government may be said to have a foreign policy 'orientation' (as opposed to a predetermined policy), which offers a guide to its current and future policy and development.

Pressures, Limitations and Choice

Ministerial statements soon revealed that the new government was obliged to come to terms with the setting in which it operated. Taking three ministerial examples – Alfred Nzo, the Foreign Minister; Aziz Pahad, the Deputy Foreign Minister, and Joe Modise, the Minister of Defence – it is striking that despite the differences between them (based on personality, experience and ministerial portfolio) a common factor was a growing appreciation of the external constraints they faced in seeking to implement government policy.

Alfred Nzo, a quiet, understated figure, was an ANC veteran, who was deeply imbued with the values and principles of the liberation movement. In his 1995 annual budget report to the National Assembly he restated the party's idealised objectives. He spoke of the country acting as a responsible global citizen, promoting peace, human rights, democracy and helping its neighbours. He confirmed the government's identification with the South and with Africa. 'South Africa', he stated, 'is an African country, actively committed to and involved in the development of our continent' (NA 18.5.95: 444). In the following year, he picked out for special mention South Africa's contributions to the UN's efforts in arms control, human rights and refugees, and spoke of the government's financial contribution of R28m to the UN peace mission to Angola; its part as a SADC member in restoring peace to Lesotho; and its co-operation with Mozambique. These were all upbeat, positive steps.

Yet even Nzo started to sound notes of caution, and to stress South Africa's own interests. In 1996 he spoke of the volatile and unpredictable international scene. In these circumstances, he stated, the government had to dedicate itself to the national interest.

> Ideological conflict [he continued] has to a large extent been replaced by economic competition, the rules for which have not yet been fully agreed upon ... Yet it is our primary task to secure and promote the sovereign integrity of the South African state, as well as the security and welfare of its citizens. These are the considerations which ultimately determine everything we do in the conduct of foreign relations (DFA 1996).

He also spoke of 'certain realities we dare not ignore'; such as the realisation that the US and the G7 'are the power bases of the world today, and essential to our economic well being'. To achieve economic development there was, he argued, no choice but to participate in the global competition for investments and markets. In summarising the government's position he struck a strong 'realist' note, stating that: 'Our primary objectives are the promotion and protection of South Africa's sovereignty and independence, as well as the security and welfare of our citizens' (NA 18.6.96: 3161).

Nzo's deputy, Aziz Pahad, was also a seasoned member of the liberation struggle, whose years in exile had brought him close to Mbeki, and left him conscious of the importance of external setting. In 1996 Pahad concluded: 'Our understanding of the international community and the dynamics of it has still to catch up with some of the realities we are confronted with.' He spoke of a rapidly changing world, in which South Africa must accept that 'interests are not the same as influence, and that influence cannot be treated theoretically'. The luxury of absolutism, he declared, was not available because South Africa's ability to gain its objectives was constrained by its limited resources and by internal and external obstacles. Despite that, the aim was to 'get results' (NA 18.6.96 –3202).

Joe Modise had been commander of MK from 1967 to the election in 1994. That experience, plus his appointment as Minster of Defence, concentrated his attention on the dangers and uncertainties surrounding the country. He did not ignore values, and underlined his commitment to the government's transparency, to civilian control, to the transformation of the armed forces, and to support for neighbouring states. However, Modise's main concern was Pretoria's ability to counter potential threats. 'We need', he said in 1995, 'to appreciate that threats, if left unchecked, can lead to a crisis', and, he added, 'the absence of an immediate war threat does not guarantee peace.' He spoke of the uncertain post-Cold War world, of competing interests, trade wars, ethnic conflicts and the collapse of states. He argued that because of this unpredictability – not least in Africa – it was essential to prepare for a range of threats. There was, Modise concluded, no hiding place from conflict elsewhere on the continent. 'Africa', he said, 'expects us to assume our regional responsibility. We are an important partner with the capability and resources to assist in the protection of our region. All threats to the region are threats to ourselves' (NA 21.6.95: 3079).

Although Modise accepted that reductions must be made in the defence budget; he queried the size of the cuts. He noted that in 1989 military expenditure had represented 4.5 per cent of GDP; whereas by 1997 it was only 1.6 per cent. Enough, he said, was enough. His constant plea was that the forces must be trained and equipped to counter new situations. He saw defence as the nation's insurance policy, 'and the extent of that insurance depends on what we invest in it'. South Africa, he argued, could not afford to have second-rate forces, because no commitment was 'too great, no premium too high to defend that freedom so dearly won and to safeguard our nation's future' (NA 21.6.97: 3081).

9
Learning the Hard Way

The constitutional achievement at home, plus Mandela's personal magnetism – 'Madiba magic' as it became known – eased the new South Africa's way into the international community. After May 1994, claimed Mandela, 'you only have to say "I am a South African", whether you are black or white, and the doors of the world are open to you'. Steps were taken to reinstate the government into the international community, and it was enthusiastically welcomed at multi-national organisations.

The new government also enjoyed some early foreign policy successes in line with its ethical principles. In the Southern African region it provided support for the 1994 Mozambique elections when they ran into problems. Then, working with Botswana and Zimbabwe – under wing of the Southern African Development Community (SADC) – it made a peaceful and successful intervention in Lesotho, where political divisions threatened to destabilise that country. As part of the Lesotho settlement, agreement was reached by which King Moshoeshoe II was reinstated as monarch. In Angola Pretoria also made several attempts to bring the warring parties together, but in this case without success. At the same time, Pretoria was prominent in SADC development schemes, such as efforts to co-ordinate the region's water resources. A start was also made in reorganising and reorientating the armed forces for peace making and keeping duties. When Alfred Nzo visited Norway in May 1995, he emphasised that the government favoured diplomacy over military power, but that, as soon as its forces were retrained, it would be eager to participate in African peacekeeping operations mounted by the UN or OAU (SAIRR 1995/6: 40).

Yet not all was success. As the ministerial statements in the last chapter indicate, the government was brought face to face with direct challenges to its hopes and ideals. Four cases of challenges are discussed in this chapter – the arms trade; the two-China policy; Nigeria and human rights, and military intervention in Lesotho. In each case the government had to seek a way through a maze of conflicting interests, values and principles, and to evaluate the resources it was able and willing to allocate.

Arms sales

In response to its international isolation and the UN arms embargo, the apartheid government had built up a substantial arms industry. Subsidised by the government, it had grown rapidly during the 1980s, with the increased military activity on the borders and the influence of securocrats inside P.W. Botha's government. By 1989 Armscor (Armaments Corporation of South Africa) – the government agency responsible for the development, production and procurement of weapons – employed 130,000 people, including many skilled scientists and technicians. It also controlled ten affiliated industrial subsidiaries, and it distributed work to 1,000 private subcontractors. In short, it was a major industrial enterprise. As well as supplying Pretoria's own forces, Armscor had developed export markets. Because of international sanctions, the scale and destinations of the sales were not revealed, but the government boasted openly about its thriving industry. Together with routine items, like small arms and armoured vehicles, Armscor established niches of excellence, including a mobile 155 mm gun, an attack helicopter, the Rooivalk, bush warfare vehicles and mine detectors, so that in some areas 'South African equipment was considered to be amongst the best in the world' (Flint 1998: 172).

In the period of negotiations (1990–94) and with the end of involvement in border wars, military activity and influence declined, resulting in substantial cuts in the defence budget. The cuts continued under the new government, which anticipated that it would live in harmony with its neighbours. As a result, between 1990 and 1999, defence spending plunged by more than 50 per cent. Inevitably that led to a marked reduction in demand for arms and military equipment for the armed forces. Purchases of arms and equipment, which had peaked at R3.6bn in 1989/90, had been cut to R1.75bn by 1996/7 (Mills and Edmonds 2000). For South Africa itself the reduced expenditure was part of the 'peace dividend', which followed from improved relations with its neighbours and the end of the Soviet threat. However, for the arms industry it meant fewer home sales. It responded by focusing more attention on commercial activities, especially exports. In 1992 it was split into two parts, whereby Armscor retained responsibility for the overall co-ordination of the industry and of procurement for South Africa's own forces; while a separate commercial organisation, Denel, was made responsible for arms sales and manufacturing. The Denel management, with slogans like 'Creating wealth, Protecting the Nation', set out to increase exports and establish joint enterprises with foreign companies.

Inevitably the ANC was suspicious of an arms industry that had served the apartheid regime, had breached UN resolutions, had kept its activities secret, and whose board, at the beginning of 1994, 'remained exclusively white, male and Afrikaans' (Batchelor and Willett 1998: 86). The industry was on the ANC's list of matters to be investigated for reform. Added to that, under the GNU, a new integrated National Defence Force (SANDF) was being moulded into shape by merging the forces of the old apartheid regime, the liberation movements and the 'homeland' armies. As a result a high proportion of the diminished defence budget went on personnel, leaving little for the procurement of arms and equipment.

Kadar Asmal (who became Minister of Water Affairs and Forestry in

Mandela's government) was among the leading ANC critics of the arms industry. In 1993 he wrote of the misery and corruption associated with the global arms trade, and the way it had debased the Third World through violence and its support for totalitarian regimes. He accepted the state's need to equip its own forces, and that arms might be sold to countries 'with democratic traditions'. However, he concluded: 'Our future foreign policy cannot be determined by shadowy merchants of death in foreign countries.' He called for an open debate about the industry. Personally, he hoped that the industry could be transformed to turn swords into ploughshares. He stated that he favoured parliamentary supervision of arms sales, and added that the sales should be limited to countries that respect human rights. Nor was Asmal alone in his concern. Shortly after taking up office, even the militant Ronnie Kasrils, the Deputy Defence Minister, spoke of the 'foul state' of the apartheid regime's arms industry (SAIRR 1993/4: 308). Kasrils also wrote of the need for stricter control, as the old South Africa had been accused of sales in 'grey markets' and to states with poor human rights records.

There were attempts to introduce an ethical dimension into sales even under de Klerk's government. In 1993, for instance, Denel was refused permission to sell arms worth R45m to Rwanda and Burundi, where bitter civil wars waged. It was, however, under the new government that the issue came to the fore. From the beginning there were counter-pressures. Criticism within the ANC was balanced by views setting the industry in a wider context. Ronnie Kasrils exemplified this, for while he pointed to the industry's murky past, he also noted that it was a repository of expertise in high technology, a major employer of labour and an earner of foreign currency. He concluded that the defence industry should be considered 'as a national asset', which can be of 'significant value, both economically and strategically' (Kasrils 1996: 124/5). Encouraged by such views, and helped by the lifting of the UN arms embargo in 1994, and by the continuation of government export incentives (perhaps from bureaucratic inertia or from the right hand of government not knowing what the left hand was doing), the industry was now able to sell aggressively and openly. For example, in November 1992 it launched Dexsa (Defence Exposition of South Africa), and in the following year participated at arms exhibitions at Dubai and Lima (Flint 1998: 175). The result, as Jacklyn Cock noted, was that arms sales continued to rise despite the change of government (Cock 1996: 23).

However, the ANC's concern intensified again when it was discovered that the industry was continuing its old clandestine ways. In one case a naval officer, Commodore Willem Ehlers (a former Private Secretary to P.W. Botha) negotiated sales worth US$40m, ostensibly for Zaire, but probably for transfer to Rwanda (Ellis 1996: 178). Then, in September 1994, it was discovered that Denel was covertly shipping guns to the Yemen without government approval. Outraged, the government responded by appointing a commission, under Justice Cameron, to investigate the production and sale of arms. When the commission reported it gave a damning indictment of the industry's practices, its secrecy and duplicity. The commission found an organisational culture 'steeped in the duplicity of the arms embargo and its consequent evasions and untruths' (Cameron 1995: 64). Calling for a comprehensive review of the industry, the report concluded that Armscor's values were so flawed that in searching for markets it had shown little or no concern about the final destination of the arms. The commission recommended that three senior Armscor officials be prosecuted for fraud and negligence (in the event all three were allowed to resign). Looking to the future the commission underlined the importance of ensuring respect for human rights and democracy, by banning sales to repressive and authoritarian regimes. 'The ethical, political, legal and strategic reasons for exercising restraint', it concluded, 'should take precedence over the economic and commercial motivation for selling arms' (Cock 1996: 26).

The Cameron Commission had endorsed values proclaimed by the ANC. However, that left the government with a dilemma that confronts all states that have arms industries: that of finding a balance between its values and its economic interests. Following receipt of the commission's report, the government tried to bring the industry under much tighter control, by creating a cabinet committee to oversee the industry, and a weapons control body – the National Conventional Arms Control Committee (NCACC), with Kadar Asmal in the chair. Yet, while those moves encouraged the critics, the arms trade also had its supporters, outside as well as inside the industry. The supporters pointed to its importance for the domestic economy; to its record in terms of employment, to the technological skills and industrial development it fostered, and to the foreign currency it earned. They claimed that a doubling of export sales would bring the country an additional R1bn and create 50,000 more jobs. To the economic arguments were added diplomatic and security considerations. Joe Modise, the Minister of Defence, claimed 'that the backbone of a going and independent state is a robust military, supported by a vibrant arms industrial base' (Batchelor and Willett 1998: 115). Kasrils asserted that the industry helped to deter aggressors and so contributed to the country's safety, while enhancing its political influence and stature (Gutteridge 1996). Encouraged by such support, Denel announced plans to expand exports by 300 per cent in five years, thereby capturing 2 per cent of the global arms market instead of the current 0.4 per cent.

The situation was, therefore, one of tension between critics who wanted a tight ethical framework for arms exports, and those who favoured a more flexible approach with an emphasis on increased sales. The result was confusion. In its attempts to regulate matters, the NCACC decided to classify both the arms that were for sale and the states that wanted to buy them. The arms were divided into four categories – from 'A' (sensitive equipment of major significance) to 'D' (non-lethal equipment). Despite the new regulations, it transpired that more than half the new sales were in category 'A'. There was further dispute over the categorisation of states. At first the committee decided to divide them as 'acceptable' or 'not acceptable', based on their human rights record, their compliance with international law and their internal situation. It was not an easy task, and when it drew up its first lists it included as 'acceptable' Rwanda, Kenya, Thailand, Chile, Colombia, and both the People's Republic of China and Taiwan; whereas the 'not acceptable' included Nigeria, Afghanistan, Burundi and Sudan. Further attempts at fine-tuning included an evaluation of the type of arms to be supplied in the light of local circumstances, and South Africa's 'national interest' was added as a further criterion, which smacked of 'realpolitik', not of ethics. Controversy and confusion reigned.

The classification was soon abandoned as too rigid and complex, and instead a 'case by case' approach was introduced. Even then difficulties and uncertainty arose. For example, in 1995 the NCACC turned down a R1.2bn arms deal with Turkey because of human rights concerns. However, early in 1997 Kadar Asmal announced that the ban had been lifted because politically it was in the national interest. The saga continued, for when in August 1997 Turkey again applied to buy 12 helicopters, the NCACC rejected it. Further confusion followed in the case of Syria. In January 1997 the cabinet gave conditional approved for a R3bn arms sale, but the US, which viewed Syria as a 'terrorist state', protested strongly, and threatened to withdraw all foreign assistance if the sale went ahead. Pretoria was deeply resentful, viewing the American intervention as arrogant and as an infringement of its sovereignty, but reluctantly it decided that its interests were best served by bending to the superpower. It pocketed its pride, and put the Syrian order on ice. There were, however no US objections when Denel opened negotiations with Saudi Arabia to sell G6 (155 mm) artillery units in a deal that was rumoured to be worth up to US$1.5bn.

The Syrian sale was not the only problem with the US. Although Washington was now dealing with a new government it continued to impose arms sanctions against South African because of illegal trading during apartheid days. In October 1991 the US Justice Department brought a case against a subsidiary of Armscor, in which (between 1978 and 1989) it was accused of conspiring with an American company (International Signal and Control Company) to smuggle more than $30m of military technology – including missile components, and night vision equipment – to South Africa, and subsequently to sell some on to Iraq. The hard line taken by the Americans in the case may in part be explained by Pretoria's continued contacts with 'rogue states'. Whatever the reason, as the court case and the US sanctions dragged on, so difficulties arose for the South Africans. For example, Pretoria believed that it lost the chance of selling the Rooivalk helicopter to Britain because vital components that were needed to bring it up to required Nato standards were subject to American export controls (Flint 1998: 177/8).

Despite such problems South African weapons continued to be spread widely. In 1998, for example, sales (in descending order of spending) were made to the following: Algeria, US, Thailand, Switzerland, Rwanda, Peru, Denmark, Colombia, Brazil and Australia (Mills and Edmonds 2000). At first it was assumed that Mandela would be numbered among the opponents of the industry, and certainly he believed in tight civilian control and supervision. However, shortly after taking office, he told a television audience that it would be unfair to say that the country should not sell arms. 'Arms are for the purpose of defending the sovereignty and integrity of a country. From that angle there is nothing wrong with having a trade in arms' (Batchelor and Willett 1998: 128). Subsequently he opened the first Dexsa exhibition, stating that arms sales could help to fund development, and he was prepared to promote sales on his trips abroad. That led to controversy. In July 1997 he visited Indonesia, a country with a poor human rights record. Although he urged the Indonesian leader, President Suharto, to extend democratic rights to the people of East Timor, who were then living under Indonesia's oppressive control, Mandela agreed to supply arms for 'external defence'. He may have hoped to use the sales to gain influence with Suharto, but critics pointed out that not only had he agreed to sell arms to a corrupt, dictatorial regime, but the equipment could be used against the people of East Timor.

A further source of dispute arose over whether to sell arms to neighbouring Southern African states. Pierre Steyn, the Secretary for Defence, argued in favour, claiming that it was both economically and politically advantageous to do so. It would, he argued, reduce Africa's dependence on US and European arms suppliers. It would also help to 'expand South Africa's influence across the continent', thereby providing greater political leverage. If used judiciously, he argued that 'arms sales can prove valuable both economically and politically', nowhere more so than in Africa (Steyn 1996: 129). Opposed to that view were those who believed that encouraging neighbours to buy arms would divert their resources away from development, lead to greater regional instability and intensify concern about Pretoria's hegemonic ambitions. In the event the neighbours resolved the issue by not purchasing from South Africa, perhaps because of their fear arising from its past domination (Batchelor and Willett 1998: 129/30).

The internal arms sales controversy was never fully reconciled, but the balance moved in favour of an export drive. By 1997 the industry had become the country's second largest exporter of manufactured goods (Shelton 1998: 2). South African arms continued to find their way to many parts of the world – especially mid and north Africa and the Middle East. The NCACC reported that in 1999 arms worth R1.1bn had been sold to 53 countries. Among the main purchasers that year were Algeria (more than R300m), India (R205m) and the United Arab Emirates (R101m). At the same time the UN Security Council named South Africa among the states that had violated sanctions by supplying weapons to the rebel Unita movement in Angola. Further embarrassing reports claimed that South Africa had sold arms to both sides in the conflict in southern Sudan, and to the warring factions in the Democratic Republic of the Congo (DRC) – including Zimbabwe and Namibia on one side and Rwanda on the other. When Pretoria was accused of breaking a UN resolution in Angola, it responded by denying sales to Unita, but noted that 'with the approval of the Angolan Government, mine-protected vehicles were supplied to private mining companies for the protection of personnel'. It further stated that no lethal weapons had been sold to combatants in the DRC (*Sunday Independent* 26.3.00). But Pretoria's disclaimers were not entirely convincing because it did not have full control of the situation. Alongside the legal trade, which itself was difficult to supervise, was illegal trading of unrecorded proportions. The arms might be exported via remote airfields and busy ports, with false documentation and the connivance of corrupt officials. Because of illegal sales the total trade was uncertain, but the figures that are available indicate that after 1994, 'legitimate' exports continued to grow, even if unevenly.

Arms Exports 1990–1999 (R million at 1990 prices)

Year	1990	1991	1992	1993	1994	1995	1996	1997	1998	1999
Sales	163	758	438	739	641	721	345	c.1,300	c.1,000	c.1,270

(Batchelor and Dunne 1998; and Mills and Edmonds 2000).

Controversy over arms continued to plague Mandela's government. To add to the divisions over external sales, differences arose about the purchase of naval and air force equipment for its own forces. This led to further divisions. Inside and outside the government squabbles arose: first, over whether it was necessary at all; second, if it was, what type of arms should be bought; third, how much should be spent, and finally, from whom should the arms be purchased. These disputes, which persisted into Mbeki's presidency, were exacerbated by the shady world of arms sales, with its corruption and underhand dealing.

'Universality' and the Two-China Policy

Among the new South Africa's inheritance from the NP government were diplomatic, trade and investment links with Taiwan. The relationship had been forged in adversity, as they were drawn together by their pariah status. In Taiwan's case this came as a result of its irreconcilable dispute with 'Mainland China' – the mighty Peoples Republic of China (PRC). For the NP government there had been nothing to lose and something to gain in the relationship. There was no chance of the PRC establishing relations with the apartheid regime, whereas, in contrast, Taipei was eager to create links, and was prepared to offer substantial economic benefits in return. As a consequence, by 1994 280 Taiwanese firms, employing 45,000 people, were operating in South Africa. Direct investment from Taiwan was already over a billion Rand, with the prospect of more to come, including support for the petro-chemical plant at Mossel Bay. Trade with Taiwan was also larger than with the PRC, and the balance was in South Africa's favour. In 1994 total trade (imports and exports) with Taiwan was R4475m, compared with R1869m for the PRC (Geldenhuys 1995).

Aware of the changing political scene in South Africa, the Taiwanese were not averse to cheque-book diplomacy. When, before he came to power, Mandela visited Taipei in August 1993, the Taiwanese treated it as a state occasion, and rewarded him with US$10m for the ANC's election expenses and US$36m for a vocational training school (*Mail and Guardian* 22.3.02). Mandela's message at the time was tolerant, pragmatic and in the spirit of 'universalism'. He laid emphasis on the importance of existing and future economic links, and added that the ANC 'would not abandon its friends who helped during the days when we needed assistance'. However, he made clear that in government the ANC would never turn its back on Beijing. 'It's unthinkable', he told a press conference, 'that we can abandon relations with the People's Republic of China' (*Report* 13.8.93). Later, when in office, Mandela revealed that Taiwan had also pledged more than R1bn to the ANC's economic flagship policy – the RDP.

There was, however, an obvious downside to the relationship with Taiwan. From the beginning Beijing made its position clear. There was only one China: the PRC. Taiwan was part of it and would in time be fully reintegrated into it. Meanwhile Beijing would not countenance a dual recognition policy – it was either them or us. That was the blunt message given to a somewhat resentful

Nzo, when he visited Beijing in 1994. To ram home the point, Beijing cut all ties with Burkina Faso, when the West African state tried to practise its two-China policy by retaining diplomatic relations with both. With this background, it was widely assumed that, despite Taipei's efforts, the new government would follow the practice of most others by establishing formal relations with the PRC at the expense of Taiwan. That did not happen. Instead, Pretoria committed itself to 'the Two-China Policy'. Repeating the ANC's commitment to 'universality', Mandela stated that the government would not 'break relations with countries unless a country does something wrong which causes us to do so'. In February 1995, Nzo confirmed the links with Taiwan and added: 'This is a matter which should be resolved by the Chinese themselves.'

Presumably Mandela believed that South Africa could succeed where others had failed, because of its special status – from the struggle against apartheid; the political miracle at home; its the powerful position in Africa, and the international standing both of the government and Mandela himself. Yet, despite the government's public stand, the policy never gained whole-hearted support either in the ANC, or the government, even at cabinet level. Its opponents believed that the policy was against South Africa's interests. They pointed to the PRC's great size and potential power, to the already strained relations with it, and to the hurdles it would create for Pretoria's future ambitions. If, for example, South Africa had hopes of playing a prominent role in the UN it could not afford to offend the PRC, one of the 'big five' in the Security Council.

For more than two years matters hung in the balance. In that time, and despite the differences over Taiwan, contact was retained with the PRC. Early in 1996, for example, two South African delegations visited Beijing – one from the SACP, and an ANC group led by Cheryl Carolus. In between the Chinese Minister of Foreign Trade, accompanied by a business delegation, attended the UNCTAD meeting in Johannesburg. Supporters of the two-China policy, argued that these contacts revealed that Beijing's bark was worse than its bite. However, there were no signs that the PRC would change its position, nor was the situation static. In particular the economic equation was changing. In the longer term, the PRC, with its vast population, its recently impressive economic growth and its increasing participation in global activities, had the potential to become a major world economic player, and even the immediate picture was changing. In particular the PRC had reached agreement with Britain to take over control of Hong Kong from July 1997. That altered the calculations. Hong Kong already had long-standing links with South Africa. In terms of trade these were smaller than those with Taiwan, but when added to those with the PRC they were greater. In 1995, for example, their combined total made them South Africa's fifth most important trading partner (R6,478m), while Taiwan was eighth (R5,774m). Equally important were Hong Kong's investments in South Africa, which, following Japan, were the second largest from Asia. To round off the picture, Beijing made clear that when it took over from the British those who did not have full diplomatic relations with the PRC could expect no sympathy in renegotiating their links with Hong Kong.

To those in Pretoria who doubted the two-China policy the question was not whether it had to be abandoned but when and how. In their view the links with

Taiwan, which may have been of immediate use, were untenable in the long term. The challenge, as they saw it, was how to effect a 'soft landing', so that, while drawing closer to Beijing, not all the Taiwanese economic benefits would be lost. Yet Mandela seemed unmoved. In October 1996, he restated that it would be immoral to cut off diplomatic ties with Taiwan. The following month he did just that. Without consulting either the Taiwanese or the Chinese, or even the whole cabinet, he announced that in a year's time Pretoria would cut its diplomatic ties with Taiwan and establish formal relations with Beijing. Despite strong pleas from Taipei he was adamant. Pretoria followed up by saying that it wanted to maintain good relations with Taiwan – retaining economic links, and representation short of diplomatic status – but formal recognition would end.

Mandela's change of direction came about because the PRC's unflinching stand forced him to recognise that South Africa's interests were best served by abandoning the old policy. However, the way he went about it was ham-fisted. The sudden, apparently impulsive reversal was far from the desired soft landing. It has been suggested that Mandela decided to act when President Li Teng-hui of Taiwan requested an early visit to South Africa, thereby forcing him into a quick, clear decision. Alternatively, Mandela may have been so embarrassed at having to go back on his word that he acted impulsively – to get the nasty business over. Whatever the reasons, once the decision was made matters turned out well for South Africa. Perhaps its special status came into play. Beijing was generous. Three weeks before the transfer of power in Hong Kong, the Chinese agreed, in negotiations with Aziz Pahad, that Pretoria could retain its mission in Hong Kong, that South African citizens could visit there without visas, that South African Airways could both retain its landing rights and in future could overfly mainland China to shorten the flight to Japan. For its part Taiwan's initial reaction was one of anger and frustration. It recalled its ambassador, and announced the suspension of 17 aid projects, worth an estimated US$840m. However, in the longer term it continued its trade and commercial ties, although inevitably with less enthusiasm and fewer generous side gestures than before.

In May 1999 Mandela paid an official visit to PRC, where he was greeted with full ceremony. During the visit he made no mention of Chinese abuses of human rights, either in China itself or in Tibet.

Nigeria and Human Rights

When Mandela's government came to power, Nigeria was under a military regime headed by General Sani Abacha. In a country with a record of corruption and abuse of human rights, Abacha's regime was noted for both. A particular problem arose in Ogoniland, in the Niger delta, where the Shell Company had extracted large quantities of oil. A local protest movement, led by the flamboyant Ken Saro-Wiwa, claimed that while both the government and Shell had derived great benefit from the exploitation of the oil, the Ogoni people had gained nothing but misery and poverty, and had their environment ruined. They demanded redress. In October 1995 the Abacha regime arrested Saro-Wiwa and several of his followers, accusing them of conspiracy to organise a political coup and of murdering political opponents. After a summary trial by a military court Saro-Wiwa and his companions were sentenced to death.

While these developments were taking place Pretoria set out to play a mediating role. According to Aziz Pahad, it had three aims in mind – to prevent the Ogoni executions, to encourage a return to civilian rule, and to secure the release of Chief Abiola – who had won the previous Nigerian election but was now a political prisoner. Pretoria decided to pursue these ends through quiet diplomacy and contacts – including visits to Pretoria by Chief Tom Ikimi, Nigeria's forceful Foreign Minister, and to Nigeria by Archbishop Desmond Tutu and Thabo Mbeki – who had served there as ANC representative for three years in the late 1970s.

That was the situation in November 1996 when President Mandela arrived in New Zealand for his first Commonwealth conference. The Commonwealth – which had committed itself to promote democracy, the rule of law, and human rights through the Harare Declaration of 1991 – was alert to the Nigerian problem. However, despite reports that the death sentences on the Ogoni prisoners had been confirmed, Mandela remained sanguine, believing in the efficacy of Pretoria's diplomacy. When, on his arrival in New Zealand, he was asked whether it was time to act against Nigeria, he replied: 'If persuasion does not succeed it will be time enough to consider options.' Mandela's confidence was unfounded. News arrived that the prisoners had been executed. The conference exploded, and Mandela lit the fuse. He felt betrayed and admitted to being 'hurt and angry' at the appalling behaviour of an 'insensitive, frightened dictator' (Sampson: 1999: 557). He accused the Nigerian regime of 'judicial murder', called for the severance of diplomatic ties, the imposition of economic sanctions and Nigeria's expulsion from the Commonwealth. In response the conference suspended Nigeria and set up a Ministerial Action Group (including South Africa) to take the matter further.

Mandela's sense of betrayal and personal humiliation was further exposed as opponents of the Nigerian regime accused him of doing too little, too late, and branded his quiet diplomacy as complacency; of being no better than the despised Western 'constructive engagement' policy towards the apartheid regime. A supporter of Saro-Wiwa wrote to Mandela saying that had the opponents of apartheid confined themselves to quiet diplomacy 'I doubt if you would be alive today' (Sampson 1999: 557). On his return home, therefore, Mandela set out to generate further action. He recalled Pretoria's High Commissioner from Nigeria; urged the UK and US to impose oil sanctions; summoned the local Shell manager before him to ram home the message; and requested a special SADC meeting to examine what further steps could be taken against Nigeria. None of this led anywhere. The Western companies continued to extract oil; Western governments did not declare an oil embargo or reduce their heavy investment in Nigerian oil, which in the case of the US was more than US$5 billion annually (Stremlau 1998/9: 66).

Similarly in Africa there was no support for action. Other SADC members refused to take the matter further; and a similar response was found elsewhere in the continent. The African states saw Nigeria less as an offender against human rights than as a continental leader which had been a doughty opponent of apartheid, a strong supporter of liberation movements, and which contributed up to a third of the OAU's income. They simply did not want to confront or criticise the West African giant. They wanted to display African unity not its divisions, and were critical of Mandela for undermining the continent's solidarity. The reaction of the Liberian Government captured that spirit, when it stated: 'To see President Mandela who has been in jail for 27 years ... set out a campaign against Nigeria is very shocking ... [Liberia] is calling on other African countries to prevail on President Mandela not to allow South Africa to be used in the division and undermining of African solidarity.' The Nigerians themselves described Mandela's attitude as 'horrific' and 'terrible', and called on all Africans to persuade him 'not to allow South Africa to be used in the division and undermining of African solidarity' (Venter 1996: 2 and 1997: 92).

In the Commonwealth further activity was muted. At a 'dialogue' meeting between the Action Group and a Nigerian delegation led by Tom Ikimi, the Nigerians expressed their resentment at their treatment, and accused other members of having much worse human rights records. In response the Action Group, which quickly became divided, reached a pusillanimous compromise whereby punitive sanctions were held in reserve while further discussions took place. Nor did the fires of indignation burn bright in South Africa itself. Even in his own government there was no enthusiasm to push matters forward, as Mandela had hoped. The DFA, for example, did not want Pretoria isolated from other African states, especially as it needed their support in South Africa's bid for a UN Security Council seat. Similarly, reaction within the ANC emphasised the need for concert with fellow African states. It too pointed to Nigeria's anti-apartheid record, and its financial contributions to the ANC – rumoured to be US$10m for the 1994 election. Tony Leon, the DP leader, commented: 'Our whole foreign policy is based on the electoral debts of the ANC' (Sampson 1999: 560).

Soon the government was vigorously back-pedalling. Thabo Mbeki told the National Assembly that while South Africa should do what it could to help return Nigeria to democracy, it could not dictate terms. It must not become arrogant by over-estimating its ability and strength. He accused those who had real power (by which he meant Western states) of failing to act. Instead he accused them of using Mandela, and exposing him to ridicule. South Africa, claimed Mbeki, had no leverage in the case – it bought no Nigerian oil, nor did it act as Abacha's banker – while those who did, had pushed Mandela forward knowing he would fail. Mbeki concluded that: 'We should not humiliate ourselves by pretending that we have a strength which we do not have.' The aim must be to understand Nigeria, not confront her. 'Slogans are not going to help' (NA 17.5.96: 1458/9). Mbeki had steered the government away from an attack upon Nigeria in terms of principles and values to an attack on the West in terms of exploiting a situation to its own ends. Soon South Africa withdrew from the Commonwealth group.

Military Intervention in Lesotho

On 21 September 1998 (in what was named 'Operation Boleas') troops of the South African National Defence Force (SANDF) entered Lesotho – the small mountain kingdom surrounded by South Africa. The troops were despatched following an appeal from the Prime Minister of Lesotho, Pakalitha Mosisili, that his elected government was in danger of being overthrown by a military coup. He requested help from SADC in general and South Africa in particular.

Lesotho's history since its independence from Britain in 1966 was one of instability, in which political parties, the monarch and the army were involved in a complex competition for power. Late in 1993 an internal crisis erupted, which continued into 1994 and reached its peak in August 1994, when King Letsie III, backed by part of the armed forces, staged a coup by dismissing the government of Prime Minister Dr Ntsu Mokhehle. The SADC and the OAU refused to recognise the new government, and invited a troika – consisting of the Presidents of South Africa, Zimbabwe and Botswana – to resolve the situation. In doing so the leaders adopted a diplomatic approach. They condemned the coup and threatened economic sanctions unless the legitimate government were restored. Yet, despite the stranglehold that South Africa had over the Lesotho economy, the coup leaders did not immediately give way. However, by continued pressure and threats, plus a military demonstration by South Africa on the border, agreement was reached early in September to restore the Mokhehle government. A Memorandum of Understanding was drawn up, whereby the troika became the guarantors of Lesotho's democracy. It was on the basis of that the new PM made his appeal in 1998.

The 1998 crisis followed an election in Lesotho in May, when the ruling party – the Lesotho Congress for Democracy (LCD) now led by Mosisili – had been declared the overwhelming winner. The opposition parties responded by accusing the LCD of rigging the polls. Pretoria attempted to settle matters by sending a delegation to Maseru, made up of Mbeki, Nzo and Modise. They persuaded the LCD to accept an independent review of the election, headed by a South African Judge (Pius Langa), with members from Botswana and Zimbabwe. In his report Langa concluded that although there had been administrative irregularities, they were not serious enough to invalidate the overall result, which reflected the wishes of the Lesotho people. However, when there was a delay in publishing the report, opposition parties accused the LDC of using the delay to doctor the findings. Up to 6,000 opposition supporters marched to the royal palace, where they appealed to the King to appoint a Government of National Unity, which was outside his constitutional powers. The crisis deepened as angry crowds surrounded government buildings, barred civil servants from their offices, took over the state broadcasting service and threatened to kidnap the cabinet. It deteriorated further when elements of the army came out in support of the opposition, and ousted the commander in chief and 28 senior officers. Following a vain attempt by South Africa's Defence Minister, Joe Modise to restore army discipline, the Lesotho premier made his appeal for help.

Lesotho's request came when, by chance, Mandela, Mbeki and Nzo were all out of the country in different parts of the world. In their absence, Buthelezi, who was acting President, consulted by phone all the major figures abroad and the Botswana and Zimbabwe governments. With their agreement, and based on the 1994 troika undertaking, Buthelezi ordered the SANDF into Lesotho, with an undertaking from Botswana, but not Zimbabwe, to send support troops. Buthelezi stated that the aim was 'to neutralise a brewing military coup which would have prevented the majority party, the opposition and the monarchy from performing their respective roles' and would have endangered them all (Van Nieuwkerk 1998). It is probable that the decision would have been the same, whoever had made it, but the absence of the three major figures when the crisis reached boiling point, presented an image of poor intelligence, weak co-ordination and indifference to regional problems within the government, so that senior figures in the DFA learned of the invasion on their radios.

The operation began when 600 South African troops crossed the border into Lesotho to be followed the next day by 200 troops from Botswana. The specific tasks were to secure the Katse Dam, to isolate the Makonyane military base (which was thought to be at the centre of the troubles), and to secure the Royal Palace, government offices and the central business district in Maseru. Expecting little or no resistance, the South African troops were lightly armed, and arrived handing out leaflets, which said they had come to prevent anarchy and to help restore law and order. Those expectations proved to be false. Not only did they meet armed resistance from elements of the Lesotho army, but order collapsed in the main towns, as mobs looted and burnt shops and offices. In the fighting and violence that ensued more than 100 soldiers and civilians were killed, including eight South African troops. The centre of Maseru was badly damaged, with more than a thousand shops and businesses destroyed at an estimated cost of R97m (Peters 2000: 34; SAIIA 1999/2000: 99). Pretoria responded by sending reinforcements with heavier arms. Eventually up to 4,000 South African troops were deployed, and they soon restored order. A political settlement followed, nursed by South Africa, whereby an Interim Political Authority was installed to oversee affairs until new elections were held within 15 to 18 months. South African troops remained in Lesotho until the end of the year.

The government claimed the operation as a success. Mbeki and Nzo defended it before parliament as a timely and necessary intervention (NA 4.3.99: 1133). They stressed how, within the SADC remit, the government had responded to an appeal from a neighbouring state; how by preventing a military coup it had saved democracy in Lesotho and created a situation in which negotiations could be resumed. They also underlined that the troops had secured strategic installations, which were important for South Africa's as well as Lesotho's future, including the mighty Highlands Water Project. Yet, alongside the government's claims of success was criticism. In South Africa, the military were accused of poor intelligence, and of failing initially to deploy in sufficient strength, so that unnecessary deaths followed. The troops were further criticised for poor discipline leading to abuses of human rights, including accusations of attacks on defenceless soldiers and civilians. Critics also pointed to the destruction of property and the economic costs that had resulted from the intervention.

In Lesotho itself, Dr Khabela Matlosa, of Lesotho University, drew a picture of the SANDF wreaking havoc, and standing aside while armed gangs were 'confiscating vehicles, looting shops and burning business and private homes', and militant youths turning parts of towns into 'no go' areas. He claimed that the result had not been favourable either to Lesotho or South Africa. Instead of gratitude the intervention had led to the rise of a Lesotho 'nationalistic campaign, heavily imbued with xenophobia'. Most of the ire had been directed against foreigners, especially South Africans; as illustrated by their flight across the border, led by their High Commissioner. He went on to question Pretoria's motives. Was the intervention, he asked, intended to reinforce the principle of sovereign equality of all African states, or was it to reduce Lesotho's status to that of a province of South Africa? At a conference of political analysts and representatives of civil society from Lesotho and South Africa many saw the intervention as a demonstration of Pretoria's hegemonic ambitions. 'The intervention was a typical case where countries use the pretext of international organisations [SADC] to further their own interests', said one speaker. Another claimed that South Africa's policy makers 'have assumed that they could make reality fit their ideas'; while a third stated: 'In situations of crisis, they [the South Africans] go back to military solutions, showing a reassertion of *realpolitik*' (Lambrechts 1999).

Learning from Experience

Mandela's government – consciously and unconsciously – absorbed lessons from its experiences in the cases discussed above. One lesson was the difficulty of implementing principles. Principles often proved to be ambiguous, and/or to clash with other principles, and/or with established interests. In the arms sales case the decision – based on principle – to try to limit sales by strict controls ran into opposition from a mix of principles and interest. Obviously it conflicted with the interests of those who were employed in or who benefited from the arms industry, but broader concerns also same into play. For instance – partly from principle and partly from interest – the government was committed to maximising domestic employment as part of the RDP. In the event the policy outcome was a pragmatic compromise in which an uneasy and shifting balance was struck between interests and principles. The Nigerian case provided another example of clashing principles, and principles competing with interests. The principles were concerned with human rights, but they were matched by respect for the sovereignty of individual states. 'Sovereignty' has a special resonance among African states because of their determination to demonstrate independence from their colonial past, and because it offers formal equality to poor and weak states.

Sovereignty was also an issue in the Lesotho case, where the principle of non-interference in the internal affairs of another state clashed with the principle of upholding democracy. Further, while Pretoria claimed it was intervening in Lesotho under SADC's banner, critics accused it of pursuing its ambition to absorb Lesotho and to protect its interests and investments there. In the Nigerian case, Mandela's stand against the abuse of human rights and in favour of democracy failed to attract support elsewhere in Africa, or among his own colleagues, because they put a higher priority on sovereignty and the brotherhood of African states than individual human rights. Mandela discovered that it was a thankless task to challenge the convention of African solidarity. The OAU concluded that to call for sanctions against Nigeria was 'not an African way to deal with an African problem' (Vale and Maseko 1998b: 272). Mbeki, in his speech to the National Assembly on Nigeria, underlined that 'the sense of being an African had an impact which went beyond the merely rhetorical level. Derived from commonalities of race and historical experience, this imposed on African rulers a sense that, at any rate, they *ought* to act in harmony, and that Africans in one part of the continent had some kind of claim or obligation on those in another' (Clapham 1996: 107).

Such clashes between the concepts of individual human rights and state sovereignty are certainly not confined to Africa. Hedley Bull has underlined the tension that exists across the board. A human rights agenda, he pointed out, based on the centrality of the individual, crosses state boundaries and overrides the claims and interests of the state. Human rights assumes the rights of the individual within a 'community of mankind', based on personal equality. Thus, concluded Bull, when state representatives discuss human rights they do so with muted voices, for if individuals have rights separate from and beyond the state, state powers are limited, and the state cannot count on their loyalty (Bull 1977: 84).

Another lesson gained from the cases was to underscore that differences inevitably arise within the government itself – between departments and individuals (ministers and officials) – over the interpretation and implementation of principles and interests, and the priority to be given to them. In the case of arms sales the spectrum of views among ministers stretched from 'doves', like Kadar Asmal, to 'hawks', like Joe Modise. It was also in part a debate between those who put their faith in principles versus pragmatists, who, with world-weary resignation, argued that if South Africa sacrificed its own interests by restricting arms sales, others would take advantage by expanding theirs. The two-China policy also led to internal differences, and the recognition that global power realities can override principles. The decision to cut formal relations with Taiwan undermined 'universalism' in favour of accepting the strength of the PRC. Although Mandela was reluctant to abandon existing links with Taiwan, others in the government had believed from the beginning that it was both impractical and against South Africa's interests to retain them. Further, as Aziz Pahad admitted, the issue of China's poor human rights record was not raised during the negotiations. In the light of that Deon Geldenhuy concluded that the recognition of the PRC, when 'expressed in the familiar "power versus principle" terms', had 'everything to do with the former and nothing with the latter' (Geldenhuys 1995: 6/7).

Yet human rights were not entirely forgotten by the new government, even in the case of China. In 1997 South Africa, unlike other African and non-aligned states, supported a motion from West Europe for the UN Commission on Human Rights to investigate the situation in China. When the motion failed to gain enough support, the Chinese attacked the European sponsors but ignored South Africa's part in the challenge. The military intervention in Lesotho also revealed internal differences. At the time of the intervention a draft White Paper on South Africa's contribution to international peace missions was in its final stages of wide-ranging discussion within the government. The paper recommended a diplomatic approach, with the emphasis on 'peace making and keeping', rather than 'peace enforcement' by military means. Yet, Lesotho was an example of the latter. Rocky Williams wrote that, despite the White Paper, which stressed the need to address the causes rather than the symptoms of a crisis, the government failed to adhere to its own guidelines. In Williams's view 'the Lesotho intervention highlighted the disjunction that exists between a good policy (in the form of the White Paper) and its implementation' (Williams R. 2000: 86/101).

The cases further obliged the government to recognise that its self-perception and its espoused values were not necessarily shared by others. In Pretoria's view it had acted benignly to preserve Lesotho's democracy and a legitimate government, within the terms of the SADC remit, and at the request of the legitimate government. However, that perception was challenged by critics inside and outside Lesotho, who accused Pretoria of bullying and harbouring hegemonic ambitions. Differences of perception also arose in the Nigerian case. When Mandela made his stand against the abuse of human rights he believed he was speaking on behalf of all right-minded people, and for Africans in particular. He was not. Not only did he fail to gain support for further action, he was accused of acting as though he were the keeper of the continent's conscience. The bitter Nigerian response envisaged Mandela as the black leader of a white state – implying that his white officials and the white Commonwealth leaders had led him by the nose, and that he had imbibed Western rather than African values. Mbeki appeared to endorse this view when he spoke about Nigeria in parliament. That speech was a far cry from a foreign policy based on the principle of human rights. Instead Mbeki gave voice to what Maxi van Aardt called an 'unwritten law', by which 'African states do not turn on each other in international fora ... but close ranks when attacks are made against one or more of them' (Van Aardt 1996).

Finally, the government had failed to appreciate the importance of sound intelligence and planning prior to action. This stood out clearly in the military intervention in Lesotho. Following the campaign Lieutenant General Deon Ferreira claimed that the intervention had been badly planned and initially inadequately equipped and armed. The commander of the operation (Colonel Robbie Hartslief) himself stated that he had led the troops into Lesotho on the basis of poor, even false information. They had had inadequate knowledge of the political situation, of the strength and disposition of the Lesotho troops, and of the attitude of the Lesotho people. They had crossed the border believing that the vast majority of the population would welcome them, and that there would be little or no resistance from the Lesotho forces (SAIRR 1999/2000: 100). Also, although much broader than in Lesotho, there had also been poor interpretation of intelligence in the Nigerian and China cases. In these the failures were of perception – of the inability or reluctance to see the situation as others saw it.

10

Bends in the Road: Readjustment & Renaissance

Based on its experiences and in response to criticism at home that it lacked a coherent foreign policy, the government took steps to readjust its position. In doing so it recognised that constraints as well as opportunities lay ahead, and that principles could not be pursued in isolation. In 1996 Raymond Suttner, the chair of the Parliamentary Portfolio Committee on Foreign Policy, admitted that there was no automatic relationship between the violation of human rights and the ability to combat it, and that some states with poor records, like Nigeria and Indonesia, were protected by their wealth and power. Action, he said, 'cannot be determined by principle alone', but must take account of constraints 'on a case by case basis'. At the same meeting Abdul Minty, a senior DFA official, stated that: 'There are institutional, systemic, economic and political constraints on a state wishing to conduct a human rights based foreign policy.' The challenge, he said, was to be effective, to pursue human rights while 'taking into account economic, political and alliance factors'. Perhaps with the Nigerian case in mind, he also spoke of the need to understand the psychology and historical background of the developing world (Minty 1996: 56).

Even if initially the government could be criticised for being too sanguine, it could not be accused of complacency. Policy was under regular review. However, not all differences could be ironed out, and the problem of co-ordination persisted. The reviews were not a combined enterprise, but rather a number of separate initiatives. The first came in 1996, when the Department of Foreign Affairs (DFA) published a discussion paper with the intention of promoting a debate about foreign policy, while in the same year the Department of Defence issued a White Paper outlining its views on future security. They were followed in 1997 by an ANC document, entitled 'Developing a Strategic Perspective on South African Foreign Policy'. Also in 1997 came a change in economic policy with the introduction of the Growth, Employment and Redistribution (GEAR) programme. Three further major government papers followed before Mandela's retirement – one from Jackie Selebi, the new Director General of the DFA, another 'Defence Review', and finally, in 1999, a White Paper on participation in peace missions. In parallel with the publication of these documents, Thabo Mbeki was outlining his vision of an African renaissance.

The debates on foreign and defence policies, traced below by reference to major government and party papers, provide only part of the picture. As with all governments, there were gaps between policy and implementation. Further, foreign policy is shaped by day-to-day events and developments, as well as the formal statements and publications. In the case of Mandela's government the day-to-day reactions and the formal papers revealed changes. However, they did not represent a complete policy 'U turn', but rather bends in the road, as the government readjusted its position in the light of the challenges and experiences of international life. It did not abandon its original principles and aims, but it modified and added to them, and set them in context.

The DFA: Discussion Document (1996) and the Selebi Paper (1998)

The stated objective of the DFA's 1996 paper, 'South African Foreign Policy: Discussion Document', – was to stimulate a debate, which would assist the government in its task of 'shaping, directing and executing South Africa's foreign policy'. Nzo said the aim was to achieve a foreign policy framework based on a 'national consensus'. He identified what he saw as the DFA's two main tasks – first, representing South Africa positively abroad, and second, analysing the world around to ensure 'the security and prosperity of our country and all of its peoples'.

The paper started by outlining the international setting: with the uncertainty of post-Cold War relations; globalisation; the information revolution, and the development of regional blocs. When it turned to South Africa's own situation, the paper spoke of 'the need for a codified foreign policy', and quoted Nzo's hopes of developing a 'predictable foreign policy, in line with the kind of nation we seek to be and the kind of world we wish to live in'. In taking that theme further the paper reiterated the commitments to 'the South' and Africa in particular, to reducing the gap between the global rich and poor, and to acting as 'an example to others in Africa and elsewhere'. Looking to the future, it listed the old 'idealist' principles but then added more 'realist' aims – such as the pursuit of 'the national interest', and 'promoting the security and welfare of South Africa's citizens'. Finally, it noted departmental concerns, such as the DFA's eagerness to help promote business activities abroad.

The department followed up the paper by organising workshops and meetings, for people outside as well as inside government. It met a mixed response. While the DFA pointed to its willingness to listen to different views, commentators claimed that the paper revealed that it had gained little from experience. In Greg Mills's view the paper was 'an ambitious but misguided wish-list', which undervalued the limitations of the external environment, and overvalued the country's resources and its capacity to act. Mills noted that at one point the paper stated that Pretoria's foreign policy 'should be modest and not over ambitious', whereas later it fell into that very trap, by claiming that the 'insecure, flexible and still evolving nature of the new global environment provides a favourable climate for South Africa to play a more proactive and assertive foreign policy'. That was to be achieved by promoting human rights and democracy, helping to secure disarmament and world peace and generally acting as a global citizen (Mills 1997: 6). Mills's comments were justified. The paper failed to identify priorities. It read like the minutes of a committee in which all views had been recorded without distinguishing between them. Yet, despite its limitations, the 1996 paper revealed that the DFA was ready to debate policy and to respond to a changing situation.

The second DFA paper, 'Thematic Review: Strategic Plans', was prepared in 1998 by Jackie Selebi, who, in the previous year had succeeded Rusty Evans as Director General. Selebi had already distinguished himself as Ambassador to the UN in Geneva, where he had steered through a treaty limiting the use of land mines, and chaired the UN Human Rights Commission. Like Evans's 1993 paper Selebi's concentrated attention on the interests of the state. However, while Evans had been mainly concerned with the international setting, Selebi emphasised the interlocking of foreign and domestic issues. For him the department's 'core business' was to create wealth for the country and offer security for its citizens, while its principal goal was: 'To ensure South Africa's sovereignty and to enhance its international capability to promote the well being of its citizens.' To achieve that Selebi stressed the need for 'good governance', which, he claimed, was based on respect for human rights and democracy. He urged South Africa to take a lead in this field. Well-being also rested on 'security', which Selebi saw in terms both of the state and the individual. For the individual it meant the provision of basic needs for food, water and fuel. At the same time he recognised that the state's wider concerns (from nuclear disarmament to countering cross-border crime) could only be achieved through co-operation with other states and international organisations (Landsberg 2000: 75–81).

Selebi was aware of the criticism directed at the DFA. Accusations of inadequacy started at the top, with claims that Nzo would not assert himself, and that Evans had been conservative and was tarred with the apartheid brush. Selebi, therefore, set out to revitalise the department's role within the government. He opposed a suggestion to merge the DFA and the DTI (Department of Trade and Industry), based on the increasing importance of economic relations, and the DFA's weak performance in that field. The DTI had dominated economic relations. At ministerial level Alec Erwin, the Minister of Trade and Industry, had 'completely taken over the trade negotiations with the European Union', and departmental rivalry had led to confusion in 'the haphazard way talks to renew the Southern African Customs Union were being conducted' (Muller 2000: 14/15). Selebi aimed to improve the DFA's performance and status. Thus he wanted it to play a leading part – together with the DTI and the private sector – in attracting investment and trade. He suggested that on overseas trips the President and cabinet ministers should be accompanied by business and trade delegations, and that all DFA staff (including Heads of Missions) should be trained in seeking trade and aid, and in business promotion.

Finally, in the broader international setting, Selebi was eager for South Africa to play a prominent part. He too identified with 'the South', and advocated a global agenda 'that suited the developing world'. In doing so he wanted South Africa to assume 'a higher, more assertive profile', and to concentrate on 'organisations from which we gain the greatest benefit', so that 'maximum benefit [is achieved] for South Africa, our region and the South'. He proposed seconding DFA staff to international bodies (UN, OAU and SADC) to extend their experience, and 'to increase South Africa's influence'. He wanted Pretoria to persuade the OAU to change its position on reform of the UN Security Council, from a rotating African representation, to a permanent seat for South Africa.

To induce a new sense of purpose and direction into the department Selebi followed up his paper by calling a ten-day conference of senior DFA officials and all Heads of Missions from abroad. The aim was to refine DFA business, while appreciating that 'domestic policy must be translated into foreign policy' (Muller 2000: 2). A 'mission statement' was agreed, whereby the DFA would seek to enhance South Africa's international capability, to ensure her security, to further the African renaissance, to create wealth and to improve the quality of its citizens' lives.

An ANC View

The ANC (as a party distinct from government) also contributed to the foreign policy debate, through the findings of a research group. In 1997 it produced a paper entitled 'Developing a Strategic Perspective on South African Foreign Policy'. This stated that the overriding objective should be 'to deepen and consolidate the national democratic revolution', and more specifically to 'advance our struggle' by increased understanding of the international environment and the 'empowerment of our general membership'. The group reiterated the 1993 'idealist' principles, and added two more: the first – which it placed 'at the top of the international agenda' – was to develop a just and equitable world order, by tackling the problems of the Third World; the second was opposition to imperialism, colonialism and neo-colonialism These represented a change of priorities, for while support for human rights was not abandoned, it no longer held the prime place. Rather, it was seen as a means to achieve a more equitable world than as an end in its own right.

The ANC group did not shy away from the complexities of foreign policy. It recognised that experience had revealed the difficulties of translating principles into action and the limitations of South Africa's capabilities. Taking human rights as an example, the group noted the diversity of the 'interpretation and relevance among different societies and cultures and among countries at different levels of development'. Nor, it warned, should we 'overestimate ourselves as a small middle-income country'. The Nigerian/Saro-Wiwa case was cited as an example of the danger of acting alone. In future the aim should be to work through multilateral bodies. This was especially important in ANC eyes because the Western states were forming powerful regional and trade blocs. Unless the South was prepared to work together injustice would grow even more. Yet, co-operation was difficult to achieve, because the South in general and Africa in particular was plagued by contradictions, over matters of principles – like human rights – and major policies, such as nuclear arms and international trade. As a result, the group concluded, South Africa would not always be able 'to act in a way that satisfies the expectations of other countries, particularly those on the African continent'.

The group regretted the collapse of the Soviet Union, leaving a world dominated by capitalist states. It accused the West of assuming that its current dominant position rested on universal verities, whereas it was based on 'values derived from one culture or stage of development' (Clapham 1996: 193). The West, and institutions like the World Bank and the IMF, were imposing unsuitable conditions on the developing world, especially Africa, by insisting on Western values and ideas such as good governance, the promotion of civil society, and multi-party systems. For example, multi-party systems, claimed the group, had in Africa 'weakened the capacity of governments to stop the explosion of ethnic wars'. Yet, while the group regretted Western dominance, it recognised that it could not be ignored. Nor could globalisation, which was politically and economically 'at the heart of international relations today'. In countering the potentially malign impact of globalisation, the group concluded that the best option was to 'empower the continent to act for itself and its interests' through an African renaissance. The key elements of this were the economic recovery of the continent, the breaking of neo-colonial relations, and 'the mobilisation of the people of Africa to take their destiny in their own hands' through 'people-driven and people-centred economic growth'. These, concluded the group, should be 'the main pillars of our international policy not only relating to Africa, but in all our international relations globally'.

The ANC group's views exposed an unresolved debate, and a contradiction within the party and the government. The ANC regretted the collapse of the Soviet bloc, with its alternative set of values and principles to those of the West. It resented the dominance of the West and identified itself with the underdeveloped South. Yet, as the group recognised, Western pre-eminence was a reality, which had to be accepted. What, however, the group did not say was that the new South Africa had embraced many Western values and principles. Thus Selebi's ideas of 'good governance', and indeed the constitution, in which the ANC took such pride, were built on Western principles. Was the group simply letting off steam against the powerful West, or had it simply failed to appreciate the contradiction?

Defence White Paper (1996); Defence Review (1998); White Paper on Peace Missions (1999)

Interlinked with foreign policy were readjustments in defence and security policies. In May 1996 parliament accepted a Defence White Paper, which was intended to bring the military into line with the new political situations at home and abroad. The paper's main theme, said Minister Joe Modise, was 'transformation'. The new South African National Defence Force (SANDF) was to be built on non-racial and non-sexist lines, and would broadly reflect the diverse composition of the country's population. In line with the government's principles and the new constitution, the forces would respect human rights and democratic processes, encourage transparency, and be subject to parliamentary control. Although the White Paper identified SANDF's primary function along traditional lines – as the preservation of the state's sovereignty and its territorial integrity against external aggression – the forces would adopt a defensive posture, while the government would pursue peaceful relations with other states and co-operation in Southern Africa. The White Paper concluded that: 'The size, design, structure and budget of the SANDF will therefore be determined mainly by its primary function. However, provision will be made for special requirements of internal deployment and international peace support operations' (DD 1996: 16).

The publication of the White Paper promoted a debate on defence, involving non-government as well as government participants. That led to another document – the 'Defence Review' – that was tabled in parliament in May 1998. Far from ending the debate, the Review gave it renewed vigour, because of the government's decision to place a major order for foreign arms. The order was predicated on the first of four options. This option, which was favoured by the Department of Defence, assumed that the forces' primary task would remain defence of the state and its geographical borders. (Secondary functions were also identified, such as ensuring order at home, and helping neighbours in times of natural disasters). With the primary task in mind, a large order was placed abroad – initially estimated at R5bn – for advanced, sophisticated weapons, including fighter aircraft, helicopters, surface vessels and submarines.

Controversy followed. The arms order was challenged both in terms of its cost and the type of equipment to be purchased. The controversy reflected fundamental differences about the nature of threats to the society and the use to be made of the armed forces. These differences were exposed by the publication of another White Paper on 'South Africa's Participation in International Peace Missions'. In October 1998 this paper, which was jointly prepared by the DFA and the Department of Defence, also gained cabinet approval. Yet, it made different assumptions about the future role of the armed forces, and therefore the training and equipment that was needed. The earlier White Paper's 'secondary functions' for the forces – support for peace operations, maintaining civil order, border protection, disaster relief, fisheries protection, and socio-economic development – became the principal tasks in the new paper, rather than the physical defence of the state.

The Peace Missions paper, after noting international expectations of Pretoria's participation, went on to stress the complexity of such operations. To underline the point it went on to give nine interpretations of the generic term 'peace mission' (including preventative diplomacy, peacekeeping, peace building and humanitarian intervention). The paper noted that the government's approach to the resolution of conflict was 'strongly informed by our own recent history', with the emphasis on negotiations, and it added that any contribution must 'depend on how closely the mission relates to our national interests' and whether appropriate resource are available. The paper set out conditions which had to be in place before undertaking a peace mission. They included a mandate from a multi-national body, agreement from the parties involved, and a minimum use of force, so that in some cases only civilians would be involved.

Too often, stated the paper, the international community had dealt with the symptoms, not the causes of conflict. South Africa's contributions should be to take a long-term view, by helping to create stable, peaceful societies. To achieve those ends six key principles were identified, which closely matched the earlier ANC's ideals – with commitments to Africa, and to greater global economic equality. 'In short', the paper concluded, 'it is in the South African national interest to assist peoples who suffer from famine, political repression, natural disasters and the scourge of violent conflict' (DFA and DD 1999: 18)

The Growth, Employment and Redistribution Programme (GEAR)

The bends in the road were not confined to foreign or defence matters; they also included economic policy. At the time of its election victory the ANC adopted the RDP as its socio-economic policy flagship. Initially there were signs of progress. Domestic investments and exports increased in the first year by 5 per cent, inflation was at its lowest for twenty years, and foreign indirect investment was healthy. However, the RDP soon fell on hard times. There were a number of reasons for this. In the first place it became clear that it was failing to reach many of its targets. As ever, it had proved easier for the government to announce grand plans than to implement them. Growth was slower than anticipated, direct foreign investment was disappointing, and in some policy areas, such as housing, land redistribution and education, delivery fell far short of promise. In part these problems were caused by bureaucratic in-fighting, as departments resisted the overarching role allocated to the RDP. Mandela had misjudged the implications of giving Naidoo such a wide and potentially powerful role. According to Hadland and Rantao, Mbeki in particular found the situation intolerable, and set out to undermine Naidoo and his ministry. They quoted one cabinet minister saying that: 'Thabo gave off strong indications that he hated Jay Naidoo' (Hadland and Rantao 1999: 110). The outcome was the abolition of the RDP ministry in March 1996.

Three months later the Department of Finance announced the government's new macroeconomic policy – Growth, Employment and Redistribution (Gear). It was introduced without the elaborate consultation that had characterised the introduction of the RDP. Instead Gear was the product of an inner circle, in which Mbeki and Trevor Manuel (the Finance Minister) were prominent, supported by senior departmental officials, academic advisers, and officials from the Reserve Bank of South Africa, the Development Bank of Southern Africa and the World Bank (Kotze: 2000: 70). As well as departmental opposition, the policy shift has been explained in several ways. Rukhsana Siddiqui argued that it was a response to globalisation: 'an explicit response ... to the challenges of an open global economy'. At the core of the new strategy was, she stated, an attempt to 'increase savings and also attract more foreign inflows in order to increase levels of investment' (Siddiqui 1999: 17, 18).

Jesmond Blumenfeld identified three more immediate reasons. The first was the publication of a strategy paper, 'Growth for All', from the South Africa Foundation, a body representing the views of major private companies. Although praising some aspects of government activity, the paper criticised others, including poor performance in the public sector, the size of the budget deficit, the failure to counter crime, and rigid labour laws, which deterred job creation and undercut the country's competitive edge. Despite counter-blasts against these views from two of the ANC's alliance partners – Cosatu and the SACP – the government responded sympathetically to the Foundation's paper. A second reason was an attempt to revive confidence, following a sharp drop in the international value of the Rand in 1996, which reflected continuing external doubts about the country's economic health and prospects. Finally, Blumenfeld pointed to the increasing influence of the Department of Finance, and a 'technocratic policy-making elite', with its stress on fiscal discipline. Whatever the reasoning GEAR was the product of top-down decision making, which in the growth/redistribution debate represented a ratchet towards growth and the market economy. The agenda, wrote Blumenfeld, signalled 'the government's acceptance of market-imposed criteria for the conduct of macroeconomic policy' (Blumenfeld 1998).

GEAR's principal aim, according to a government statement, was to create a 'fast growing economy [providing] sufficient jobs for all work-seekers'. To achieve that required an export-led economy, with tight budgetary control, a stable exchange rate, low inflation, relaxation of exchange controls, reduction in tariffs, tax incentives for new investments, and restructuring of state assets with some privatisation. Pursue those policy criteria, stated the paper, and substantial direct foreign investment would follow. Like the RDP before it, GEAR started with ambitious targets. These included an average GDP growth rate of 4.2 per cent per annum over the coming five years; inflation at 8.2 per cent and the creation each year of 270,000 new jobs in the formal sector. The policies proposed to achieve these ends reflected increased business influence, with incentives for domestic and foreign investors; tariff reductions to meet World Trade Organisation (WTO) targets, and public service restructuring. The business community acclaimed its market orientation and its emphasis on tight government control of expenditure.

Although GEAR became official policy, the economic debate was far from over. Inevitably it created tensions inside the ANC. To its advocates, who included Mandela and Mbeki, GEAR was a measured response to global developments. Mandela declared that the new policy was 'non-negotiable', and he defended it against critics within the alliance; while Mbeki rejected the argument that it favoured a minority at the expense of the majority, and instead saw it as a means to the 'twin goals of growth and equity' (Kotze 2000: 70). To its critics it was the equivalent of a self-imposed but misguided, IMF structural adjustment programme. Hein Marais noted how it 'shocked many in the ANC alliance', because it favoured business at the expense of the working masses, by supporting wage restraint, and reductions in public expenditure (Marais 1998: 161/2). Cosatu dismissed GEAR as 'conservative' and biased in favour of the private sector.

Doubts were voiced elsewhere. The National Institute for Economic Policy concluded that GEAR, with its budget cuts and tight monetary policy, relied too much on the private sector. It was too anxious to embrace the global economy; while the 'trickle-down factor' simply had not worked and would not work in South Africa (Arnold 2000: 65). Academics joined the fray. Paul Williams claimed that GEAR would contribute to insecurity among the poor. He wrote of a 'neo-liberal mindset' prevailing among officials, who derided socialists as 'idealistic utopians', while the officials themselves suffered from 'a fetishism of the "investor"'. He argued for an understanding of wealth creation 'in broader developmental terms rather than the pursuit of a technical profit-focused 'economic growth' model'. He suggested that an emphasis on growth only exacerbated 'the insecurity of the poor and the weak'. Williams advocated rejecting the principles embodied in GEAR and concentrating on policies that deal with 'the problems of poverty, unemployment and growing inequality'. How, he concluded, 'can a government which claims to promote human rights abroad be taken seriously when nearly a quarter of its own citizens live in poverty and the evidence suggests the situation is likely to worsen before it gets better?' (Williams P. 2000: 73–91).

Thabo Mbeki and the African Renaissance

The continuing debate on South Africa's future orientation took on a wider dimension through the concept of an African renaissance. Mandela first spoke of it at an OAU meeting in June 1994. He suggested that instead of repeating that the continent is poor and unstable, 'we must say that there is no obstacle big enough to stop us from bringing about an African renaissance' (Mills 2000: 139/40). Yet, while Mandela initiated the idea, it was Thabo Mbeki who developed it as a rallying cry for the benighted continent. As with Mandela and Steve Biko before him, Mbeki set out to foster a sense of pride and confidence in being African. 'I am an African,' he proclaimed, in proposing adoption of the new South Africa's final constitution in May 1996. He identified himself with the triumphs and tragedies of his native land – of past wrongs, when 'the strong had annulled the injunction that God created all men and women in his image'; when race and colour were 'used to determine who is human and who is sub human'. That immoral society, said Mbeki, had deprived many people of their self-esteem, and made them victims, 'the beggars, the prostitutes, the street children', while others became criminals, 'who have learned to kill for a wage, who have no sense of the worth of human rights; rapists who have absolute disdain for women ... animals who brook no obstacle in their quest for self enrichment'. Then, projecting his vision across the whole continent, Mbeki said that 'the pain of violent conflict is a pain I also bear. The dismal shame of poverty, suffering and human degradation of my continent is a blight that we all bear.'

Despite that catalogue of suffering and evil, Mbeki's message was of hope. 'I am born', he declared, 'of a people who will not tolerate oppression', who will not allow 'fear of death, torture, imprisonment, exile or persecution to result in the perpetuation of injustice'. He spoke of the patience of ordinary people, 'who do not despair when things go wrong; nor triumph when things go well', and who will not permit the behaviour of the few to 'result in the description of our country and people as barbaric'. He praised the new constitution, and foresaw a future 'society which ... enables the resolution of conflict by peaceful means, [and] rejoices in the diversity of our people'. He finished on a high note, claiming that, phoenix-like, Africa 'is rising from the ashes. Whatever the setbacks of the moment, nothing can stop us now. However improbable it may sound to the sceptics, Africa will prosper' (Mbeki, quoted in Adenauer Stiftung 1998).

That theme – a continent that would prosper despite past agonies – was developed in Mbeki's call for an African renaissance. He used the concept broadly and flexibly, so that he was able to stress different aspects to different audiences. In April 1997, for instance, he challenged members of a US business conference to examine their stereotypes of Africa. He asked whether they had anticipated the peaceful elimination of apartheid, or the current spread of democracy across the continent, or the campaigns against corruption. These new developments, he claimed, had created opportunities for Western business to help in 'the economic regeneration of the continent', and to reduce poverty. With your help, he told his audience, the revival could be based on the liberalisation of trade, the reform of financial and commodity markets, and the transfer of resources from the developed to the developing world. 'Africa's time has come' – no longer would it offer 'a message of regression and underdevelopment. The new century must be an African century.'

A year later Mbeki spoke about the renaissance to a very different audience in a radio broadcast to fellow South Africans. The subject was the same, but not the content or tone. Now he spoke of the violence and instability that still plagued the continent. The time has come, he stated, to banish this shame, to say 'enough and no more'. He attacked African leaders, who, through a 'pungent mixture of greed, dehumanising poverty, obscene wealth and endemic corrupt practice' had made themselves rich at the expense of the poor. They were the scourge of the continent; the source of military coups, civil wars and instability. We must, urged Mbeki, purge ourselves of such evils, through 'the rediscovery of our soul' – a soul that had previously flourished in the civilisations of Egypt, Axum, Carthage, Zimbabwe and Benin. The call 'for an African Renaissance', concluded Mbeki, 'is a call to rebellion. We must rebel against the tyrants and the dictators, who seek to corrupt our societies and steal ... We must rebel against ordinary criminals who murder, rape, and rob, and conduct war against poverty, ignorance and the backwardness of the children of Africa.'

In May 1998, Mbeki spoke about the renaissance to another South African audience – this time to members of parliament. To them he put the renaissance in the context of the international system, which he said was divided into two distinct parts – the rich First and the poor Third Worlds. That same division, he declared, was found inside South Africa in the form of two nations: one prosperous and mainly white, the other living in poverty and predominantly black. Quoting the Freedom Charter – that 'South Africa belongs to all who live in it, black and white' – Mbeki committed himself to closing the gap between rich and poor through 'people-centred development'.

Mbeki's renaissance speeches (and there were many more of them) had a grand, inspirational ring. They created a positive image founded on hopes and ideals. Despite Africa's current problems, despite the poverty, instability and corruption, their message was of faith in the future. As he spelt out his future vision based on an idealised past, Mbeki set out to capture the enthusiasm of others, inside and outside the continent. However, the precise policy implications of the renaissance were clothed in ambiguity. As Peter Vale and Sipho Maseko commented, they were 'high on sentiment, low on substance' (Vale and Maseko 1998b: 279). Mbeki's vision was so broad – embracing past glories, present concerns, and future hopes – that it could be (and was) understood in different ways. It was an exercise in constructive ambiguity. Further, although shaping the emphasis to match the audiences had the advantage of allowing diverse people to identify with the vision, it created uncertainty and confusion. Added to these were different doubts – about the appropriateness of South Africa leading the charge, not only because of its apartheid past, but the new government's values and policies. How, asked Chris Landsberg and Dumisani Hlophe, can a society, 'encumbered [from the past] by racism and white supremacy, spearhead a Renaissance in the rest of Africa?' To do so, they argued, implies an attachment to the land, people and customs of Africa, combined with a desire to revitalise its culture, traditions and spirit. Yet, for many Africans, the new South Africa not only carried sins of the past, but now attempted to introduce Western ideas on to the continent (Landsberg and Hlophe 2001: 23–40).

The grand sweep of Mbeki's ideas opened up a rich field for scholars. Peter Vale and Sipho Maseko argued that Mbeki's ideas could be classified in two distinct ways – 'the globalist' and 'the Africanist'. The globalist placed Africa in the context of a changing world economic order – of new technologies, massive flows of capital and information, computers and the internet. Its prevailing values were those of the free market, privatisation and cuts in public expenditure, thereby eroding the power of governments. Within this context South African ambitions would be as a leader of a Western-style continental economic revival, which in the long term would lead to equality for Africa with the other continents. In contrast, the Africanist concept was based on values drawn from within the continent, which, said Vale and Maseko, were 'rooted in largely hidden and unexplored links in culture, in literature, in folk-lore'. Seen in this light the renaissance was less a policy agenda than a broad aspiration, in which traditional values were reinforced by political awareness, while the future was based on self-help and respect (Vale and Maseko 1998b: 273).

Graham Evans offered a different interpretation. He argued that one way to understand Mbeki's renaissance was to set it in a Third World context, which is 'rooted in the notion that every aspect of the game is rigged, so that the poor ... have been created by, and are now deliberately constrained by the global hegemony of the rich'. Although the West claims that the international system has no controlling structure, seen through Third World eyes it is a hierarchy, controlled by Western institutions and governments. In this light Western colonialism had given way to new forms of inequality and oppression. Yet, Evans too was uncertain about Mbeki's motives. He offered three possible interpretations. First,

Mbeki was a cynical politician, playing the populist African card to bolster his personal position at home and abroad. Second, he was a modernist, whose aim was to develop and integrate Africa (and South Africa in particular) into the global political economy. Third, he was a radical, who – in the tradition of Marcus Garvey's 'back to Africa' movement of the 1920s and Steve Biko's Black Consciousness of the 1970s – identified himself with African concepts of consensus democracy, and 'ubuntu' (community). If he followed that third path, argued Evans, Mbeki would distance himself from Western concepts of democracy, with its acceptance of a vigorous opposition, an independent media and individual rights (Evans 2000).

A final example of the diverse interpretations is that of Vusi Mavimbela, who, as Mbeki's political adviser, was in a strong position to offer an insight into Mbeki's thinking. Mavimbela saw the renaissance as the third phase of Africa's liberation. The first had started with Ghana's independence in 1957, and went on to the demise of the socialist states in the late 1980s. The second was the current changing scene of the 1990s. The third – the renaissance – had yet to come, when empowered African people would deliver themselves from the legacies of colonialism and neo-colonialism. To achieve that would require stable societies and responsible, democratic leadership, leading to sustained economic growth. All Africans would contribute: whether proletariat, rural masses and entrepreneurial middle class. The renaissance would emancipate African women, capture the enthusiasm of youth, bring in a revolution in education based on information technology, and see new roles for the OAU and NAM (Mills 2000: 313).

To summarise, therefore, Mbeki's renaissance was built upon an idealised view of both of what had been and what was to come. It offered a vision; a new hope for the continent. However, while it might help to inspire, its policy implications were uncertain. The ambiguity was both a strength and a weakness. It was a strength in the sense of helping to enlist a variety of supporters, and in motivating people, irrespective of Mbeki's motives. It was a weakness in that the vagueness failed to offer a clear policy guide. In part the ambiguity reflected the continuing attempt by the government to square the circle of marrying together its acceptance of many Western values and policies with its commitment to the aspirations of post-colonial African society. To implement Mbeki's vision implied that South Africa could sustain a mixture of values at home, and promote them across the continent. It was a difficult task, as is discussed further in Chapters 14 and 15.

11
Domestic/Foreign Affairs Interlocked: Migration, Aids, Crime & Visitors

Despite internal disputes the ANC alliance held together. The recognition of strength through unity came as a by-product of its experience as a liberation movement, when its very existence and the fate of its members depended on their supporting each other. Loyalty to the movement and to colleagues persisted when the alliance came to power, and was reinforced by the privileges and patronage of office. Anthony Sampson wrote that Mandela 'relished his personal patronage, offering old friends jobs like ambassadorships and watching their surprise' (Sampson 1999: 506).

While the ANC held together the GNU did not. In May 1996 de Klerk led the NP ministers out of government. There were two main reasons for this decision. The first was related to what de Klerk, and most party members, saw as the NP's anomalous position, whereby it was part of the government, in that it occupied cabinet seats; yet, at the same time, it was the main opposition party in parliament. De Klerk described the GNU as 'unnatural' – because there was a dominant party (the ANC) with a clear majority both in parliament and the cabinet, and yet the parties in government had not agreed a policy framework. According to de Klerk, things went reasonably well in the GNU's first year, but then tension increased as differences arose along party lines. He accused the ANC of forcing decisions through cabinet, and becoming increasingly autocratic and resentful of criticism. The policy differences were mainly over domestic issues – such as handling the continued violence in KwaZulu-Natal; the NP's doubts about the establishment of the Truth and Reconciliation Commission, and, ironically, the ANC's refusal to commit itself to share power under the permanent constitution. De Klerk went on to complain about the weak performance of his NP cabinet colleagues, who, he said, were either too timid to challenge the ANC or too consumed in their departmental duties to see the bigger picture. As a result de Klerk claimed that he had to act as the lone critic within the cabinet.

De Klerk's second set of reasons were more personal. First, he admitted that after being President he found it difficult to play second fiddle. He further complained about his treatment by Mandela and the ANC in general. Although, he stated, he always defended the government's record in public, he was never asked to represent the country abroad, nor did Mandela seek the benefit of his experience and advice: 'no matter how sound that advice might be it was nearly always resented'. In short, the mutual distrust between de Klerk and Mandela persisted. After a relatively tranquil first year in the GNU the clashes started again. De Klerk complained that Mandela had a 'habit of flying off the handle without properly checking his facts beforehand', and papering 'over problems with charm and promises, without taking effective remedial action' (De Klerk 1998a: 352). To add to these problems of political relationships de Klerk was also faced by a matrimonial crisis (see Chapter 6).

In May 1996 de Klerk confronted the NP caucus with the GNU issue – asking whether the party should continue with the power-sharing arrangements. There was disagreement. Most of the members holding cabinet posts were keen to continue; whereas a majority of backbenchers favoured withdrawal. De Klerk himself had had enough. After listening to the discussion he announced that his choice was to leave the government now, giving as one reason that there would be ample time for the NP to establish itself as a distinctive alternative to the government before the 1999 election. In any case, whatever the caucus's decision, de Klerk stated that he intended to resign as Deputy President, but that he wanted to continue to lead the party in parliament. Although he claimed that he was giving the NP the option of remaining in the government by appointing someone else as Deputy President, in reality it was an ultimatum, not a choice. The party would have split apart had it selected another Deputy President to sit in government, while its world-renowned leader sat as leader on the opposition benches. If it was to remain a single party it had no choice but to leave the government. Therefore, after only two years, 'power sharing' – which the NP had so strongly advocated during the negotiations – collapsed. Even some ANC ministers regretted this, claiming that de Klerk had undermined the camaraderie that had developed in the cabinet.

In fact an emasculated form of sharing power continued. De Klerk had hoped that the IFP would follow his example and leave the GNU, but Buthelezi and his colleagues decided to remain in office, despite a continued dispute with the ANC over the future status of KwaZulu. This arose from one of the last-minute efforts to persuade the IFP to participate in the 1994 election. It was mutually agreed that, following the election, an international commission would be asked to investigate the future status of the province within the new South Africa. Subsequently the ANC back-tracked, claiming that the new constitution, as agreed by the Constitutional Assembly, had removed the need for any international input. Although the IFP hotly disputed this, it remained in government, where Buthelezi retained his ministerial portfolio and occasionally acted as President in the absence of Mandela and Mbeki.

In contrast, not only did the NP leave the government it started to fall apart. In August 1997 de Klerk announced his retirement from politics. In doing so he claimed that he wanted to give his successor time to settle in before the 1999 elections. However, as well as the reasons noted above – the stress of his personal life, his dislike of being subordinate to Mandela, and the ANC's attacks on him – there must be a suspicion that the man who had led South Africa from the evil of apartheid, found that he could not entirely discard the luggage of the past either for his party or himself. Despite his earlier advocacy of power sharing, de Klerk discovered that the new politics was not to his taste, that he had no stomach for the give and take and the compromises that had replaced the dominance of his party, and his own position as leader.

De Klerk was replaced as NP leader by the little-known Marthinus van Schalkwyk. Mandela showed no regrets at the change. With the experience of two years in office, he was now confident that the ANC could function without the NP. An encouraging sign for him was the lack of adverse international reaction to the break-up of the GNU. De Klerk disappeared from the political scene with hardly a whimper. He had become the Kerensky of the South African revolution. Like Kerensky in Russia, de Klerk had set in motion a process that he thought he could control and shape to his own aims; whereas in the event, as with Kerensky, the force of the revolution threw him aside. The muted international reaction to de Klerk's departure was an indication that Mandela's government had succeeded in establishing a base for itself.

Following the break-up, Mandela withdrew a step further from detailed administration, leaving Thabo Mbeki, now the sole Deputy President, to oversee much of the business of government. Mbeki attracted both admirers and critics. His admirers pointed to his intelligence, dedication and hard work, and to his service and loyalty to the ANC. The critics accused him of surrounding himself with 'yes men', of paranoia over political rivals, and they alleged weaknesses as an administrator – accusing him of poor time-keeping, of failing to delegate, of taking on too much himself and leaving loose ends (Hadland and Rantao 1999: 100).

The Flow of People

While the demise of the GNU was a product of domestic politics, South Africa's return to the international fold had an impact on issues that lay across the permeable border between foreign and domestic policies. Among these was a growth in the flow of people in and out of the country. Increased population mobility was a worldwide trend, which in South Africa's case was enhanced by the internal settlement and the return to the international fold. The flow posed a series of challenges for the new government, both of principle and practice. Should it seek to control the flow – in and out of the country? If so how? What should be its attitude towards illegal immigration? How would the movement of people affect relations with neighbouring states? Was there the danger of a brain drain? Were human rights issues involved?

During the 1990s there was a striking increase in the number of people entering the country. Among them were those who previously had shunned it because of apartheid. In 1993 20 airlines were flying into South Africa; by 1997 there were 120. The airlines brought in those who came as tourists, or on business, or to study. In a country of great beauty and diversity of people, with magnificent scenery and beaches, world-renowned game parks and a fine climate, tourism made giant strides. More than half the tourists came from Europe – with the British and Germans in the lead – followed by Americans. Tourism would have flourished even more if South Africa had not gained a reputation for violent crime. Even so it became a major industry. In 1998 six million people entered the country as tourists, creating an estimated 737,000 jobs, and generating an income of R53bn, accounting for 8.2 per cent of GDP (SAIRR 1999/2000: 516).

At the same time some South Africans were permanently leaving the country, but the numbers involved were uncertain. The uncertainty was reflected in a sharp differences between the official South African figures and those of the countries that received the emigrants. In the years 1989 to 1997 Pretoria recorded 82,811 permanent emigrants, whereas the combined figure given for South African immigrants by the five main receiving countries – Britain, Australia, New Zealand, Canada and US – was 233, 609 (McDonald and Crush 2000: 3–9). Presumably many emigrants disguised their intentions when they left, or changed their minds on arrival at their destination. Looking to the future there was further uncertainty over the number of people who were still resident but had rights of settlement elsewhere. That was most marked with British passport holders. The total was unknown, even to the British High Commission, but it was estimated that up to 350,000 South African residents held (or had rights to) British passports. Together with their dependants that could imply that between 700,000 to 800,000 people had UK rights of settlement. The assumption was that short of a catastrophic political/economic collapse, the bulk of them were most unlikely to exercise that right but the numbers involved highlighted the scale of the uncertainty.

Even so, the exodus during the 1990s raised controversies – about the motives for leaving, the impact of the exodus on the country, and the efficacy of government policies in dealing with the situation. The exodus became something of a political football, on two counts. First, it included a significant proportion of skilled workers, prompting fears of a brain drain, and second, it had a racial element, as most of the emigrants were white. The reasons they cited for leaving included: increased crime, heavy taxation, political uncertainty, positive discrimination favouring blacks, and concern about future job opportunities, especially for the young. As more people joined 'the chicken run', dramatic newspaper headlines spoke of 'Exodus as Rainbow Nation's Iridescence Fades' and 'Most Skilled South Africans Ready to Quit the Country'. At a SADC conference Mandela criticised the emigrants, stating that 'the real South Africans are being sorted out in the process'. Requests were made to advanced countries not to recruit skilled South Africans. Sir Raymond Hoffenberg, a former President of the Royal College of Physicians in Britain, on returning to his native South Africa, wrote to *The Times* appealing to the British National Health Service to stop recruiting South African nurses and doctors. It was, he stated, immoral to try to attract them (*The Times* 15.2.96).

Concern about the loss of skilled personnel was genuine, but McDonald and Crush claimed that it was exaggerated. They presented a mixed picture, with skilled people entering as well as leaving the country. They pointed to earlier inflows, when skilled whites had moved south as colonies – notably Mozambique and Zimbabwe – had gained their independence. Further they noted than an estimated 7,000 African professionals (from countries like Uganda and Ghana) had previously taken up posts in the old Bantustans, and that skilled Taiwanese workers had settled in the country. The inward flow, helped by removal of apartheid, had continued in the 1990s. In 1992, for example, almost 200 Zimbabwe medical doctors had settled in South Africa, and more recently Cuban doctors had filled posts in rural areas.

Looking to the future, McDonald and Crush concluded, from an attitude survey they had conducted, that 'the alarmist rhetoric of crisis that pervades discussion of the brain drain in the popular press is misplaced'. Although they accepted that thousands of skilled people were leaving each year, they claimed that with the exception of information technology, employers had few problems in filling posts. They argued that the sense of panic arose from inadequate information and stereotyping. Among the stereotypes was a belief that English-speaking white males were most likely to want to leave, but their survey indicated that they 'are just as likely to want to stay, and that black South Africans, women and Afrikaners are just as likely to say they would leave'. In fact, they concluded the greatest hurdle to attracting skilled immigrants came from the government's own red tape and confused decision-making (McDonald and Crush 2000: 5/6). However, these views did not go unchallenged, not least in questioning the reliability of an attitude survey on such a contentious topic. For many inside and outside the government, emigration remained a matter of concern.

The Flow of Labour into the Country

Since the great mineral discoveries of the late nineteenth century South Africa had drawn in migrant workers from neighbouring African territories. They were predominantly male, many worked in the mines (often under bilateral government agreements) and most returned to their countries of origin. Large numbers were involved. In 1974 the official figures were 485,100 workers – of whom 148,856 came from Lesotho, 139,714 from Malawi and 127,198 from Mozambique. By 1986 the total was still substantial, but had fallen to 385,405 – with 138,193 from Lesotho and 73,186 from Mozambique. Alongside these legal workers 'illegal migrants' had come seeking a better life.

During the 1990s two broad changes were discernible in the scale and pattern of those entering the country for work. First, the formal demand for foreign labour fell. Second, the number of Africans illegally entering the country increased. The drop in formal demand was explained by greater mechanisation of industry, the closure of some mines because of declining mineral prices, and increased competition from South African workers, as domestic unemployment increased. Between 1994 and 1999, about 500,000 jobs were lost in the formal sector, at a time when each year more than 300,000 South Africans were coming on to the job market. By 1999 the official estimate was that 23 per cent of the workforce was unemployed, and that was probably an underestimate. Even the 1.5 million people who were said to be more or less active in the informal sector could not compensate for that (*South Africa at a Glance* 2000).

Despite the government's tough immigration policy, the flow of immigrants steadily increased. Some came through formal channels seeking asylum. Others came on temporary permits but stayed on. By 1995 the official estimate was that 750,000 of those who had entered on temporary permits had remained when the permits expired (SAIRR 1996/7: 46). However, most entered without formal entry requirements. Again this was part of a worldwide phenomenon, as waves of people sought to escape from wars, ethnic conflict, grinding poverty, natural disasters and state oppression. In South Africa's case it was an old problem that became acute, as the end of apartheid removed some obstacles for Africans entering the country, while at the same time, some neighbouring states were suffering from poverty and instability. Inevitably in these circumstances there was great uncertainty about the numbers involved. The picture was so confused that by the late 1990s estimates of 'illegals' living in South Africa ranged from two to eight millions (or between 5 per cent and almost 20 per cent of the total population). Even a study by the Human Rights Research Council could not put the figure more precisely than between 2.5m and 4m (SAIRR 1999/2000: 23). What was clear was that South Africa, with its relative prosperity and stability, acted as a honey pot, attracting people from other poor, unstable parts of the continent.

Within this context of labour flows at first the government made little effort to counter the brain drain, by trying to attract skilled immigrants. A sluggish bureaucracy, union fears of increased competition for scarce jobs, and public xenophobia combined to produce a restrictive policy. By the late 1990s, however – under pressure from business, which was concerned about skills shortages – it started to pay attention. In 1999 a White Paper on 'International Migration' proposed making entry easier for skilled workers, and letting market forces determine the skills that were needed. In homage to the market the White Paper stated that: 'Only industry knows what it needs, why and for how long,' and it flirted with the idea of delegating the power to issue entry visas to private companies, but in the end it was decided that the final word must remain with the state. To aid in this task an Immigration Review Board was created, and a geographical pecking order was suggested for skilled immigrants – first the Southern Africa region; second the rest of Africa; and only then the rest of the world (DHA 1999).

Illegal Immigration

It was not the brain drain but illegal immigration, which involved conflicting principle and policy, that most taxed the government. Buthelezi, as Minister of Home Affairs, had responsibility for immigration. In 1995, he declared: 'If we South Africans are going to compete for scarce resources with millions of aliens who are pouring in then we can bid goodbye to our Reconstruction and Development Programme' (Christie 1997: 45). In May of the following year, Mandela, in contrast, stated that South Africa should not be 'very tough' with illegal immigrants, especially from those countries that had supported the ANC in the years of struggle. They should be regarded as 'brothers and sisters' (SAIRR 1996/7: 47).

Buthelezi's 'tough' approach was based on the rights of South African citizens, and linked to a narrow interpretation of the national interest. In this he had support from the majority of South Africans, who accused the 'illegals' of increasing competition for jobs, of undercutting wages, of swamping social and health services, of spreading disease, and of promoting crime. An opinion survey in October 1996 'confirmed that South Africans are generally parochial and look upon undocumented migration with suspicion, if not open hostility'. Sixty-five per cent of those questioned regarded illegal immigration as 'bad' or 'very bad', and 80 per cent favoured stronger border controls (Schutte *et al.* 1997). Buthelezi could, therefore, claim to be voicing the will of the majority.

In contrast, Mandela's view (although it had an element of special pleading because of past support for the ANC) was based on an assumption that the rights of individuals could override other considerations (Hill 1997). Based on that assumption, Mervyn Frost has argued that, although a majority of South Africans may have said that now they opposed illegal immigration, they had already committed themselves to the principle of individual human rights by their acceptance of the new constitution, which included such rights. Therefore, maintained Frost, if immigrants genuinely believe that their life, liberty, or health are threatened they carry their rights with them and should not be rejected. Breaking a law or opposing the will of the majority cannot deprive the immigrants of their individual rights. 'Does', Frost asked rhetorically, 'the existence of the internationally recognized boundary between South Africa and its neighbours imply that [South African] citizens are morally entitled to be less concerned with the rights of people beyond those boundaries?' (Frost 1997).

The immigration controversy was widely debated inside the country – in the media, among academics, group leaders and politicians at local and national levels. In the Gauteng Legislature, for instance, Humphrey Ndlovu of the IFP accused immigrants of responsibility for much of the crime and social ills, and called for strong measures to restrict them. His views were endorsed by Daryl Swanepoel (an NP member), who accused immigrants of retarding housing and educational developments, of criminal activities and of spreading disease. However, outside the legislature, such views were opposed. For instance, Ravi Moodley of the Institute of Artisans, and Sheena Duncan of the Black Sash, argued that immigrants should be seen in a positive light, as they provided a pool of skill and talent, and accused the government of wasting resources on a futile policy (SAIRR 1996/7: 44/45).

Pretoria's attempts to square the circle of defending citizens' interests while recognising the rights of immigrants included the appointment in 1996 of a Labour Market Commission. This advised that the treatment of immigrants should conform to international standards, and that a more liberal approach should be adopted toward skilled immigrants, especially those from SADC countries. To balance against these 'liberal' moves, the commission recommended increased sanctions against employers of illegals, and argued that a proposed SADC Protocol for the free movement of people was politically and economically unsustainable in South Africa. The government agreed and refused to sign the protocol. In a further attempt to match efficiency and flexibility a 1997 Green Paper recommended that a clearer distinction be drawn between refugees and work seekers; that an independent Review Board be appointed, and a points system be used that was not simply based on market criteria. In June 1996 Buthelezi told parliament that the SADC had agreed that citizens from other member states now illegally living in South Africa could be granted permanent residence, if they could meet a set of criteria – including five years' continuous residence and engagement in fruitful economic activity. More than 200,000 people applied under the scheme (SAIRR 1996/7: 35).

Policy implementation on the ground to counter illegal immigration was often robust. The Home Affairs Department, which had responsibility for executing policy, worked with legislation (the 1991 Aliens Control Act and the 1994 Refugee Act) that emphasised state security rather than individual rights. Measures taken by the old regime to keep out 'illegals' were maintained, such as the use of police and military patrols and border fences (although power was turned off in sections that had been electrified). People who were caught were usually deported, with numbers steadily rising –90,692 in 1994; 157,085 in 1995; and 181,286 by 1998 (SAIRR 1999/2000: 24). The government realised, however, that it could not succeed alone. If it was going to make real inroads into illegal migration it needed support from its neighbours.

On the face of it the SADC – the regional organisation – seemed the obvious vehicle to use. However, the SADC's stated aim was to foster a common market, which implied more not less movement of goods, capital and people. As a result when the SADC issued a draft Protocol in 1998, it proposed fewer restrictions on movement, and Pretoria refused to sign (Moore 2000). Instead, in the absence of broad regional co-operation, the government set out to reach bilateral agreements with its neighbours. For example, in January 1997 it decided that, as the civil war had ended in Mozambique, immigrants from there should not be treated as refugees. This was followed up in February when Joe Modise, the Minister of Defence, signed an agreement with Mozambique, which allowed troops from both sides to cross the border in hot pursuit of illegal immigrants and drug smugglers (SAIRR 1996/7: 44). Yet, for all the effort illegal immigration remained a problem throughout Mandela's presidency. It was like trying to stop an incoming tide with the walls of a sand castle

Human Immunodeficiency Virus (HIV)/Acquired Immune Deficiency Syndrome (Aids)

Among criticism levelled at immigrants was that they were responsible for the spread of HIV/Aids. When the problem was first identified in South Africa in the 1980s it appeared to be on a small scale, and largely confined to white, homosexual men. During the 1990s that changed. The scourge of HIV/Aids lay across the land, as a new virulent strain established itself predominantly among the black heterosexual community. By the end of the decade it was a major crisis for sub-Saharan Africa – with 70 percent of the world's known cases – and for South Africa itself, with an estimated 4 million sufferers (Heinecken 2001). The accusation that migrants were responsible was understandable but misplaced. Like other people on the move they may have made a contribution to the spread of the contagion, but many others were involved. For example, armed forces carried it with them as they moved across the region. Greg Mills wrote: 'Estimated prevalence in the Angolan and Congo armies runs between 40% and 60% ... while some have suggested that it is as high as 80% in the Zimbabwe

Army.' The South African National Defence Force (SANDF) acknowledged that between 10 per cent and 12 per cent of its troops were infected, but that was almost certainly an underestimate. When tests were made during a training exercise in April 1999 the figures were much higher. One unofficial report suggested that 'the rate of infection in the SANDF may be as high as 60–70%' (Mills 2000: 101–3). A contagion that had marched across the continent was not going to stop at South Africa's border, migrants or no migrants.

Not only was the full extent of the HIV/Aids pandemic unknown, its future economic, social and political implications were wrapped in uncertainty and controversy. Part of the explanation for the uncertainty came from the reluctance of individuals and governments to admit the full scale of the problem. It was inherently difficult to gather accurate statistics about a matter that involved such intimate personal behaviour, added to which it touched on the prosperity, security and pride of the state as well as the individual. However, the evidence that was available left no doubt about the seriousness of the threat to society. While uncertainty surrounded future implications, the speed at which HIV/Aids was spreading was apparent. In 1990 tests at South African antenatal clinics revealed that only 0.73 per cent of pregnant women were HIV positive. By 1995 that figure had leapt to 10.5 per cent and by 1999 had reached 22.4 percent. By then, the best estimates were that more than 4 million people (or one in nine of the population) were HIV positive, and that South Africa had more people with the disease than any other country in the world (Van der Vliet 2001: 151–84). The disease also intruded into relations with neighbouring states. For instance, both Malawi and Mozambique complained that their nationals employed in South Africa had been obliged to undergo tests and were repatriated if they were found to be HIV positive.

To add to the individual suffering the broader social implications were immense. It was not a problem that would peak and then disappear. Its impact was likely to be felt for generations. Even in the medium term Marcus Haacker of the IMF estimated that South Africa would suffer a loss of at least of 5.8 percent of GDP per capita, with dire social consequences and potential political instability (de Waal 2003: 9). In 1998 the US Census Bureau stated that already life expectancy in South Africa had fallen from 65 to 56, that population growth had been revised down to 1.4 per cent per annum and that Aids had accounted for a million deaths (SAIRR 1999/2000: 10). The future was even bleaker. The spread of the virus was most pronounced among young adults – the more economically (as well as sexually) active part of the population – thereby undermining the country's future development and welfare. The Minister of Health, Dr Nkosazana Zuma, calculated that that by 2005 Aids would have accounted for more than 7 million deaths; that nearly a million children would be motherless, and that by 2010 more than 6 million South Africans would be infected (Schonteich 1999).

The government floundered in the face of the pandemic. In the early 1990s, as de Klerk's administration began to appreciate the danger, it had introduced a National Aids Plan. However, its efforts were largely frustrated, as many Africans scorned the white government's advice, dismissing its 'Safe Sex' campaigns as an attempt to reduce black numbers. 'Aids' was said to be an acronym for 'Afrikaner Intervention to Deprive us of Sex'. The advent of Mandela's government did little to improve matters. Its approach was hesitant and controversial, and it became caught up in a series of disputes – with international drug companies in their failure to make cheaper drugs available; with provincial administrations for deviating from central policy, and with NGOs that accused the government of vacillation and inactivity. Mandela himself played little part. Perhaps because of his generation and cultural background, he tended to shy away from public discussion of sex. Elsewhere in the government there was discord and confusion. Disputes arose over such issues as government involvement in making and funding (R10.5m) of an ineffective play about the epidemic; a bogus miracle cure (Virodene) that for a time had official backing; the government's refusal to supply drugs to pregnant women, and the dismissal of the Aids Advisory Committee in 1997, after it had criticised government policy. At the same time Mbeki personally became caught in controversy when he questioned the basic nature of the problem, and the prevailing medical opinion. The disputes and obfuscation meant that the government's efforts were largely failing to translate themselves into safer sexual practice (Van der Vliet 2001).

Mary Crewe concluded that the epidemic was characterised by three main features. First, its 'rapid and unchecked growth'; second, a lack of clear government policy, and third, 'the failure of public prevention campaigns to have any impact'. She argued that the problem was not lack of awareness, for many had suffered personal loss and all knew of the potency of Aids, but the awareness had not resulted 'in personal behaviour change and support and care for those who are infected' (Crew 2000: 23/4).

International Crime

Among the flow of people into the country were international criminals. Criminals with international links had operated in South Africa before the 1990s, but once again the scale of the activity increased significantly in the 1990s, and while this too was part of a global trend, the increase in South Africa was sharper than most. By 1999 Peter Gastrow could write: 'Organised crime is thriving in South Africa' (Gastrow 1999: 58). The police reported that 192 crime syndicates were operating in the country, of whom at least 32 operated internationally. A syndicate, wrote Mark Shaw, is 'a well organised and structured group, with a clear leadership corps, that is involved in criminal activities' (Shaw 1997: 1). These criminals were from a wide range of countries, and, preferring those they could trust and communicate with ease, they tended to operate in ethnic/national groups – Nigerians, Russians, Chinese, Moroccans and Italians.

With modern communications and transport facilities, international criminals are more ambitious in their activities and increasingly difficult to catch. They constantly seek convenient bases from which they can operate at a profit with relative safety. South Africa in the 1990s provided such a base. It was attractive, because it boasted advanced communication, transport, banking and business systems; it was politically stable; it was well placed geographically as a conduit between East and West; it had multiple entry points along its extensive coastline and land borders (including numerous small, unregulated airports); the government, the security services and the courts were inexperienced in dealing with international crime, and they had their hands full with domestic crime and internal reorganisation, while some officials were open to bribery.

The police, customs and court officials were often overwhelmed by the scale and sophistication of the criminal activity, and had difficulty in gathering adequate evidence for successful prosecutions. Commenting on West African groups, Mark Shaw wrote: 'Relationships are built on trust or long association and it is almost unknown for an individual West African to serve as witness for the state' (Shaw 1997: 16). The government's efforts to counter the criminals by its National Crime Prevention Strategy was further weakened by poor co-ordination among the agencies involved – including police, customs and court officials, military intelligence and the secret service. It was further weakened by the vast sums of money involved, leaving the poorly paid police and officials vulnerable to corruption. Overall, concluded Gastrow, the new, more democratic South Africa 'created opportunities for both the indigenous and international organized criminal groups to exploit the new low risk environment' (Gastrow 1999: 59).

The activities of the international gangs included car and cattle theft, transporting and trading drugs, prostitution, banks raids, cash heists, money laundering, game poaching and smuggling illegal immigrants. Although there was overlap, syndicates tended to specialise. The police reported that 96 syndicates concentrated on drugs, 69 with car theft, and 46 commercial fraud (SAIRR 1999/2000: 65). There were links between types of crime and ethnic groups, so that Nigerians (mainly Igbos) were prominent in drug smuggling, Russians in trading guns and Chinese in smuggling ivory and rhino horns. Two examples of criminal activities – game poaching and drug smuggling – will serve to illustrate the scale and nature of the problems faced by the government.

Game Poaching

South Africa was already involved in the struggle to preserve game animals before 1990. Its record was mixed. The white government had been among the first to establish and maintain game parks, so that the country could boast of the richest stocks of game in the world. Yet there had always been game poaching. During the 1980s this involved military officers in the special forces and intelligence units. Most of their poaching took place outside South Africa as Pretoria pursued its aggressive regional policy. According to Stephen Ellis, during the 'secret wars in southern Africa, officers under the command of the SADF's Chief of Staff (Intelligence) were systematically demanding from their allies payment in whatever commodities lay to hand, including hard wood, gold, diamonds, rhino horns and ivory'. Although the full scale of the trade was unknown, it was substantial. In 1985, for example, the total weight of ivory from official elephant culls in South Africa was 7 tons, and yet 49 tons was exported. Ellis concluded that 'the import and re-export of ivory and rhino horns from South Africa was a substantial trade which was growing in size', and came as a direct result of the destabilisation policy. A US agency also found evidence that in Angola the South Africans were buying ivory from both sides in the conflict, and that Cuban troops were also illegally trading ivory. In 1989, following the Angola/Namibia settlement, General Arnaldo Sanchez, the Cuban commander, was welcomed home as a hero. Later, however, he was convicted of corruption, including smuggling ivory, and executed (Ellis 1994).

In the 1990s, following the end of the border conflicts, the struggle to preserve endangered species entered a new phase. Game poaching became part of what Kathleen du Bois called the 'inter-relatedness of crime'. She noted how syndicates involved in poaching became enmeshed in a network of other criminal activities – car theft, gun running and the drug trade (Du Bois 1997: 28–41). With its rich reserves of wild animals, South Africa was in the forefront of the battle to preserve them. The main trade in species was in rhino horns and elephant tusks, and as South Africa boasted the world's largest stocks of both animals, it was a natural target for poachers. Rhinos (both white and black varieties) were in particular danger because in parts of Asia their horns were reputed to have aphrodisiac qualities. So great was the demand that more than 80 per cent of the world's rhinos were killed between 1970 and 1999. South Africa became central in attempts to save those that were left. Based on the best estimates, from a stock of 100,000 black rhino in Africa in 1960, only 2,200 survived by the late 1990s, of which 900 were in South Africa, and of the remaining 6,800 white rhino no fewer than 6,300 were in South Africa.

The government's efforts to counter poaching were in the hands of the Endangered Species Unit, which it inherited from the white government. Inevitably there were complaints of lack of resources, but the unit had its successes. Between the beginning of 1991 and mid-1995 it recovered 403 rhino horns and more than 4,000 elephant tusks. To take a particular example: in 1995, in co-operation with the Zambian authorities, a gang of 14 men was arrested, and convicted. They had with them ten elephant tusks, four rhino horns and three AK–47 rifles. However, such successes were again only the tip of an iceberg. Most of the poachers were Africans, including men who had fought in the border wars of the 1980s. Many worked for or traded with Asian syndicates, including members of the Taiwanese community. In dealing with the situation the game guards faced many difficulties against smugglers who operated in remote areas and were usually heavily armed, for guns were cheap in a region that had been flooded with them during the liberation struggles. Further problems arose because the poachers operated across international boundaries – with Botswana, Mozambique, Zimbabwe and Zambia. This created difficulties in pursuit, and with different legal systems when poachers who had crossed borders were caught. Nor were all the neighbours able or willing to devote many resources to game preservation, but there was little Pretoria could do to remedy such deficiencies.

The Drug Trade

During the 1990s South Africa was drawn into the international illegal trade in drugs. Previously the trade had been on a small scale. In August 1994, Lee Brown, the US Drug Control Director, stated that even 'a few months ago South Africa did not appear on the radar screen, but that has changed' (Baynham 1995: 150). In 1996 a Johannesburg magistrate, in sentencing a Nigerian dealer to eight years' imprisonment, commented that previously drug cases had been rare in South Africa, but now it had become 'the new world drug Mecca' (Baynham 1998: 91). It became a haven for traffickers, as they found that they could route and store drugs there with relative safety, whereas they faced improved enforcement measures in their old haunts.

Although South Africans themselves were involved, much of the drug trade was controlled by foreigners – West Africans, East Europeans, Russians and Pakistanis. Some groups specialised within the trade. Cannabis was mainly obtained from local and regional sources; cocaine and its derivative 'crack' were controlled by Nigerians, and heroin, which came largely from East Asia, involved Indians and Pakistanis as well as Nigerians. Overall the Nigerians were the main drug operators. The official estimate was that 'some 50,000 Nigerian immigrants are in the country, some with long histories of contraband smuggling ... Cocaine was the biggest problem' (Baynham 1998: 92). The most successful Nigerians bought houses in Johannesburg's wealthy northern suburbs, but the bulk congregated in the more central areas of Hillbrow and Yeoville, which, according to a British customs officer, 'are under the control of criminal gangs ... On every corner the effects of the drugs trade are visible to all' (Manhire 2000).

Other Southern African states were drawn into the trade, as entry and exit points for the illegal narcotics and gang members. The two small, landlocked kingdoms of Lesotho and Swaziland, with their porous borders, were used in this way. After extensive research across the region, Mark Shaw concluded that Swaziland was 'a significant trafficking route for drugs into South Africa, and for stolen goods leaving the Republic', while Lesotho provided an attractive base for operating inside South Africa, and 'has become an important transit country for West Africans, particularly Nigerians, to enter South Africa'. Shaw also discovered that Mozambique's three main ports were major 'transit zones for drugs on their way to both South African and European markets', and were controlled by Pakistani, Nigerian and local Mozambique criminal networks (Shaw 2002: 305).

To succeed the drug dealers had to be flexible and seize what opportunities arose. As a by-product of their main activity, therefore, they became involved in money laundering, and the clandestine production of illegal passports and travel documents, to enable them and their couriers to move about freely. Shaw identified two defining features of these groups. 'The first', he wrote, 'is that they are highly fluid, resembling ... the complex interactions of a network of individuals and small groups. The second is that they are engaged in multiple criminal activities, all of which are closely connected' (Shaw 2002: 315). The trade had a local impact, by increasing the use of drugs, by linking with other criminal activities

– including prostitution, car theft and arms smuggling – and by bribing and corrupting officials. Mandela warned that the trade in drugs could undermine the government's authority and its ability to maintain peace and order.

South Africa became a matter of concern to other authorities, to the extent of the US and Britain giving direct support. In 1997 the US Drug Enforcement Agency established an office in Pretoria, to help with intelligence gathering, training and joint operations. The government, itself increasingly aware of the problem, extended its efforts at home through the African Narcotics Agency, and in 1998 announced that it would post officers to South America and Asia in an attempt to undermine the trade at its sources (Oosthuysen 1998: 121).

The complex international networks of the drug trade can be illustrated by three cases in which the authorities came out on top. The first, in 1999, was an operation controlled by a Nigerian gang involving a large shipment of cocaine, which was concealed by suspending it in a barrel of rum. The rum was dispatched from Colombia by air to Johannesburg. From there the plan was to extract the cocaine in South Africa, from where it was to be taken to Swaziland, for global and regional distribution. However, the scheme was foiled through prior intelligence work; customs officials arrested the couriers and confiscated the drugs.

A second case concerned a Dominican woman who was living in New York. She too was controlled by Nigerians. At the start of her journey she was sent to South Africa with her own passport under the guise of being a tourist. On her arrival at Johannesburg she was issued with a false passport and sent to Bangkok, where she picked up a consignment of heroin. She then returned to South Africa where she handed over the drugs, and, armed with her original passport, stayed for a further week behaving as a tourist. Finally she flew back to New York with more drugs. There she was arrested by US Customs officials.

The third case illustrates that South Africans were also sucked into the trade. Some became international traders in their own right, others were recruited to play subordinate roles. One of these roles were to act as couriers. Couriers were paid about R20,000 plus expenses for a successful trip (Shaw 2002: 300). One such was a white man, who was recruited in Durban by a Nigerian syndicate. He flew to Zurich, where he was met by another syndicate member. From Zurich he flew to Ecuador to pick up cocaine, which according to the plan, he would deliver to Zurich via Madrid. He was arrested in Madrid, following effective intelligence work.

However, as with game poaching, such successes were only scratching the surface of the illegal trade. Despite its efforts Mandela's government, like others around the world, was often in retreat in the drugs war.

Day-to-Day Business and Visitors Galore

While the government struggled with chronic problems – such as migrants, HIV/Aids and crime – the day-to-day business of foreign policy continued. Alongside the conscious attempts of any government to shape developments, foreign policy is also the product of an accumulation of day-to-day decisions – the outcome of bureaucratic routine, reactions to and of other international actors, and the impact of events, both inside and outside the country. The outcomes are not always thought out, but rather come as responses to unforeseen happenings. However, recording a full sequence of day-to-day activities is impossible and even a synopsis carries the danger of becoming just 'one damned thing after another'. And so, instead of attempting 'the impossible', here a small taste of the issues that faced the South African government on a daily basis is offered by discussing one aspect of activities over a short time span. The aspect is foreign visitors; the period is the early months of 1999, just before the second democratic election.

With an election imminent the main attention of the political leaders was focused on domestic affairs. Yet foreign visitors were received, decisions made, ideas advanced and responses given. January 1999 was a particularly busy month. Ambassadors and senior members of the DFA assembled in Pretoria for their 'indaba' to discuss Selebi's paper (see Chapter 9), and Mandela attended the World Economic Forum at Davos in Switzerland (see Chapter 13). However, the first foreign visitor was Tony Blair, the British Prime Minister. On his previous visit in October 1996, he had been leader of the opposition. At that time he had vigorously advocated new Labour's concept of 'a third way', which trod a path between unbridled capitalism and old-style socialism, and was based on discipline in public finances combined with economic liberalism. He advised South Africa to follow the same path. In 1999, when he returned as Prime Minister, he had several objectives in mind – to pay homage to Mandela before he retired, to renew links with Mbeki (as Mandela's successor), and to discuss matters of mutual interest.

The diverse mutual interest included bilateral trade; British aid and investment; Pretoria's negotiations with the European Community; Mandela's mediation with Libya over the Lockerbie air disaster, and the venue for the 2006 Football World Cup. To demonstrate the UK's continuing support, Blair announced an increase in the aid programme, and a continued British contribution to training the security forces. In return he encouraged Pretoria to be active as a continental peacemaker and keeper. Blair also tried to iron out differences over controversial issues, such as Iraq and Kosovo, and he defended Britain's decision to sell part of its gold stocks. In South African eyes, the sale created the danger of other central banks and financial institutions following suit, thereby depressing the gold price, and so closing down marginal mines, leading to increased unemployment. It was a situation that underlined South Africa's part in and exposure to the rigours of the international economy. As it transpired the outcome was not too serious – the price fluctuated, reaching a low of US$256, but steadied later around the $290 mark.

Despite such differences Blair's meetings with political leaders went well, and he left expressing confidence in the country's future. However, during his stay he faced the ire of two groups of demonstrators – one recalling the past, the other opposing current British policy. Those who drew Blair into the past were Afrikaners, reminding him that a century before – during the South African (Anglo-Boer) war – Afrikaner women and children had been forced to endure the appalling conditions in British concentration camps. In contrast, most of those protesting about current policy were Muslims objecting to British and US policies in the Middle East. The police, in a ham-fisted attempt to control the Muslim crowd resorted to firing rubber bullets and birdshot. One person was killed and five were injured.

In February, South Africa played host to the representatives of two major powers – the People's Republic of China (PRC) and the USA – who remained divided ideologically despite the end of the Cold War. The Chinese were led by Zhu Rongji. They came, in part, to prepare the ground for Mandela's official visit to the PRC later in the year, but, at the same time, they took the opportunity for talks with Mbeki, in which they agreed to establish an intergovernmental co-ordinating body. Further discussions covered economic and technical co-operation, the creation of a trade commission and an agreement on civil air transport. This public display of friendship was a clear demonstration that the 'two-China' dispute was dead and buried, and with it the policy of 'universality'. That was underlined in May, when Mandela paid his visit to Beijing, where he was warmly greeted by the head of state, Jiang Zemin. The visit – which followed a major Chinese trade mission to South Africa in March 1998, and a 'stop over' in Beijing by Mbeki in April 1998 – went smoothly. It crowned the new relationship following the abandonment of the two-China policy and the opening of full diplomatic relations in January 1998. Nor did Mandela endanger his reception by raising the issue of human rights in the PRC, and in Chinese-occupied Tibet.

Of greater immediate importance were the Americans. Their delegation was led by Vice President Al Gore, who was accompanied by five members of President Clinton's cabinet, plus a small army of officials. They came for a meeting of the Binational Commission. As seen by Washington, the commission was part of a growing relationship and an indication of its commitment to South Africa. This commitment was further reflected in exchange trips by leading figures, including President Bill Clinton, who in March 1998 had become the first serving US President to visit South Africa. Clinton was accompanied by Robert Rubin, the US Secretary to the Treasury, who was keen to promote trade, and he urged Pretoria to adhere to a market economy. Shortly afterwards William Cohen, the US Secretary of Defence, came to discuss security issues.

The 1999 meeting of the Binational Commission enhanced the already warm personal relations between the joint chairmen, Gore and Mbeki, thereby cementing links between the two governments. Among its tasks the commission was to promote common interests and to consult on new developments. For example, before Clinton sent it to Congress, the Americans asked for comments on the US African Growth and Opportunity Bill, which was designed to reach free trade agreements with countries that were committed to democracy, liberal economies and good governance. However, the bonhomie of the 'Gore–Mbeki show' could not iron out all bilateral differences. Even the Africa Growth Bill ran into problems in the US Senate, where it was opposed by supporters of labour and the textile industry, who feared that it would undermine their interests.

In more general terms the US advocated development by trade rather than aid, whereas Pretoria wanted both. Within that broad framework the two sides had specific differences. They included a bitter dispute over the behaviour of US pharmaceutical companies, and a US court case against Armscor (see Chapter 12). Yet, while these disputes disturbed the harmony of the relationship, they were also an indication of the strength and diversity of day-to-day contacts between the two states. Those contacts bore more fruit when, in March 1999, Mandela achieved a breakthrough in the long-standing dispute between Libya and the US/UK about the terrorist bombing of a Pan Am aircraft over Lockerbie in Scotland in 1988. Through the patient and persistent efforts of Mandela and Professor Jakes Gerwel (Director General of the President's Office) Libya agreed to hand over two suspects for trial by a Scottish court, sitting in the Netherlands. In this case, at least, Mandela had shown that, despite Western criticism of his links with 'rogue states', those links had paid a handsome dividend. The result also underlined the skill of Mandela and Gerwel as mediators and 'go betweens'. All sides trusted them, and so they could move forward on the basis of mutual confidence. The advantages for the West were obvious, while for Colonel Gadaffi, the Libyan leader, the agreement held out the prospect of reducing Western pressure, and of gaining South African support for his ambitious plans to help create a United States of Africa.

Also in March, after more than three years of protracted and often frustrating negotiations, an accord was reached with the European Union for a Free Trade and Development Agreement. It had been hoped that the agreement would be signed before Mandela's retirement, but even at this late stage snags arose. Some European states dragged their feet over what seemed petty issues, but in which the interests of powerful domestic groups were affected (see Chapter 13). These snags were annoying but came as no surprise to Pretoria's negotiators, who had learned that, for all the talk of helping the new democracy, the Europeans made few if any concessions when their domestic interests were at stake. In the tough, detailed negotiations, the South Africans had learned that they could not rely on broad, general claims or on sympathy from the EU bureaucracy. They needed well-researched, closely argued briefs, and dogged determination.

The 1999 Election

In June 1999 the second post-apartheid election confirmed the political pre-eminence of the ANC. It won 66 per cent of the vote and continued in government. There was, however, a shift of ranking among opposition parties. Following de Klerk's retirement the NP had steadily declined; while the DP, led by Tony Leon, strengthened its position (mainly but not exclusively among whites) and became the leading opposition party in parliament. Next in size came the IFP, which retained its core support in KwaZulu-Natal. The 1999 election, therefore, left the party political map largely unchanged, with the ANC in a dominant position. Even the mixed composition of the government remained. With the end of the interim (five-year) constitution, formal 'power sharing' also came to an end. However, although he was no longer constitutionally obliged to offer cabinet seats to other parties, Mbeki did so for the existing IFP ministers.

IV

South Africa Gains an International Identity: Its International Roles

12
The Prodigal Returns as a Middle Power

Although the 1999 election did little to change the complexion of domestic politics, viewed from outside it marked an upheaval: Mandela had retired. In his five years in office he had established himself as a major international figure. Inevitably most of the questions that followed the election concentrated on a future without his leadership. How would the government perform without him? Would South Africa gain less international attention and support? What would be the impact on the economy? How would Mbeki fare as President? Here, however, a different set of questions is discussed – by examining what had been achieved by the end of Mandela's presidency. In short: what international inheritance did the great man leave behind? The final part of the book attempts to answer that question by identifying four broad international roles South Africa had established by the end of the 1990s – 'The Prodigal Returns as a Middle Power'; 'The Bridge Builder'; 'The African Power and Accommodation'; and 'The Regional Giant'.

International Roles

The roles a state plays are in part created by itself and in part shaped by the response of others. A compound of factors are involved – the state's geo-political setting; its aims; its values and interests; its resources and how they are employed; its political leadership; its response to experiences; its perception of itself and how it is seen and treated by others. In South Africa's case, for instance, two of its roles relate to Africa. Its geographical position determines that it is involved in the continent, irrespective of the political complexion of the government. Yet – as is demonstrated by comparing the continental policies and relationships of P.W. Botha's government with those of Mandela's – the nature of the roles is dependent on the values and interests that the state pursues, the resources it employs and how successfully it employs them, and the response of other African states and organisations.

A state has more than one role, and is judged in different ways, according to the role it is filling within a particular setting. The 1996 DFA discussion paper recognised that in saying that:

> States are often allies and competitors at the same time. They may co-operate at the WTO to reduce tariffs in a third country, but their industrialists may be in fierce competition for market access to the same country (DFA 1996: 9).

Although states play more than one role, no state can lay down a precise foreign policy (or set of roles) in advance. It can declare its aims, principles and perceived interests, but, in seeking to implement them it has to deploy what resources it has within the context of the time and in response to the reactions of other international players. In doing so it will often have to modify its original aims and/or give priority to others. It will have to find its way through the vagaries of international affairs, with its unexpected events and developments. Nzo once mused about the possibility of a 'codified foreign policy'. That was a pipe dream. If an analogy is drawn with a legal system, foreign policy is more like common law than codified law. Common law is based on broadly agreed principles, which are applied and interpreted case by case, taking account of the particular circumstances. Over time a general, but flexible pattern emerges. Similarly foreign policy combines intention with experience and the capacity to build on experience. It cannot be fixed, but over time an 'orientation' can be identified, based on the state's main roles, as derived from the compound of factors noted above.

The Return of the Prodigal

The biblical story of the prodigal son involves three men – a father and his two sons. The younger son, eager to leave home, asks his father to give him his inheritance there and then. The father agrees, and the younger son sets off to lead a wild, dissolute life. In contrast, the elder son stays behind to help his father. The younger son, his inheritance spent, falls on hard times and lives a wretched life. Eventually he decides to return home – to confess his faults, throw himself on his father's mercy and seek a humble job on the family estate. In the event the father, on seeing the returning prodigal, is overjoyed. Far from being content to find his son a humble job the father greets him with love and forgiveness, celebrating the son's return by throwing a great feast at which he kills a fatted calf, kept for a special occasion. The elder son is much less enthusiastic. He asks his father why there is such rejoicing at the return of a son who has behaved badly, while his own faithfulness has not been so rewarded. St Luke's story – which might be better entitled 'The Forgiving Father' than 'The Prodigal Son' – ends there. We are not told what happened later – how the relationship developed between the two sons, whether the prodigal behaved well, or whether his past caught up with him in one form or another (St Luke 15).

There are parallels between the biblical story and South Africa's return to the international fold. On the South African side there was repentance for past sins, and within the international community much rejoicing at the prodigal's return. Yet, it would be a mistake to push the analogy too far. While, for instance, the younger son remained the same person, the South African state that re-entered the international community was very different from the one that had been condemned for its racist policies. Further, South Africa's story did not end with the triumphant return. Instead the new state became immersed in the changing international scene, in which alongside the welcome and acclamation were new problems and challenges.

South Africa's welcome took diverse forms – the lifting of sanctions, increased trade and aid; the growth of the tourist industry; diplomatic links; and Pretoria's enthusiastic admission to international organisations. 'We all stood and cheered. It was like the second coming', said a witness to South Africa's readmission to one of these bodies. One measure of change came in the expansion of diplomatic posts. In 1989 South Africa had 30 diplomatic missions abroad; by 1995 that had risen to 124, covering 163 countries, most of whom established their own missions in South Africa. At the same time Pretoria was admitted or readmitted to the major multilateral organisations, their agencies and off-shoots. By any standards it was a remarkable transformation.

Nor was the welcome confined to formal recognition. As far as South Africa was concerned killing the fatted calf came in the form of international aid. Foreign states and organisations were eager to help, and be seen to help. The UN committed itself to support 'the completion of the process of peaceful political transition and the establishment of sustainable democracy', through such measures as the reform of the civil service, the restoration of security, and the reduction of inequalities in health, education, housing and employment (Geldenhuys 1998: 95). Towards those ends UN agencies – Unesco, WHO, Unicef and ILO – made their separate contributions. For example, Unicef allocated R80m for primary health care and to help women and children, and the UN Development Programme offered R56m for the advancement of human resources. In addition the UN cancelled most of South Africa's outstanding debt to it of US$95m. The debt had built up since September 1974 – when the apartheid regime had been suspended from the General Assembly. After that Pretoria had refused to pay its full UN dues. Following discussions a compromise was agreed, whereby the new government was liable to pay only US$3m, the sum that had been incurred prior to suspension from the Assembly. In return Pretoria agreed to make a contribution to UN peacekeeping operations in Africa.

Other international organisations and individual governments were equally active in offering development aid, and, unlike apartheid days (when the small amounts of aid had been channelled through NGOs), most of the aid was now directed through the government. The provision of aid was a clear indication of international approval, especially as by the usual criteria South Africa was too wealthy to qualify for much support. In 1990 its GDP was US$90,720bn or three times the size of its nine African neighbours combined, and its per capita income was US$2,530, compared with an average of US$647 for the neighbours (Bischoff and Southall 1999: 155). In the general enthusiasm for the new state, that hurdle was crossed by treating it as a special case; whereby aid was given to bolster the new democratic order and to help those who had suffered under apartheid. The US Ambassador, Princeton Lyman, explained that it had been given 'to compensate for the country's relative isolation throughout the sanctions years, which deprived it of help, for example in housing and education'

(Kornegay 2000). Added to which the context for aid had changed. While during the Cold War it had often been linked to support for one of the power blocs, now it was replaced by a commitment to Western-inspired values of democracy and good governance. What better candidate of such virtues could be presented than South Africa, with its political 'miracle', its liberal constitution and its venerated leader?

Finally, donor states and organisations, like individual political leaders, were eager to be associated with the new South Africa. In October 1994 representatives of fifty governments attended a Commonwealth and UN sponsored donors' conference, following which a total of R4.7bn (US$1.3bn) was pledged in grant aid. The bulk of aid came from developed Western states and international organisations. Alongside a substantial contribution from the EU, there were separate contributions from its member states, including aid 'packages' of R7bn from both France and Britain. The US allocated US$600m over a three-year period, for trade, investment and development (Geldenhuys 1998: 95–8). Princeton Lyman, the US Ambassador, pointed out that in per capita terms South Africa was receiving twice as much aid as Russia. However, he underlined again the main American theme, that the driving force of economic success was private enterprise and not aid from the government.

Although Pretoria welcomed the support, there was room for doubt and misunderstanding on both sides. The donors were eager to help, but they expected thanks and appreciation, and to further their own interests and values. The South Africans were equally determined not to become lackeys of the West. Mandela on one occasion angered the Americans by dismissing US aid as 'peanuts', by which he meant that it was little compared with America's wealth. To add to the potential for misunderstanding and administrative muddle, much of the aid came in the form of 'packages': a mixture of grants, loans, credits, investments, export guarantees and tax incentives.

Japan provides an example of what it (as donor) regarded as generous gesture, only to find that it was seen in a different light by the South Africans. In May 1994, shortly after the formation of Mandela's government, Japan offered an aid package of US$1.3bn, the largest it had ever put together and the largest offered by a single state to Pretoria. It consisted of US$500m for export-import loans, US$500m as investment credits for Japanese companies, plus US$300m in grants. Access to the aid was subject to precise procedures, which were laid down in Tokyo through its Overseas Development Assistance Programme. The Japanese were shocked when Jay Naidoo (then a Minister) dismissed the package as mainly a propaganda exercise, with 'the bulk of the finance devoted to supporting Japanese business concerns rather than towards grant aid or concessional loans'. So deep was the misunderstanding that meetings between officials from both sides 'broke down in acrimony'. However, the Japanese persisted, because they saw South Africa both as a good cause in its own right, and as the best way to gain influence and markets in the continent. Thus, following the Asian financial crisis of 1997–98, the only foreign aid proposal Tokyo put forward was a revised package for South Africa, which had larger grant and loan elements, and was consciously targeted at ANC priorities. Even so Pretoria's response was lukewarm, based on the continued belief that the package was designed largely for Japanese interests. As a result Tokyo started to explore ways of bypassing the government and channelling its support through NGOs (Alden 2002: 378/9).

Further criticism of aid programmes was voiced by radical figures, such as Charles Nqakula, the General Secretary of the SACP. He too claimed that aid was designed primarily to meet the interests of the donor states and their commercial companies. 'The great bulk of this money', he said, 'is very often earmarked as special subsidies for British, or Japanese or US exporters. Or it is spent on fees for foreign consultants of all kinds' (Nqakula 1994: 9). There was further resentment when some donors claimed that as a relatively wealthy country South Africa should not need such support. The Americans led the way in this respect. In 1996 USAID Administrator, Brian Attwood, said that if South Africa 'gets its economic policies right and invests in people there shouldn't be a need for aid'. These US doubts were not confined to South Africa, but reflected an increasing scepticism about the efficacy of aid in general. Washington kept preaching the gospel of trade and the market. It was in that spirit that Ronald Brown, the US Secretary for Commerce, explained why the US aid programme was confined to three years. It was aimed, he said, to help 'make South Africa a more productive, consumer-orientated, competitive society' (Geldenhuys 1998: 96/97).

International Organisations

One clear sign of acceptance of Mandela's government came from international organisations. These bodies, which had rejected the apartheid regime, now enthusiastically courted the new South Africa. There was equal enthusiasm on the South African side. Soon South Africa was up to its neck in international organisations, with their plethora of initials and acronyms – UN, WHO, Unesco, NAM, ILO, SADC, OAU, IAEA, WTO, UNCTAD. By 1999 Pretoria was a member of 45 international organisations. The joy of such bodies in welcoming the new South Africa was enhanced by their own past record – their sense of achievement; of having contributed to a just cause (against apartheid) and having won. Nor did their enthusiasm end there. Like Mandela's government, international bodies espoused idealistic aims. In the post-Cold War setting, they shared a language of values and principles, in their pursuit of 'democracy', 'human rights', 'good governance', and 'the rule of law'.

The Commonwealth exemplified this. During the 1980s – with apartheid still in place – its summits had been dominated by sustained attacks on Pretoria, and on Britain's refusal to impose further sanctions. In the 1990s the focus shifted, as the end of apartheid both rejuvenated the organisation and led to a new agenda .The Harare Declaration of 1991 spoke of 'the protection and promotion of the fundamental political values', of 'democracy, democratic processes and institutions which reflect national circumstances, the rule of law and the independence of the judiciary, just and honest government [and] fundamental human rights' (Commonwealth Secretariat 1995). Then, in 1999, shortly before

Mandela's retirement, at a Commonwealth summit in Durban, the members added to the Harare Declaration a 'Framework for Principles Promoting Good Government and Combating Corruption', based on policies which were to be credible, tangible and visible.

The International Middle Power

Having been admitted to the inner international circuit Mandela's government was not content to be passive, to sit back and enjoy its new-found status. Instead it saw itself as a mover and shaker, and behaved in a way that was characteristic of an active 'middle power'. As the name implies, 'middle powers' are those that stand in the international hierarchy between the 'great' and 'small' states.

Andrew Cooper and colleagues – recognising that such a broad definition left the concept of 'middle power' vague and contested – have suggested four ways of giving it greater precision. The first, and the most common, was to measure the state's position in the global hierarchy by quantifiable assets such as its area, population, economy and military capability. A second definition was derived from a state's geographical situation, in which its relative power within its own region came into play. A third definition was based on a normative approach, whereby middle powers were seen to be wiser, more virtuous and trustworthy than other states. Cooper was sceptical of the third definition, and favoured instead a fourth approach, whereby 'middle powers are defined primarily by their behaviour: their tendency to pursue multilateral solutions to international problems, to embrace compromise positions in international disputes, and to embrace notions of "good international citizenship".' (Cooper, Higgott and Nosell 1993: 21).

On all four counts there is a case for classifying South Africa as a middle power, although its position in the international hierarchy is not entirely clear cut. If quantifiable resources – such as the economy, and the size and skills of its population – are the criteria, it is not as well endowed as such middle powers as Australia and Canada. (In GDP per capita South Africa is similar to such countries as Mexico and Turkey, but has a smaller population.) However, if the status of 'middle power' is based on Cooper's fourth definition – a state's behaviour, taking account of its capacity and willingness to act, and the effectiveness of its actions – then the new South Africa is firmly in the frame. The capacity to act depends not only on the state's resources but its geo-politic situation, its aspirations, its leadership and the attitude of other states towards it. What South Africa lacked in resources it made up in other ways. In regional terms it was the most advanced and powerful country in Central/Southern Africa. It was politically stable, it held the moral high ground; it was eager to use its position and resources in pursuit of its aims, and in Mandela it had a major statesman. In the international arena South Africa was able to 'punch above its weight'.

The claim to middle power status was reinforced by Pretoria's active participation in multilateral organisations. 'At its core', wrote Cooper, 'the concept of middle power diplomacy signifies a certain content of foreign policy based on an attachment to multilateral institutions and a collaborative world order' (Cooper 1997: 4). Similarly Robert Keohane stated that: 'A middle power is a state whose leaders consider that it cannot act alone effectively, but may be able to have a systemic impact ... in an international organisation'. (Keohane 1968: 296). In line with such claims Pretoria set out to use its influence in multilateral bodies by combining the pursuit of global principles with its ambitions to be a leader of 'the South'. Selebi saw South Africa as a 'key supporter of a rule-based international community ... [enabling] the weak to have the same voice as the powerful'. Nzo spoke of building a 'more equitable, democratic international order', which, he told parliament, 'allows the weaker and smaller countries to participate on an equal footing on the world stage' (Mills 1999/2000: 8 and NA 4.3.99: 1138).

Pretoria's multilateral commitment was also motivated by attempts to counterbalance the emergence of powerful economic blocs of advanced states, such as the EU and the North American Free Trade Area (NAFTA). Its efforts in this direction were not confined to Africa, but included attempts to create new patterns of contact with Latin America and states around the Indian Ocean rim. There was an air of experiment in these efforts – a sense of throwing bread upon the water, in the hope but not the certainty that rewards would follow. The Indian Ocean initiative exemplifies this. The broad idea of forming such a group/community of states was raised by Mandela when he visited India in January 1995. He spoke of history and geography providing a foundation on which to build a co-operative venture around the ocean's rim. The Indian government responded warmly, and was soon joined by Australia. The outcome was an exploratory meeting of seven states in Mauritius in March 1995. That was so encouraging that a further meeting was held in the following year, with seven more states attending, including Indonesia and two from Africa – Mozambique and Tanzania. Again there was progress, as they agreed to form 'The Indian Ocean Rim – Association for Regional Co-operation' (IOR-ARC). According to its charter the IOR-ARC was 'designed to set directions for the economic and trade policies in the Indian Ocean' (Mills 1999: 149). While the main focus of attention was economic co-operation, a research network was set up, and plans made for joint educational activities.

Following that encouraging start, however, the IOR-ARC ran into problems. Other states – including Pakistan, Iran, Egypt, Bangladesh and France – expressed their interest in joining. In one sense their enthusiasm to participate was a sign of success, but the number and diversity of the applicants led to confusion about the criteria for entry. Even the association's geographical scope was in doubt, so that, depending on interpretation, it could embrace anywhere between 24 and 60 members. Further uncertainty arose because of existing antagonisms (notably between India and Pakistan); questions of human rights (for example, Indonesia's poor record); and ideological commitment (as in the case of Iran). In an attempt to preserve the early progress and to avoid quarrels it was decide to put all new applicants on ice. Even so, the momentum declined, as existing members revealed their reluctance to commit resources to IOR-ARC activities. For example, the Indian Ocean Research Network was soon in financial difficulties, with only Australia making its full contribution. While, therefore, bread had been thrown on the water, it had not, during Mandela's presidency, led to a significant catch.

The Campaign Against Personnel Mines

A more successful example of South Africa's role as a middle power came in its contribution to the campaign to ban anti-personnel mines (APM). These mines, which troops often left behind without proper records of their whereabouts, had proved to be a menace to civilians. The Red Cross reported that more than 80 per cent of those who were killed or maimed for life were civilians, and so the mines were increasingly seen as a humanitarian as well as a military concern. The scale of the problem was immense, with estimates that an average of one to two million mines were planted each year, while fewer than 100,000 were lifted. Because of its wars and instability, Africa, and Southern Africa in particular, had the world's greatest concentration of mines. An OAU report stated that six of the world's most mined countries were in the continent, with estimates of between 9 and 15 million mines in Angola alone, and more than 2 million in Mozambique.

By the beginning of the 1990s little progress had been made in limiting the use of AP mines. However, early in 1994 de Klerk's government showed concern by declaring a moratorium on their marketing and export. In the same year the UN Secretary General convened a review conference, but after spending two years on meetings its achievements were modest. It certainly failed to satisfy those who were campaigning for a complete ban on the mines. Among the campaigners were South African NGOs, which came together to form the South African Campaign to Ban Landmines (SACBL). SACBL lobbied the new government, but initially it moved cautiously, with the Department of Defence reluctant to accept a full ban and more generally the government not wanting to be out of line with its SADC partners.

However, under continued pressure from NGOs, Pretoria edged forwards by adopting a bridging role between those who favoured a complete ban and those who wanted unrestricted use. In 1995 it signed an international convention, restricting the use of AP mines, and in the following year announced its intention to discontinue their manufacture and sale. In doing so Pretoria was responding to an initiative from two other 'middle powers' – Canada and New Zealand – by giving its support for 'all efforts to achieve an international prohibition on the production, stockpiling, transfer and use of all anti personnel land mines'. In a memorandum, signed by Mandela and the Prime Minister of New Zealand, the two leaders called for 'the world wide elimination of anti personnel mines'. In October 1996, matters moved further when the government sent representatives to a conference in Ottawa, which was attended by more than 70 governments, plus a host of NGOs. At Ottawa campaigners for a ban succeeded in shifting the debate away from military issues to those related to the suffering of innocent people. The outcome – in what became known as 'the Ottawa process' – was a call for steps leading to a complete ban on AP mines.

In February 1997 Pretoria, its bridging role over in this case, announced that it was imposing a complete ban on AP mines. Leading from the front, it became a strong advocate of 'the Ottawa process', and was the first African government to destroy its stockpile of AP mines. In May 1997 it furthered the cause by hosting an OAU conference on the subject. Outside the continent Pretoria also played a prominent part. For example, its representative led a discussion about a ban at the Geneva Conference on Disarmament. Then, in a demonstration of middle power co-operation, Canada nominated Jackie Selebi as chairman of the negotiations for a Landmine Treaty that opened in Oslo in September 1997. It was a tribute both to Selebi and to South Africa (Nel, Taylor and Van der Westhuizen 2000: 43–60). The momentum paid off, so that by December, 120 governments had signed the Ottawa Convention; and although some of the most powerful states (including the US, China and Russia) were not signatories, it was an impressive achievement. Together with other middle powers, Mandela's government had succeeded in establishing a new international norm – involving a shift in values – which gained respect, even from the states that had refused to sign (Maxwell 1998).

Leadership Aspirations

A frequently stated aim of Mandela's government was to gain greater international equality by enhancing the position of developing states. As a middle power it presented its case in idealistic terms – by stressing the need for a stronger voice for the Third World, but, at the same time, it also suited Pretoria's leadership aspirations. To achieve its ends it was eager not only to be active inside international organisations but to change them. As a result – and from the UN down – it was both a strong supporter of international bodies and a keen advocate of their reform. In the case of the UN Nzo argued that the existing Charter looked too much to the past, by favouring the victorious powers of the World War II. To remedy that by looking to the future he advocated an expansion of the Security Council – from its five permanent members (the main allies of the war, each with the power of veto) – to include new permanent representatives of developing states. At the same time he suggested increasing the powers of the General Assembly, with its Third World majority. Nzo called for a debate in South Africa on whether the government should seek a permanent seat in a reformed Security Council as a representative of Africa (NA 4.3.99: 1138). Without doubt the government favoured the idea. 'Since', said Selebi, 'South Africa's main foreign policy concern is to be part of shaping the global agenda, we would want to become a permanent member of the Security Council' (Schoeman 2000: 54).

Despite such efforts little progress was made at the UN. Change was stunted by the organisation's own laborious processes, by foot-dragging from the established powers, and by the failure of developing states to match general appeals for reform with agreement on the particulars. For example, while the OAU also favoured permanent African representation in the Council, it wanted a set number of permanent African seats to be filled in rotation, and not by the same states (such as South Africa). To fulfil its UN ambitions Pretoria's first task was, therefore, to win over fellow African states; a task still to be achieved when Mandela retired.

Yet progress was made in South Africa's leadership ambitions. One step along that path was the invitation to host the 1998 conference of the Non Aligned Movement (NAM), and to chair that organisation for three years. NAM had been formed during the Cold War by a group of states (predominantly from the Third World) that claimed to be uncommitted to either East or West. With the end of the Cold War it reinvented itself, as the representative of peoples, who having been freed from the colonial yoke, were now determined to have their collective voice heard. When it met at Durban in 1998, NAM numbered no fewer than 113 states. In their eyes, the rich, developed states were out to exploit and subordinate them. Despite their great diversity in terms of development, size, culture and interests NAM members found a common bond in seeking greater equality in the distribution of global power and rewards. Mbeki told the delegates at Durban that their main task was to restructure the global economy. Yet, to achieve that, and in line with the South Africa's own principles, he stressed that they should first ensure that their own houses were in order; in relation to democracy and sound economic management; and second, that their economic aims could only be achieved by working with the developed states. Such home truths were not universally popular with NAM members. Mbeki also angered the Indian delegation by criticising Delhi's testing of nuclear weapons, along with Pakistan, and the Indians were further annoyed when Mandela offered to act as a 'go between' in the Kashmir dispute with Pakistan (Arnold 2000: 166).

Meeting the Multilateral Challenge

While the rapid increase in diplomatic links and membership of multilateral institutions were enthusiastically pursued, it imposed strains on the administrative and personnel capacity of the new government. There was a problem of finding satisfactory staff to cover the array of new posts, at a time when there was heavy demand elsewhere. The diplomats were recruited from diverse sources. Some had little relevant experience, and even those that had – who had served in the ANC's missions, or had represented the apartheid government – had to come to terms with a new situation. The ANC members had now to represent the full spectrum of a state's interests, not the narrower concerns of a liberation movement. The old DFA officials, having previously tried to defend the indefensible and been excluded from most international bodies, now found themselves representing a popular government within the same bodies.

The heavy demands on the administration, and the speed of involvement in world organisations, were graphically recorded in a report of the DFA's Multilateral Branch. The report, which covered the first half of 1995, was prepared by Abdul Minty, a senior DFA official, who previously had been a leading figure in the British Anti Apartheid Movement. Minty recorded a list of new commitments, starting in February 1995 when South Africa entered the International Maritime Organisation (IMO), and its representative was elected Vice President of that body. In March it became a founding member of the Indian Ocean group (IOR-ARC) at its meeting in Mauritius. In April a delegation led by RDP Minister, Jay Naidoo, attended the UN Economic and Social Council (ECOSOC) in Geneva, to discuss African development issues. In the following month South Africa was elected to serve on the UN Commission for Narcotic Drugs. In June it gained a seat on the International Atomic Energy Authority (IAEA); and, in the same month an area office of the International Labour Organisation (ILO) was established in Pretoria. Meanwhile, Pretoria was active in discussions on the control of weapons of mass destruction, including nuclear arms, and a South African (Zach de Beer) became chair of the UN Committee for the Prohibition of Chemical Weapons. In Africa, South Africa was made a member of the OAU's Central Organ for Conflict Prevention, Management and Resolution, and joined an OAU mission to the Comoros, following an abortive coup. Looking to the future, Minty noted that South Africa had been chosen to stage UN World Environment Day, and nominated to host and chair the UN Conference on Trade and Development (UNCTAD) in May 1996. Looking even further ahead, it was to chair the Non Aligned Movement (NAM) from 1998 to 2001.

That was a formidable agenda for any administration but especially for one as new and undergoing such change as in South Africa. The report also indicated how quickly South Africa had become a prominent player in international organisations. As an active and trusted middle power it gained a reputation both for commitment and even handedness. Those characteristics led to invitations not only to attend meetings but to chair them – including UNCTAD; NAM; the Nuclear Non-Proliferation Treaty (NPT); the Oslo conference on personnel mines; the 1998 UN Commission on Human Rights; and the 1999 Commonwealth Conference. Further, it was voted unto the executive of UN bodies, such as the Children's Fund (Unicef); the Educational, Scientific and Cultural Organisation (Unesco); the Development Programme, the Population Fund, and the Commission for Refugees (Nel, Taylor and van der Westhuizen 2000: 43–60). The prodigal South Africa had not only been welcomed back into the international community it had been given positions of trust and responsibility, to the extent of acting as an international 'go between'.

13
The Bridge Builder & Accommodation

Before leaving for the 1999 meeting of the World Trade Organisation (WTO) at Seattle, Alec Erwin, the Minister of Trade and Industry, stated that 'South Africa is something of a bridge between the developed and developing world'. He explained this in terms of the country's economic structure with its First and Third World sections, its geographical position astride the Atlantic and Indian Oceans, and the range of its domestic and international interests. All these, he claimed, helped South Africa to understand and articulate the views of both sides in the world's economic divide, between the 'developed North' and the 'developing South'. Yet, although South Africa had a foot in each camp, Erwin reiterated that it identified itself with the South. The real challenge, he said, was to ensure that future development took place across the board, benefiting the poor as well as the rich. In pursuing this end Erwin rejected the notion that the South should slavishly follow the model of the affluent North. Along that road, he argued, lay stagnation – the best prospects for long-term future growth lay with the developing world. Within that context he believed that 'South Africa has a major interest in giving leadership'. It should, he argued, be confident enough to seize initiatives, including a major revision of the world's trading system. Progress, he concluded, could only be achieved and sustained through a broad approach (embracing economic, social and political policies), which offered equality of opportunity and rewards, the recognition of human rights, just labour laws, fair trading regimes and effective financial systems (Muller 2000: 9/10).

The part that Erwin envisaged for South Africa in the global political economy was that of an active middle power, and one that – reinforced by the expectations of others – was ready to adopt a leadership role. Time after time, claimed Selebi, 'countries, organisations and peoples have looked to us to provide leadership, new ideas and breakthroughs' (Schoeman 2000: 50). With its new-born confidence, Pretoria believed it could play a bridge-building role, which would enable it to fulfil its ambitions to narrow the gap between rich and poor; to reduce the threat of war; to act as a peacemaker (particularly in Africa); to forge new alliances; and to ensure that Africa was not marginalised by the international community.

It was in that spirit that the government acted. Two 1996 trade conferences illustrate the point. The first, which met in South Africa, was the United Nations Conference on Trade and Development (UNCTAD) at which Alec

Erwin was elected President until 2000. For the states of the South, UNCTAD had acted as a watchdog and supporter, but it was in danger of being eclipsed by other bodies, such as WTO, IMF and the World Bank, which were dominated by the richer states. With Erwin in the chair, South Africa supported UNCTAD in the spirit of its bridging role, by such steps as stressing the need for co-operation, and by giving assistance to poorer states in their relations with the WTO.

The second conference, held at Singapore in December 1996, was a meeting of the WTO itself. Again the South African delegation, which contained both business and labour representatives, set out to further the interests of the South, without alienating the developed world. For example, it sought a middle path in a dispute over international working conditions. At issue was the question of the acceptance of universal standards, to cover such matters as labour and safety standards. The poorer countries suspected that the rich were trying to protect their own industries by imposing costly regulations to remove the Third World's cost advantages. Guided by the South Africans, acting in their bridge-building/middle power role, the conference eventually agreed a compromise, which renewed existing labour standards, but rejected their use as a protectionist device (Kuper 1997: 263/4).

The International Political Economy

Erwin was not the first to envisage South Africa as having a special niche to act as a bridge between 'the haves' and 'the have-nots' of the international political economy. In March 1995, Nzo had stated:

> The position in which South Africa finds itself is that it has features both of the developed and developing worlds. It is truly at the point of intersection between both worlds – an industrialized state of the South, which can communicate with the North on equal terms to articulate the needs, the concerns and the fears of the developing world. Conversely we can interpret the concerns and fears of the developed world (DFA 1996: 12).

Some other middle powers had a mix of First and Third World elements, but South Africa was the only one in Africa, and so offered a link between the advanced economies and the world's poorest states. In relative terms Africa was falling even further behind in the economic stakes. Measured in GDP per capita the continent had 18 of the world's 20 poorest states. Its share of world trade, which had always been small, fell further from 3 per cent in the 1960s to less than 2 per cent in the 1990s. As a result Africa's voice was weak in the organisations and institutions that shaped the world's economy. Pretoria aimed to change that (Gelb and Floyd 1999). With a foot in both camps, it was ready to use its new-found status and prestige to seize the initiative when opportunities arose, as happened when South Africa was chosen to chair bodies like UNCTAD and NAM.

Although the government saw itself promoting greater understanding and acting as champion of the underprivileged, it had to operate in a setting dominated by the rich and powerful. It was their values and interests that shaped the financial and trading agendas, via bodies like the World Bank, the IMF and the Gatt. Although determined to demonstrate its own independence and its championship of the South, Pretoria realised that to succeed it had to work with the developed world. As early as 1993 the ANC's International Department had noted that: 'Our future relations with the international community will have to be based on economic and trade considerations rather than on ideological considerations' (Alden 1993: 77). In its attempts to build bridges, the government therefore pursued a policy of 'accommodation' – which its opponents derided as a form of appeasement. For instance, in 1997 it invited, for the first time, the US, Britain, France and the EU to send representatives to the NAM meeting. Mbeki explained this as a way of gaining co-operation in restructuring the world economy, so that NAM members became stakeholders rather than suppliants.

Yet, for all its good intentions, South Africa could not escape an inbuilt tension in its bridge-building/accommodation role. The government argued that having a foot in each camp provided the opportunity to seek an agreement between them, but alternatively it could be seen as a source of tension and conflicting interests. To secure its ends – at home and abroad – Pretoria needed an expanding international economy. Despite Erwin's long-term faith in the developing world, in the immediate future expansion largely depended on the wealth and drive of the advanced states. The Parliamentary Committee on Foreign Affairs concluded that although South Africa's future was linked with the South, 'there are certain realities that we dare not ignore', including the economic dominance of the wealthy G7 countries, which are 'essential to the economic well being of the developing world'. The committee went on to note the generous support being given to South Africa by the richer states. 'For this', it concluded, 'we are grateful, and will continue to build on this sound foundation' (NA 18.3.95).

Another part of 'reality' was 'globalisation'. In Greg Mills's view, it was 'an irreversible fact of life', in which the new South Africa had to operate and look for support (Mills 1999: 110). The 'irreversible fact' was reflected in the extension of the General Agreement on Trade and Tariffs (GATT) – in which during the 1950s only 30 countries had participated, whereas by the 1990s there were more than 130 member states. The wealthy kept assuring the poor that globalisation – with its emphasis on the market, tariff reductions, the information-based revolution, deregulation, privatisation and fiscal conservatism – was the best, indeed the only way forward. Pretoria had reservations about these assurances. It pointed, for instance, to the agricultural protection policies of Western states, but it accepted that to be an active player it had to accommodate itself to the prevailing norms and rules, even if its aim was to change them. Government ministers defended themselves by claiming that it was only through co-operation and facing up to economic realities that they could achieve greater global equality and satisfy South Africa's own interests.

Such assumptions were not always popular even inside the government. An official claimed that to attract foreign investment and aid South Africa had to parade like a beauty queen before Europeans and Americans 'who will say "yes, beautiful" and therefore we will invest in you or give you aid'. As a result, South Africa could finish up as a dependent creature of the rich (Taylor and Williams 2001: 265). Critics inside the tripartite alliance were more vociferous. They claimed that globalisation, far from narrowing the gap between rich and poor, was enlarging it. For them the government's policy of accommodation smacked of hypocrisy and appeasement. They accused it of talking 'left' and acting 'right', and of being in the pocket of the local business community, whose interests, experience and culture orientated it to the North. In the eyes of the critics the North's dominance was a threat to the developing world and to South Africa itself. Their criticism was sharpened by the economic crises of the 1990s, when countries like Mexico and even some of the 'Asian tigers' ran into problems, because, argued the critics, they had followed the route mapped out by the IMF. Ben Turok claimed that integration into the global economy was undermining the state's commitment to social development and its management of the economy. He accused Pretoria of accepting too readily the prevailing neo-liberal consensus. He challenged the efficacy of trade liberalisation and the 'reality' of globalisation (Turok 1999: 4/5).

Mandela personally experienced the conflicting tensions when he attended the World Economic Forum at Davos, Switzerland in January 1999. Most of those attending this annual meeting were from the world's richest governments and private companies, but South Africa was also invited. Mandela saw his presence there as part of Pretoria's bridging role, but for the critics it was mere tokenism – an invitation to ward off criticism that only the wealthy went to Davos. Seen by the critics, the meeting smacked of the rich parading their economic dominance. Nor were the critics confined to the developing world. In 1999 a demonstration against globalisation was staged outside the meeting. It was a modest affair of about 60 people, drawn from affluent societies, who claimed that the rich were exploiting the poor, and called for a fairer deal for the poor, the writing off of Third World debt, taxation on capital flows, and the elimination of capitalist tax havens. While the 1999 demonstration was small it was the forerunner of larger, more militant protests of the future. Meanwhile critics feared that Pretoria was kow-towing to the capitalists. Was Mandela, they asked, becoming a rich man's poodle in his search for investment and aid?

Mandela would have none of that. He rejected the view that he should boycott the Davos conference. Instead he took the invitation at its face value, as an opportunity to span the global economic divide. 'Such', he said in his address 'is our approach to the international business community that our new democracy never hesitated to accept your kind invitation.' He went on to thank the participants for their support. 'What', he stated, 'has stood out in all our interactions with you is your profound good will towards South Africa.' He explained that to progress South Africa must defeat racism, and to achieve that required not only stable democratic institutions and a culture of compassion, but a strong economy. He admitted the difficulty of achieving economic and social reconstruction, because it involved structural changes across the whole society. However, in South Africa's case he found encouragement in civil society's engagement in the process of social transformation, and he picked out for special mention the co-operation between business, labour and the government. 'Such partnerships of social forces', he continued, 'give our society a resilience and stability that keep it on a steady course whatever the vagaries of the political mood.'

Mandela then broadened his canvas, and in doing so attacked aspects of the existing global economic situation. He spoke of building a system that would benefit all by forging links between North and South. He repeated that his government was committed to helping the developing world, if for no other reason than self-interest. South Africa, he reiterated, could not prosper unless its neighbours prospered. Characteristically, however, Mandela staked his claim on more than self-interest. He argued that South Africa could not turn its 'back on those that helped liberate us, often at great costs to themselves'. Finally, he spoke of building a new global economic structure, which, unlike the present, would benefit all. While globalisation had been hailed as an economic panacea, Mandela pointed to recent Asian experience, which had led to economic and financial turmoil and the undermining of national economies. Globalisation, he concluded, was no panacea, but if harnessed efficiently it could contribute to development. He did not underrate the tasks that lay ahead, but regarded it as essential that 'the prodigious capacity of the world economy shall satisfy the basic needs of all people' (SAGMC 29.1.99).

The South African Economy

Meanwhile at home the government had replaced its Reconstruction and Development Programme (RDP) with the Growth, Employment and Redistribution Programme, (GEAR), based on a mixed economy, with the aim of the public and private sectors operating in harmony (see Chapter 10). As with its predecessor the new policy fared unevenly; the government again failed to achieve its targets. However, it was not all gloom. Trade had increased substantially from R140bn in 1993 to R290bn by 1998. Although growth was slower than anticipated some was achieved – with increases of 3.1 percent of GDP in 1996, 1.7 per cent in 1997, and less than 1 per cent in 1998. While direct foreign investment was disappointing, the outflow of capital had been reversed and domestic savings increased. In terms of the daily life of the mass of poorer people there were also some successes to report, particularly in the provision of electricity and water in both urban and rural settings. Finally, despite its inexperience and the problems it faced, the government's sound management of the economy helped it to avoid the major crises that struck some Asian and Latin American states. Yet, major problems persisted. As Blumenfeld noted, when Mandela retired in 1999

> the economy was again in recession, there had been relatively little new investment, especially by foreign firms, the number of jobs lost still exceeds the number created, and, despite the processes of transformation, economic empowerment and affirmative action which had benefited a growing number of black households – average income had not risen discernibly (Blumenfeld 2000: 33).

A major problem for the government was the gap between expectations and performance. It had inherited a flawed economy, which, distorted by apartheid, had bred inefficiency, social and economic inequalities and layers of bureaucracy; and it had failed to develop the potential of the majority of people. At the same time it had brought down international sanctions that had further held back development. The apartheid regime's response had been to pursue inward-looking, protectionist policies, leading to more inefficiency, and leaving local industries vulnerable when exposed to the global market. The stamp of apartheid could not easily be erased, and it left the new government with numerous problems and dilemmas. Was it, for example, to persist with protectionism, or put emphasis on the global market? The government decided to reduce protectionism, not simply because of the link with apartheid, but because it saw economic stagnation along that path. It reasoned that the economy depended heavily on trade, and as such, could only prosper by facing the rigours of the international market. Added to that were hopes – too optimistic as it proved – that the wave of good will that had greeted the political transformation would be translated into substantial, direct foreign investment.

South Africa's main economic partners – both in trade and investment – were in the developed world, with the European Union (EU) in the lead, followed by the United States and Japan. The government's recognition that these rich states dominated the global economy did not imply that it was blind to their double standards. While they preached the market economy and free trade they practised protection of some industries, not least agricultural. The contradiction was so marked in Japan's case that 'breaking into the Japanese market was believed by most [South African companies] to be impossible' (Alden 2002: 382).

The European Union and the Free Trade, Development and Co-operative Agreement (TDCA)

By the 1990s the EU was the world's largest trading entity – accounting for 40 per cent of total trade (including that between its members). It was also South Africa's main trading partner, with Britain and Germany in the lead. The EU link was therefore central to the government's economic and development policies. As Aziz Pahad said: 'Our European policy is essentially an outward projection of South Africa's domestic imperatives – economic and social' (Spence 1995). In 1994 the EU and South Africa set out to negotiate an agreement covering trade and development policies. From the beginning the EU – with an economy that was almost 40 times larger than South Africa's – was in the driver's seat. The imbalance was reflected in trade figures. In 1996 South Africa supplied only 1.4 per cent of the EU's total imports, whereas the EU accounted for 44 per cent of South Africa's. A second factor was the difference in experience and the resources available to the negotiators. While the South Africans – led by the Department of Trade and Industry – had little experience of such negotiations, and had to learn on the job, across the table they faced EU officials who were familiar with world trade issues and were backed by a specialist bureaucracy.

Initially Pretoria anticipated a speedy outcome. It was not to be. Only in 1999 was a settlement finally reached in the 'Trade, Development and Co-operative Agreement' (TDCA). Why were the negotiations so prolonged and difficult? To start with more than 10,000 items were under consideration, and not all of them could be covered by blanket agreements. Then the two sides had different perceptions both of themselves and of each other. Initially Pretoria presented itself as a developing country of 'the South', and anticipated agreeing terms under the Lomé Convention – which shaped economic relations between the EU and 70 former colonies in Africa, the Caribbean and the Pacific (ACP). However, as seen through EU eyes, South Africa was different. While the EU was prepared to offer concessions and improved trading terms to Lomé members because they were categorised as 'developing' or 'least developed', South Africa was seen as an 'economy in transition'. It pointed out that South Africa's exports to Europe were more than a third of the total of the Lome members combined. To the EU, South Africa's economy was too large and sophisticated to be granted full Lomé terms. Instead it offered a reciprocal free trade agreement.

Another complicating factor arose because for the EU the settlement with Pretoria became a test case for future agreements, including the replacement of Lomé. Thus, South Africa was again playing a bridging role – this time 'force majeure' – by helping to shape future economic relations between the world's largest trading bloc and states outside the magic circle of the rich and developed. This was a disadvantage for Pretoria, because the EU, with its eye on the future and with the 'thin end of wedge' argument in mind, reasoned that if South Africa were given concessions, others would demand the same. A further complication arose from the nature of the EU. Although it negotiated as an entity, it had to take account of the interests of its individual members and the powerful interest groups within them. Some EU states, especially those with similar agricultural products, saw South Africa not as a country deserving support but as an economic rival. They wanted to build barriers, not open doors to South African products, while at the same time Spain was seeking enhanced fishing rights around South Africa's coast. Even when all the major issues had been resolved the final stages of the negotiations became bogged down in petty disputes over individual items, as Portugal, Spain, Greece and Italy objected to South Africa using the names 'port', 'sherry'. 'ouzo' and 'grappa'. Thus it was that the enthusiasm that had greeted South Africa's political miracle was lost amidst the noise of clashing economic interests.

Although Pretoria had to abandon ground during the negotiations, it held firm on some matters. It was incensed when the EU claimed the right to discontinue the agreement if South Africa violated respect for such matters as democracy, human rights, the rule of law and good governance. Such a clause would have given the EU the unilateral right to judge the new South Africa on the very principles on which it had based its democracy, and which it sought to promote abroad. In rejecting the proposal the government stated that to have accepted it would have been offensive to itself and to have set a precedent 'that could impact negatively on its partners in the region' (Bertelsmann-Scott 1999/2000: 109–20).

Eventually a wide-ranging agreement was reached – to be implemented in

January 2000. This covered trade, economic and social co-operation, and development assistance, whereby over a ten- to twelve-year period 95 per cent of exports from South Africa to the EU, and 86 per cent of EU exports to South Africa would be tariff free. For a limited period a degree of protection was accepted for some South African products, including automobiles and textiles. Inevitably, because of the EU's Common Agricultural Policy, agricultural products were among the most contentious items. However, through their persistence the South Africans whittled away the EU's objections, so that eventually only 27 per cent of these products were completely excluded from the deal. The dispute over the names for 'port' etc. was settled when Alec Erwin agreed to phase them out for exports, but to retain them in the domestic market for 12 years, after which the position would be reviewed. Finally, the agreement left a degree of flexibility, as both sides anticipated changes in their regional arrangements – the EU as it expanded to the East, while Pretoria had hopes of SADC developments.

Once the negotiations were over the government presented the TDCA as a 'win-win' situation, in which, although neither side had gained all its initial aims, both would benefit substantially. And, claimed Pretoria, the balance of advantage was in South Africa's favour. Alec Erwin stated that the TDCA had 'created a solid and strategic platform' for future trade and investment. The partnership was, he said, beneficial in a variety of ways: it would open up new markets; enhance productivity, stimulate exports; increase growth, create more jobs and generally help development. In the spirit of the mixed economy, in which the state and private companies were to pull together, Erwin concluded by challenging the business community to seize the opportunities the agreement had opened up (Bertelsmann-Scott 2000: vii).

Outside government, less sanguine voices were heard. Cosatu viewed the EU agreement with suspicion. To start with it saw a danger of perpetuating a colonial relationship whereby South Africa exported primary goods in exchange for high value-added products. Other fears were that tariff liberalisation and increased competition, built into the TDCA, would have an adverse effect on employment. Cosatu even questioned the basic assumptions that tariff liberalisation and exposure to the global market were in South Africa's interests. 'Rather than simply presuming', commented Cosatu, 'that industry will develop if it is exposed to the "cold winds of competition" government should nurture domestic industry through selective use of protective measures.' Nor was it 'convinced that jobs generated from increased exports to the EU would outweigh job losses from increased imports'. Instead, therefore, of concentrating on export promotion, argued Cosatu, the government should encourage import substitution. Finally, it expressed fears that the EU would not keep to the spirit of the agreement, that it would use non tariff barriers to keep out South African goods, while employing its undoubted economic strength to flood the local market. (Bertelsmann-Scott 2000: 107–26).

Further doubts about the TDCA were expressed by Professors Fred Ahwireng-Obeng and Patrick McGowan. Although the two economists recognised that the agreement added to the government's international credibility, and demonstrated its 'commitment to a smooth transition from apartheid and protectionism to democracy and liberalism', they thought it had exaggerated the advantages of an agreement that claimed to be based on free trade. 'Free trade', they wrote, 'is seldom free and fair, nor is it always beneficial.' In this instance the influence of powerful European interest groups had resulted in the EU appearing to make disproportionate gains, while the overall outcome revealed 'a considerable shift from [Pretoria's] initial objectives and commitments'. Nor were the two men convinced that the overall benefits of the TDCA outweighed the costs, because 'the expected net benefits have been eroded ... and are obscure, doubtful and problematic' (Ahwireng-Obeng and McGowan 1999: 101).

Even the business community was cautious. Although, Kevin Wakeford, the Chief Executive of the South African Chamber of Business, looked forward 'to embracing the challenges presented to business by this agreement', he went on to ask: 'How does business convert this clinical and uncreative Agreement into a more vibrant, socially pragmatic accord?' He answered his own question by saying it could only be done if the government cut out unnecessary red tape, and if business was prepared to re-examine current practices; interpret the agreement in broad social and economic terms; and maximise opportunities such as joint ventures and strategic alliances (Wakeford 2000: 99–105). Niel van Heerden – who previously had headed the DFA and had a spell representing Pretoria at the EU, but now spoke as Director of the South Africa Foundation – saw both pros and cons in the TDCA. Among the advantages he noted an improved trading environment; the stability provided by the agreement; the rewards it offered successful entrepreneurs; and the hope of future expansion, which if realised would increase employment. However, he too had fears. He was concerned about the implementation of the agreement – whether it would over-tax the skills and resources of government departments – and he was concerned that South Africa's private business sector, with its large conglomerate companies, might be challenged in Europe under monopoly regulations (Van Heerden 2000: 95–8).

Relations with the US.

'The US is simply too powerful and wealthy to be ignored or spurned,' wrote Kenneth Grundy (Grundy 1997: 139). It was a judgement the government accepted, and which Mandela underlined by his trips to America. In March 1998 President Bill Clinton reciprocated by visiting South Africa, the first serving US President to do so. Clinton was on a twelve-day visit to Africa, with South Africa at the apex of his tour. Although he saw the continent through the prism of American interests, he knew that there was no consensus within the US on the importance of Africa, or the policy to be pursued. There were prominent Americans who were concerned about the continent – including those who had led the anti-apartheid campaign; and Afro-Americans who were increasingly conscious of their African heritage. However, other leading figures were much less enthusiastic. Senator Mitch McConnell – chair of the Senate's Foreign

Appropriation subcommittee – confessed that he had 'a hard time finding an American national interest' in what for him was a 'peripheral' continent. Robert Kaplan, an academic, wrote of Africa 'falling off the world economic map' (Grundy 1997: 144). These doubts had been fortified by the painful and humiliating experience of American intervention in Somalia in 1993. That reinforced those in Washington who were eager to avoid entanglements in the continent and let Africans sort out their own conflicts.

The approach of the Clinton administration was to support Africa's own efforts, provided they broadly matched Western values and interests. In that regard South Africa was seen as a pivotal player – a continental leader, a potential ally and as a bridge between the superpower and the continent. When Clinton addressed parliament in Cape Town, he declared that the question should not be 'What can we do about Africa?' but 'What can we do together with Africa?' He spoke of the world needing Africa as much as Africa needed the world. In seeking their common interests he envisaged Pretoria and the US working together in the spirit of '*masakhane*' ('building together'): 'America wants a strong South Africa. America needs a strong South Africa' (Arnold 2000: 163).

In Clinton's entourage were business representatives. They were a reminder that for Washington the road to economic regeneration was paved with private companies seeking trade and investment, and not with governments bearing aid. Even before his tour, Clinton writing to Congress, had noted the need to open up Africa to private economic activity. In a 'time of shrinking Federal funding,' he wrote, 'any strategy to support trade and development in Sub-Saharan Africa will need to rely heavily on increased US commercial involvement' (Broderick 1997: 53). In American eyes, therefore, their main contribution to development was to encourage private enterprise and trade. Clinton's message was 'doing well for American business can ... serve the cause of liberalisation and democracy' (Stremlau 2001: 331). It was an approach that bred doubts in Pretoria. The government did not share Washington's scepticism about aid, and was concerned at the decline in US aid from US$210m in 1994 to US$47m in 1999 (Stremlau 2000: 81). Added to that was the realisation that the US would always enjoy economic dominance because its economy was so much larger than South Africa's, as reflected in the balance of trade. In 1997, for instance, the trade gap was R8,093m in favour of the US – with South Africa importing R16,036m, and exporting R7,943m.

While always stressing that private enterprise was the principal vehicle for economic development, Washington was eager to establish co-operation between the two governments. In March 1995 this led to the creation of a Binational Commission. At the time the US's only similar arrangement was with Russia. The aim of the commission was to supplement traditional diplomacy, 'by bringing together senior decision makers and officials ... to develop a familiar, committed and enduring mutual relationship' (Bischoff and Southall 1999: p.162). The Commission was jointly chaired by Thabo Mbeki and Al Gore (the US Vice President). Its main business was economic and social development – such as the provision of housing and basic services in black settlements, and the implementation of the US's new Africa Opportunity Fund.

However, Mbeki and Gore established such a good rapport that the commission's writ spread to embrace a range of topics – such as agreements on civil aviation and taxation, and an anti-drugs drive. Although the commission was effective, it attracted some adverse comments in South Africa. This included criticism of the razzmatazz surrounding it, and the disproportionate amount of time and effort it absorbed for South African officials. More fundamentally it was criticised as a sell-out to the dominant capitalist power.

The government dismissed the 'sell-out' accusation by pointing to differences that continued to arise. There was, for instance, friction over Pretoria's continuing contacts with what the Americans regarded as 'rogue states', such as Cuba, Libya, Iran and Iraq. With the exception of Iran, which supplied oil, they offered little material reward to Pretoria, but the ANC was determined to demonstrate appreciation for past support, and in doing so demonstrate its independence from the US. Mandela was blunt on this issue. Not only did he criticise US treatment of Iraq, he drew attention to American breaches of the UN Charter. He chastised the US, saying that ' as the leader of the world it should set an example to help eliminate tensions in the world', and in Clinton's presence, said that whoever criticised 'our friendship with those who helped us in our darkest hours' should 'go and throw themselves into a pool' (Mills 1998: 41/2). In a similar vein Pretoria supported the EU in 1997 in condemning the Helms-Burton initiative, by which the US imposed further trade restrictions on Cuba. Nor was Mandela slow to point out that the US and Britain were ready to use South Africa as a 'go between' in persuading Colonel Gadaffi of Libya – whom they regarded as an outcast – to hand over suspects in the Pan Am aircraft disaster over Scotland.

Other differences between Washington and Pretoria included – as noted earlier – a dispute over charges brought before the US courts against Armscor. The new government regarded this as grossly unfair, because the breach of US law and international sanctions had come in apartheid days, while the NP was in power. When a US court proposed a fine of R37m, Pretoria was furious and threatened to retaliate by revealing information about US illegal arms sales, by downgrading its diplomatic representation and by closing the Binational Commission. In the event none of these steps was needed, for eventually a compromise was reached whereby Armscor admitted guilt by entering a 'no contest' plea, which resulted in a substantially reduced fine. Another clash, which was still unsettled when Mandela retired, came over the reaction of American pharmaceutical companies to the distribution of low-cost generic drugs. Washington supported the companies' claim that their patent rights had been undermined, and accused South Africa of unfair trading. To Pretoria's anger, in April 1999, the US administration declared that South Africa was breaching international trade rules, and threatened to impose penalties (Stremlau 1999/2000: 82). In response Dr Nkosazana Zuma, the Minister of Health, publicly attacked both the companies and the US government.

However, these quarrels were more like spats between friends than signs of deep-seated animosity. They arose from a wide-ranging series of contacts, most of which were conducted without animosity or rancour. At the end of Mandela's presidency John Stemlau could conclude that the relationship rested 'solidly on converging interests, shared values, and broad public support for stronger bilateral co-operation' (Stremlau 1999/2000: 79).

Towards a Safer World: Nuclear Bridge-Building

In August 1994 the new cabinet, having endorsed de Klerk's decision to abandon nuclear weapons, went on to commit itself to a policy of nuclear non-proliferation. Already astride the moral high ground, Mandela's government was able to gain more esteem on the back of de Klerk's decision. It was the only African state to have possessed 'the bomb', but more important, it was the only state anywhere to have abandoned it. The strength of South Africa's position was demonstrated when the US successfully nominated it for a seat on the International Nuclear Support Group. It was the only NAM member.

Nor did Mandela's government sit back on its laurels. It persuaded the OAU to pass a resolution declaring the whole of Africa a nuclear-free continent. It followed that up by playing a significant part at the 1995 Non-Proliferation Treaty (NPT) conference, where it set out to bridge the gap between states that possessed nuclear weapons ('the haves') and those that did not ('the have-nots'). The conference, which celebrated the treaty's twenty-fifth anniversary, marked a turning point in the nuclear debate by reorientating the issue from a predominantly East/West to a North/South concern. Prior to the conference the US – whose interests were served by the 'status quo' – had declared in favour of an unqualified extension of the treaty. In contrast most NAM members, who formed the bulk of 'the have-nots', opposed an extension, which they saw as an ruse by 'the haves' to retain their exclusive and dominant position. The South African delegation refused to endorse either side. Instead it sought to act as a bridge and to find an accommodation. As seen by Pretoria, if 'the have-nots' tried to impose a majority vote onto 'the haves', the danger of proliferation and more nuclear weapons would increase The result, said Nzo, would be no treaty at all. He argued that the NPT – the only formal limitation on nuclear weapons to which 'the haves' had bound themselves – should not be jeopardised until it was replaced by something stronger. He then made the dubious claim that South Africa had only been prepared to destroy its own weapons 'because we saw our security being guaranteed by its [NPT] provisions'.

At the conference the South Africans lobbied widely, before producing a set of bridging proposals, which the Sri Lankan chairman described as 'brilliant'. They were a compromise whereby the NAM members agreed to support an indefinite extension of the NPT, provided their preferred option of complete nuclear disarmament was placed on top of the next agenda. On that basis two documents were agreed – one strengthening the review procedure of the treaty, the other outlining a set of principles and objectives to achieve non-proliferation and disarmament. 'The haves' went away content that the treaty remained in place; 'the have-nots' with the hope that the review and the principles would lead to future change.

Pretoria continued to be active in nuclear affairs. It persuaded other African powers to agree the Pelindaba Accord, which covered co-operation in research, development and training in the peaceful use of nuclear science and technology. In 1998 – as a member of a 'new Agenda' group, which included Ireland, Egypt, New Zealand, Sweden, Slovenia, Mexico and Brazil – it mobilised support for an evolutionary approach to the reduction of nuclear weapons. That proposal, based on a step-by-step approach, was opposed by the nuclear powers, including the US, Britain and France. However, despite their efforts 114 states supported the proposal, and twelve of the sixteen NATO countries abstained when it came to a UN vote. Thus South Africa kept nagging away. In 1999 at the Geneva Disarmament Conference it proposed that a special committee be appointed 'to deliberate on practical steps for the systematic and progressive efforts to eliminate nuclear weapons' (Shelton 2001: 123–30).

Yet, although South Africa succeeded in establishing a place for itself in nuclear diplomacy, little progress was made towards the desired goal of nuclear disarmament. The US still refused to sign the NPT and went ahead with its anti-ballistic ('star wars') system; attempts to make the Middle East a nuclear-free zone failed; France conducted nuclear tests in the Pacific; the continuing confrontation between India and Pakistan led to both acquiring nuclear weapons; more than 50 governments failed to reach safeguard agreements with the International Atomic Energy Authority; and 'rogue' states like Iraq and North Korea went their own way, ignoring international agreements (Shelton 2001: 123–30). Mandela's government had built a bridge, but like the other international bridges it had constructed, it could not guarantee who was prepared to cross it.

14
The African Power

'We share great pride in being African. Our only desire is to contribute to the great African story, to the well being of our continent.' Thus the ANC committed itself to the continent as it came to power. Within that commitment was a recognition of a particular debt it owed to neighbours in Southern Africa, who had helped and suffered in the liberation struggle. 'The region', stated the ANC, 'sustained us during our struggle and our destiny is intertwined with it; our peoples belong with each other. Southern Africa is, therefore, a pillar upon which South Africa's foreign policy rests' (ANC 1994: 9/10). In the years that followed the government never tired of acknowledging its African identity, its debts from the liberation struggle, and its mutual dependence on the continent. For example, after visiting Tanzania in 1996 Mandela told the Senate that the trip had underlined 'the centrality of Africa and Southern Africa in the foreign policy of our new democracy' (*Cape Times*, 20.3.96). There is no reason to doubt the sincerity of those views.

To add to the sense of commitment were two binding elements The first was self-interest in a peaceful and prosperous continent. Nzo stated that our economies are so interlocked that 'for South Africa to believe that it could enter a prosperous future in isolation without taking neighbouring countries [with it] ... would be unrealistic and hazardous'. South Africa could not be secure or prosperous if it were surrounded by poverty, instability and conflict. Nzo's deputy, Aziz Pahad, told parliament: 'Our role in Africa is not based simply on political emotionalism. It is in our self-interest that we have to play a role on the continent generally, and specifically in the regional context' (NA 18.5.95). The second binding element was sense of national identity. In the past the white governments had presented South Africa as a white man's country – an outpost of European civilisation in an alien continent. In contrast, when Mbeki declared 'I am an African', he was claiming a common identity with Africans across the continent for himself, his party and the government. Seen through the eyes of Mandela's government the commitment to Africa reflected more than material interests or geographical proximity; it was based on a sense of a common heritage of suffering, resilience and finally triumph.

Yet, although committed to the continent and co-operation with fellow African states, the government recognised South Africa's distinctiveness and its relative power, derived from its economic strength, its political achievement and its military potential. Added to that were international expectations. From outside the continent the new South Africa was seen not only as a natural leader, but as the best, perhaps the last chance for a continent that had generated great hopes in the 1960s as new independent states had emerged from the old colonies, only for hopes to be dashed as unstable, corrupt and inefficient regimes became all too common. Thus it was that the Western states and private companies developed dual attitudes towards sub-Saharan Africa: one for South Africa, another for the rest. Nor was Pretoria reluctant to seek a leadership role for itself and pursue its own interests. In writing of relations with Japan, Alden stated that the new bureaucracy's 'confident pursuit of self interest ... was a source of astonishment to some Japanese officials' (Alden 2002: 381). The overall result was that the government's African policy and its continental relations had an inbuilt tension, arising from the dichotomy between its sense of commitment to the continent and its claim to a common African identity on the one hand, and on the other hand its relative strength, the pursuit of its own interests and its leadership aspirations, which were backed by international expectations.

The tension was not always apparent, and in any case took time to surface. It was with new hope that Mandela's government launched itself into continental affairs – from membership of the Organisation of African Unity (OAU), to hosting (and winning) the 1996 African Football Championships. Its admission to the OAU in May 1994, as the 53rd member, formalised its acceptance into the African family. Pretoria endorsed the OAU's aims, which, as stated by Secretary General Salim Ahmed Salim, were to promote 'the unity and solidarity of the African states, as well as ensuring peaceful settlements of disputes'(Van Nieuwkerk 2001). To help implement those aims Pretoria became a member of the OAU's Central Organ of Conflict Prevention, Management and Resolution, and as such participated in peace delegations to Rwanda and Burundi, and assisted in Morocco's referendum on the future of the Western Sahara.

However, after an initial flourish, the OAU did not feature prominently in Pretoria's activities. The relationship was restricted, both by Pretoria's early reluctance to be drawn into problems far from its borders while still finding its feet at home, and by the OAU's own limitations – its bureaucratic inertia, the instability and conflict between members, and its chronic shortage of funds. For instance, at the 1998 Ouagadougou summit, delegates were told that members were again in arrears – US$48m in that year alone. Even the Peace Fund, which the OAU established in 1993 for peace and security issues, with an undertaking that five per cent of the annual budget would be allocated to it, was inadequate for the tasks it was designed to undertake. By 2001 the fund stood at US$47m., while the UN peace mission to the DRC in that year was budgeted at more than US$600m (Berman 2002: 36). As a result OAU meetings tended to be strong on rhetoric, but weak on implementation. Hamill and Spence concluded that while membership was symbolically important for South Africa, 'it is unlikely to involve deep or prolonged intervention' outside Southern Africa. They noted that at the OAU Tunis summit in 1995, Mandela had described the situation in Rwanda as 'a rebuke to us all', but had avoided any mention of South Africa becoming involved (Hamill and Spence 1997: 219).

The relationship that developed with the OAU was a pointer to the government's ambivalent continental role. It was one thing for Rusty Evans to say: 'It is clear that South Africa's first priority ... must be Southern Africa, followed by and closely connected with [the rest of] the African continent'; but it was another thing to implement it (Venter 1997: 82/3). At times Pretoria adopted a modest stance – claiming that as a new boy on the block, it needed to absorb its own internal revolution before stepping outside, and it did not yet have the appropriate resources to participate in continental-wide activities. Yet running in parallel were those, inside and outside the country, urging Pretoria to take the lead in a range of activities from stimulating economic activity to resolving conflicts. Those voices found an echo inside the government, which was ready to discuss ideas about continental development in broad geo-political regions, with Egypt, Kenya, Nigeria and South Africa leading their respective hinterlands. In a similar vein the government was ambitious to represent the continent as a permanent member of the UN Security Council. To achieve that would have required not only reform of the UN, but strong support from fellow African states. Although it was not put directly to the test, because of lack of progress at the UN, the signs were at best uncertain. One straw in the wind was South Africa's bid for the 2004 Olympic Games, as 'the African candidate'. The bid failed partly because it did not gain strong African support.

Fairly or unfairly, the new South Africa was treated with a degree of suspicion elsewhere in the continent. The suspicion was built partly on concern about its relative power, which was reinforced by memories of past aggression by the apartheid regime, by the continued influence of white officials and businessmen, and by its economic and cultural links with Western states and companies, from which it was accused of gaining advantage over the rest of the continent. The overall implication was that, despite its claims to a common identity, the new South Africa accepted Western values and interests, to the detriment of its African heritage. Having a foot in different camps was an asset as an international bridge-builder, but in Africa it could be interpreted as having split loyalties. Thus, despite its protests, Pretoria found itself accused by some African critics of being unwilling to commit itself fully to the continent. Walter Ofonagoro, the Nigerian Minister of Information, stated that Mandela was the black president of a white state, who could not be trusted (Vale and Maseko 1998a: 3), and his colleague Adebayo Adedeji spoke of 'the emerging reality [which] indicates that South Africa appears to be increasingly distancing itself from continental Africa', while moving towards the West (Venter 1997: 80). There was concern that Pretoria could become a Trojan horse inside the continent – a tool of Western institutions helping to spread and legitimise policies that were injurious to other African states (Siddiqui 1999: 21). Yet, in contrast, Pretoria was accused by some critics in the West and some political opponents at home of compromising its values and principles in its attempts to curry favour in the continent by stressing its African identity, its experience of the liberation struggle and its racial awareness.

The Search for Continental Peace

While African states might have their doubts, the Western powers were eager for South Africa to take the lead in continental conflict resolution, both directly and by persuading other states to participate in peace missions. The main Western powers in Africa – US, Britain, and France (the self-proclaimed 'P–3') – each put forward schemes that they claimed would help to achieve a more settled continent. Their schemes came in various guises and packages – training courses, logistic support, the provision of transport facilities, communication equipment, and help in creating command structures. They were presented as enabling Africans to help themselves. Warren Christopher, the US Secretary of State, said that the object was to develop African forces that could quickly be deployed to maintain peace across the continent, with the proviso that they were drawn only from democratic states. However, whatever the situation, the Western states were unwilling to commit their own troops to action. They had no intention of repeating the 1993 Somalia experience. Kofi Annan, the UN Secretary General, admitted that the 'inability of the United Nations to restore peace to Somalia soured international support for conflict intervention and precipitated a rapid retreat by the international community from peacekeeping world wide' (UN 16.8.98). In Washington President Clinton issued a directive stating that: 'It is not US policy to seek to expand either the number of UN peace keeping operations, or US involvement in such operations', and he went on to lay down strict criteria for future US support (Herbst 1999: 221). Thus it was that the UN, the West and the rest of Africa – stood aside when the mass slaughter started in Rwanda in 1994. It was a grim end to the new world order in Africa.

For the future, instead of direct involvement, Paris proposed RECAMP (Renforcement des capacités Africaines de maintien de la paix), London, an African Peacekeeping Training Support Programme, and Washington an 'African Response Force'. The American scheme was based on a standing body of 10,000 African troops, at an initial cost of US$20m, half of which the US would cover. However, the proposal ran into opposition, not least in South Africa, where the Americans were criticised for lack of consultation, for excessive expectations of African states, and for wanting to determine the continent's security arrangements without risk to themselves. Pretoria suspected that the 'let Africans sort out their own problems' approach was an attempt to avoid responsibility. Although it was concerned about instability, and prepared to help in conflict resolution, the government did not want to be saddled with responsibilities it could not meet, and which it believed belonged to the whole international community. Nor did it want to be branded as a proxy of the West. In response to the criticism, Washington suggested a less ambitious scheme – 'The African Crisis Response Initiative'- with an emphasis on training, the provision of transport and equipment. Still South Africa would not bite, although by 1997 Washington had succeeded in recruiting Ghana, Uganda, Senegal, Ethiopia and Malawi, with budgets from the US of US$15m and US$20m for 1997 and 1998 respectively.

The government's broad approach to security issues was set out in two White

Papers – in 1996 on Defence; and in 1999 on Peace Missions (see Chapter 10). Although, when Modise introduced the Defence Paper, he stressed that the primary task was protection of the country against external aggression, he added that security could not be confined to military matters. It also rested on political, economic and social conditions, and the promotion of peace and stability through international co-operation, based on law and respect for human rights. That path was pursued further in the 1999 Paper, which was drawn up by a committee chaired by Dr Rocky Williams, a former MK leader. The paper emphasised diplomacy, and the need to treat the causes rather that the symptoms of instability. It noted that crises 'will recur if the underlying causes are allowed to persist'. Its watchwords were caution, co-operation and conciliation. To underline its caution sections of the paper were taken almost verbatim from the US Presidential Document, which followed Somalia.

Conscious of constraints, the 1999 Paper stated that the level and size of South Africa's contribution to a peace mission 'will depend on how closely the mission relates to our national interests and the type of demand [it makes]'. Before agreeing to any military deployment it identified various benchmarks, including domestic and international mandates, regional co-operation, and clear entry and exit criteria. Further it proposed that participation should only occur in the event of 'a clear threat to and/or breach of international peace and security, and/or a disaster of major humanitarian proportions and/or endemic causes of conflict, which unless addressed may cause long term instability' (Curnow 2001). Although the paper noted the importance of multilateral co-operation, a distinction was drawn between on one side the UN, where it proposed gaining a 'mandate', and on the other the OAU and SADC, where an 'endorsement' be sought 'as far as possible' (DHA 1999). In a separate article Rocky Williams stated that neither of the African bodies had 'de jure' authority to enforce mandates, and were too slow in their responses (Williams R. 2000: 94).

Pretoria's approach to continental peacemaking was, therefore, shaped by a combination of values, experience and practical considerations. The values were drawn from its political success at home. Aziz Pahad stated: 'The most important contribution South Africa can make in preventive diplomacy is [to employ] the moral authority it has derived from its own process of national reconciliation and democratization' (Cilliers 1996b: 11). Yet, although preventive diplomacy was the government's first choice, it also spoke of the possibility of using its armed forces in support of peace missions. In October 1997 Modise told a military audience in Zimbabwe: 'We will be professionally prepared to respond to an African or international demand for a contribution to a multilateral peacekeeping of peace support force. I assure you that the South African National Defence Force stands ready to play its part to the full – subject to the authority of our President and Parliament.' Yet, the provisos were important. Even the enthusiastic Modise was conscious of the limits within which the government was prepared to act, as later noted in the White Paper on peace missions. Pretoria further realised that it had so many different constituencies to please – at home, in Africa and globally – that it faced the chronic problem of being 'damned if it did act; and damned if it didn't'. It also knew that as yet 'no one had conceived of a way of intervening in a civil conflict and remaining impartial at the same time' (Mayall 2000: 81). In short, intervention was likely to create as many enemies as friends. That was the case in Zaire.

War in the Congo

The war in Zaire – The Congo war or 'Africa's Great War', as it was labelled – was a confused and confusing affair, involving three separate rebel movements and at least nine other African states (Bausch 2002: 4). Alongside the rival local parties and armies, from the start it drew in other African states, as fighting in Rwanda and Burundi spilled over the borders bringing with it a flow of refugees, plus fleeing and pursuing troops. Soon they were joined by other states and multilateral organisations – UN, OAU and SADC. The fighting inside the country fell into two main phases. The first, from late in 1996 to early 1997, saw Laurent Kabila leading the Alliance of Democratic Forces for the Liberation of Congo-Zaire (ADFL) against the venal government of President Mobutu. At that stage South Africa became involved, first because it felt it could not ignore events in a country of the size and importance of Zaire, and one that could destabilise the whole region, and second, in a belief in the value of personal diplomacy. While on a fact-finding mission Mandela met Kabila, and sought, in co-operation with the UN, to broker a settlement, with much toing and froing between South Africa and Zaire, which involved Mbeki, Nzo and Tutu among others. Mandela followed up with invitations to a peace meeting, and when difficulties arose about a mutually acceptable venue he solved the problem by having a South African naval vessel, the *Outenique*, moored off the Zairean coast, where the discussions were held. But little progress was made. George Alagiah, a BBC correspondent, drew a picture of a 'hapless' Mandela seated between a pathetic, terminally ill Mobutu, and an ebullient Kabila. Mandela, in trying to sell a peace deal, used the language of conciliation, reminding them that they were all Africans and flattering the two leaders by describing them as 'two of the greatest sons of Africa'. That drew a resentful comment from one observer, who said of Mobuto that such 'nonsense may have worked in South Africa, but it is an insult to tell Zairians that the man who has ruined their lives is a great son of Africa' (Alagiah 2002: 173).

Mandela's peace efforts failed because Kabila believed he could gain power by force. He was right. Mobuto was a spent force, and his corrupt administration and ill-disciplined army was near to collapse. With military support from Rwanda and Uganda, Kabila's forces advanced quickly against the dispirited Zairean troops, so that by May 1997 they had occupied the capital (Kinshasa) and overthrown Mobuto's regime. Kabila proclaimed himself President, renamed the massive, underdeveloped state 'the Democratic Republic of the Congo' (DRC), and promised democratic elections by March 1999 (Shearer 1999). While the Presidents of Uganda, Rwanda, Angola, Burundi and Zambia attended Kabila's official inauguration, South Africa's only representative was the ambassador to Kinshasa. In the immediate aftermath of Kabila's victory there was much talk of 'a new beginning' and 'a second independence', but that early optimism was unfounded. Kabila proved to be little better than Mobuto. One authoritarian, corrupt ruler had replaced another, and economic mismanagement again flourished. The result was renewed discontent, leading to more fighting. This time there was no quick victory. The conflict was protracted and complicated, as Kabila's regime now found itself under attack from dissident groups in the east of the country. As the situation deteriorated so external involvement increased. Uganda and Rwanda had quickly become disillusioned with Kabila, and so backed the dissidents, whereas Kabila gained support from Libya, which provided guns and money, and from three SADC states – Angola, Namibia and Zimbabwe – which sent troops and split the SADC (see Chapter 15). Other states that had not sent troops also felt the impact of the conflict – such as Zambia, which absorbed a large inflow of refugees (Cilliers and Malan 2001: 28).

The South African National Defence Force (SANDF)

A limitation on South Africa's role in peace missions during Mandela's presidency, which the government would not admit in public, was the state of the South African National Defence Force (SANDF). In terms of size and experience it appeared to be the continental leader, but for all Modise's claims that it was 'professionally prepared', it was undergoing a major internal reform, which restricted its capacity to act. Aided by a British military training mission the reorganisation and reorientation of the armed forces was in progress throughout the Mandela years. While in apartheid days most troops had been white, with many conscripts, by the late 1990s the forces were permanent and mainly black. While at the beginning of 1994 only 1 per cent of officers were black, by 1999 the proportion had risen to 32 per cent. The reorganisation was a complex and difficult task, in which the immediate impact was felt more sharply in the army than the smaller air and naval branches. It involved creating a single new force from troops that had been enemies – namely the old South African Defence Force and the liberation forces of the ANC and PAC (MK and APLA) – plus troops from the four 'independent homelands'. Not only had these men fought each other, they had been trained to undertake different tasks, and under different military cultures. Always, however, they had been trained and equipped to be aggressive, to fight to kill. Now they were being asked not only to work together but to concentrate on peacemaking and peacekeeping.

Nor could the reorganisation be divorced from the political and racial tensions of the society. In the early period of negotiation both the ANC and the NP government retained their armies, in part as security fall-backs should the negotiations fail. Only in November 1993 did serious discussions begin about the future shape of the forces. Following that Rocky Williams has identified three phases of change. In the first, which lasted to the inauguration of the new government in April 1994, the established South African Defence Force (SADF) – with its white officers, its staff skills, and its experience of state bureaucracy and politics – made the running.

The second phase, from May 1994 to March 1998, which Williams calls 'the absorption phase', saw the start of integration. It was a formidable task, with the integration of personnel numbering 90,000 from SADF, 22,000 MK, 6,000 APLA, and 11,000 from the homeland armies. In this phase the bulk of top posts remained with the SADF old guard, while many of the MK and APla officers who had been given senior ranks were shunted into the sidelines or sent on training courses. This phase also saw tension over the form and direction of the forces between the Ministry of Defence, headed by Joe Modise and Ronnie Kasrils, and the Chief of the National Defence Forces, General Georg Meiring. On broad policy issues the Ministry was largely successful, as in the 1996 White Paper, but control on the ground remained with the old guard.

The third phase, which lasted from March 1998 until the end of Mandela's government, was sparked off by the folly or gullibility of Meiring. He received a bogus intelligence report, claiming that a 'coup d'etat' was being planned, which involved an extraordinary mixture of people – including not only former MK officers, who were now holding senior positions in the SANDF, but Michael Jackson, the American pop idol. Meiring, without thoroughly checking the report, took it to Mandela. That led to 'a severe breakdown of trust between the political elite and the commander of the SANDF'. Mandela rejected the report, and shortly afterwards dismissed Meiring. He replaced Meiring with General Siphiwe Nyanda, one of the alleged plotters, who had previously served with MK. At the same time the white commanders of the Army and Defence Intelligence units were also replaced (Williams, R. 2000:17–28). Inevitably the reorganisation of the armed forces, and the internal tensions it created limited their effectiveness. It was another reason for Pretoria to tread warily in undertaking peace missions, a caution that was fuelled by the 1998 intervention in Lesotho (see Chapter 10).

In Rhodes's Footsteps: Trade and Investment

The new South Africa rapidly extended its trade and economic links with the rest of the continent. Between 1994 and 1998 its continental trade expanded from R10.9bn to R25.3bn. Even if the statistics exaggerated the growth, because covert trade had gone unrecorded while sanctions were in place, this was a substantial increase. Seen from Pretoria the expansion was an admirable example of its contribution towards the development and well-being of the continent, beneficial to all. Mandela himself said: 'I share the view of many that the forging of closed economic relations can be of great benefit both to a democratic South Africa and the rest of Africa' (Conradie 2001: 7). The government's intention, as explained by a senior DTI official, was not to exploit other African states, but to further mutual development (Games 2001: 114). However, a number of caveats must be added. First, even at the end of the 1990s South Africa's trade with the rest of Africa was still only small part of its total trade. Its main links remained with the developed Western states. Second, the balance of the continental trade expansion was strongly in South Africa's favour. During the 1990s South African imports from Africa rose from 1 percent to just over 2 percent of the total, while her exports grew from 5 to 10 per cent. Third, while the government could take some direct steps in this economic expansion – through parastatal bodies like Escom and Sasol and by encouraging and offering incentives to companies – mainly it had to rely on the private sector to respond to the new challenge. It was within the framework of South Africa's own mixed economy that a continental trade and investment drive was mounted.

Some companies already had strong continental links. Botswana's rich diamond mines, for example, were owned and operated by Debswana Diamond Company, a joint venture between the Botswana Government and De Beers of South Africa. Others had traded secretly during sanctions, but for many it was a new experience. Within that context the government was eager to present the expansion in terms of human development, whereas the nature of private companies and their very existence meant that they would and could only sustain their interest in Africa if it led to profit. Backed by government support, through financial and insurance schemes, many took up the challenge with enthusiasm. An opinion survey in 1997 revealed that 62 per cent of companies thought that Africa was their best option for foreign investment. Alongside their quest for profitable trade and investment was a sense of adventure. Some pictured themselves treading in the footsteps of Cecil Rhodes as they expanded to the north. Graeme Bell of Standard Bank spoke of 'a sense of pioneering'; the Managing Director of the supermarket Shoprite-Checkers saw it as 'an army on the move', and confirmed that 'South Africa's firms want to conquer it [Africa] before anyone else does' (Simon 2000: 392). The companies varied in their size and range of interests, but they include such major enterprises as Anglo American, South African Breweries, Escom, Toyota, Woolworths and Standard Bank. Their activities stretched over mining, retailing, banking, insurance, telecommunications, computers, and as suppliers of electrical goods, vehicles and weapons. In their search for business the South Africans not only had advantages over rivals from outside the continent, because of lower transport and labour costs, and their experience of African conditions, but often over local businesses, in that they were more advanced and sophisticated and could call on greater resources.

Successes soon followed. The clearest progress came near to home, among neighbouring states. For example, in 1997 80 per cent of direct investment in Botswana came from South Africa, and by the late 1990s it had become Mozambique's main trading partner, with a very favourable trade balance. In 1998 and 1999 South Africa's exports to Mozambique were R2,656m and R4,074m respectively, while imports were only R213m and R321m. South Africa was equally active in terms of investment in Mozambique, both private and public. It included US$1.3bn by Sasol for a new gas pipeline in Mozambique's Sofala Province; US$1bn by Murray & Roberts to build an aluminium smelter; US$ 130m by Eskom to integrate power lines to South Africa via Swaziland, and US$63m by Ilovo Sugar in a sugar mill (Naidu 2002: 28).

Although progress was most prominent among neighbours, it was not confined there. South African Breweries, for example – through buyouts, joint ventures and new subsidiaries – established itself in Kenya and Ethiopia to the north and east, and to the west in Ghana. By 1997 South Africa had replaced Britain as Kenya's main source of imports (Makgohlo 2002: 53). To add to the success of its own companies, many businesses from outside the continent saw South Africa as the safest and most developed base from which to spread into the rest of Africa. Thus South Africa attracted many of the world's largest and best-known companies that established an African presence, with the attendant benefits of drawing in capital and skilled personnel.

South Africa's economic expansion met a mixed response within the continent. In some places it was greeted with enthusiasm; in others with suspicion and hostility. The enthusiasm came from those who benefited from the relationship. The hostility arose from those who believed that their interests were being sacrificed to those of South Africa, and/or who feared that it was imposing a new form of dominance based on its economic strength. The harshest critics spoke of exploitation; of neo-colonialism; and of undermining local industries and businesses. They complained of the activities of South African companies, and that foreign businesses and investors were turning their backs on the rest of the continent in favour of South Africa. In their eyes, the new government, far from ending South Africa's hegemony, was imposing a new form through its economic strength. Some critics even introduced a racial factor, pointing out that most South African business leaders were white, and branding them as neo-colonialists in a different guise.

Strong criticism came from Zimbabwe. Alois Mlambo, of the University of Zimbabwe, accused Pretoria of committing the very sins it had vowed to avoid. After writing of its ingratitude for the help it had received during the liberation struggle, Mlambo claimed that instead of helping its neighbours it was using its economic strength to dominate them. He claimed that South African traders and investors were 'aggressive and pushed their way around, in the process taking away opportunities for local entrepreneurs'. He claimed that while putting pressure on its neighbours to open up their markets, Pretoria put up tariff barriers to defend its own economy. As an example he cited Pretoria's reluctance to renew the 1964 Preferential Trade Agreement with Zimbabwe, whereas it was uging Harare to open up for all South African goods. Mlambo accused Pretoria of fearing that Zimbabwe's efficiently produced textiles would undercut its own protected industries (Mlambo 2001: 65–73).

Zimbabwe was not alone. Complaints were heard in Kenya, where white businessmen were accused of arrogance and insensitivity to local practices, markets and customs. More serious accusations came from the Angolan government. It stated that de Beers was purchasing 'blood diamonds' from the rebel Unita movement, which controlled Angola's main diamond deposits, and used the income to buy arms. The Angolan government claimed that without that income Unita, and the rebellion, would have collapsed. The sums involved varied according to the diamond market and the fortunes of war, so that while in 1997 Unita sold diamonds worth an estimated US$600m, in 1998 income fell to US$250m, but it showed signs of revival in 1999 when US$300 million were estimated to have been sold (Dietrich 2001: 107). Yet, despite the variations the sums involved were large. It was estimated that between 1992 and 2000 the value of diamonds produced under Unita's control was US$3–4bn. Unita's leaders were as conscious as the government of the importance of the trade. Unita's former chief of staff, General Arlindo Pena, described the income from diamonds as the movement's 'lifeblood'.

In 1997 Gary Ralfe, a Director of de Beers, admitted that his company must have been involved in handling diamonds for Unita. He explained that:

> Unita has over the recent few years been responsible for most of the production in Angola. One of the essential jobs we at De Beers carry out worldwide is to ensure diamonds coming into the market do not threaten the overall price structure. Therefore although we have no direct relationship with Unita, there is no doubt that we buy many diamonds that emanate from the Unita held areas, second hand on the markets of Antwerp and Tel Aviv (Le Billon 2001: 68, 75).

Later de Beers was to change its policy and refuse to deal in 'blood diamonds', but that could not change the past nor exonerate the company's earlier behaviour.

15
The Regional Giant

Although the government identified itself with the whole continent its main concern was its immediate hinterland – the Southern African region. It was there that it had its strongest economic and social links and faced its main security concerns. While elsewhere in the continent there was an element of choice in the depth of Pretoria's involvement, that was not so in Southern Africa. Mandela and his colleagues were fully aware that South Africa's fate and that of the region were interlocked. 'Our success', said Mandela, 'is linked to the region. We [are] ... part of a family of Southern African nations, our destiny inextricably linked by geography, history and our huge collective potential' (Conradie 2001: 64). Pretoria repeatedly stated that its aim was not to dominate but to contribute to regional development as an equal partner. Ministers spoke of themselves as newcomers, eager to learn and co-operate. Mandela blamed colonialism for South Africa's regional dominance, and saw regional regeneration as a collective enterprise, in which South Africa would shoulder its responsibility 'not in the spirit of paternalism or dominance but with mutual co-operation and respect'.

In part the ANC was paying a debt of gratitude to those who, by supporting the liberation struggle, had borne the brunt of the apartheid regime's external aggression. It spoke of 'a special relationship with the peoples of Southern Africa, all of whom suffered under apartheid' (ANC 1993). However, once again a hard-headed recognition of self-interest was added. 'The stark reality', admitted Selebi, 'is that this country's regional policy is not the result of mere altruism, nor of some form of benign pragmatism. It is driven by self-interest.' Mandela explained that: 'Concern for national sovereignty and national interest, need not prevent us from planning seriously for regional growth and development – indeed they dictate that we move in that direction, because our fortunes are so interdependent. None of us can achieve sustainable growth and development or peace and stability in isolation' (Conradie 2001: 1). Alfred Nzo put it into a nutshell when he told the SADC: 'We cannot be an island of prosperity surrounded by a sea of poverty' (South African Government Media Ciculation 24.8.95). However, the prevailing international view was that South Africa had indeed been launched into a regional sea of poverty and instability.

The Giant

Despite protests to the contrary, it was naïve to suggest that South Africa was 'an equal partner' – just one of the pack. It was so much more powerful than its neighbours that it could not avoid playing a leading, even a dominant regional role. While in global terms South Africa is a small/medium power, in Southern Africa it is a giant. Its relative strength stretches across the board – in trade, transport, capital, infrastructure, services, technological development and military strength (see accompanying table). The figures speak for themselves. In 1990 while South Africa consumed 150,000 kWh of electricity, its nine neighbours together consumed 24,000m kWh; South Africa had 21,000 km of the region's 36,000 km of rail lines; and 58,000 km of its 86,000 km of paved roads; and while 111bn tons of goods passed through South African ports only 7bn moved through the rest (Esterhuysen 1994). The gap persisted, and if anything grew during the Mandela years, so that, by 1997, South Africa accounted for almost three-quarters (73 per cent) of the region's GNP.

Southern Africa (1997)

	Population	GNP (US$m)	GNP (per capita US$)	Military forces ('000)
Angola	11.7	3,012	260	110
Botswana	1.5	5,070	3,310	8
DRC	46.7	5,201	110	40
Lesotho	2.0	1,363	680	2
Malawi	10.2	2,129	210	5
Mozambique	16.6	2,504	140	6
Namibia	1.6	3,428	2,110	6
South Africa	40.6	130,151	3,210	90
Swaziland	1.0	1,458	1,520	–
Tanzania	31.3	6,632	210	35
Zambia	9.4	3,536	370	22
Zimbabwe	11.5	8,208	720	39

Source: Mills 2000: 224

While it was possible for Pretoria to treat its neighbours as equals in a formal, diplomatic sense, it could not escape the consequences of its own strength nor their weakness. However anxious it might be to avoid offending neighbours, they were among the world's poorest states, with problems of debt, political instability and corruption. While apartheid had been one source of the region's difficulties its demise did not eliminate all of them. Apartheid had gone, but Lesotho, Swaziland and Zambia remained poor and politically fragile; Malawi, and Mozambique were still wretchedly poor; Zimbabwe under Mugabe, and to a lesser extent Namibia under Njoma, were on the road to authoritarian rule; and in Angola a seemingly endless civil war was undermining the very fabric of society. Then, when a major war flared up in Zaire/DRC it drew in surrounding states, and threatened to destabilise the whole of central/southern Africa. Only

Botswana was relatively stable, prosperous and democratic. That the aggressive policies of the apartheid regime had contributed to this situation added to the new government's sense of obligation, but it did not eliminate the problems. Nor did it alter the reality that in relative terms South Africa was a giant (albeit a friendly one) surrounded by dwarfs. It could not avoid the consequences of having the region's – indeed the continent's – largest economy, and its most advanced technology and infrastructure The issue was not, therefore, whether Pretoria would play a leading regional role, but how it would fashion that role, and how other states would respond to it. Although Mandela's government would not or could not admit it, seen from the outside, the region was a millstone around South Africa's neck. The implications of this perception were negative for the whole region, not least in the search for foreign investment. At Davos in 1999, the leader of a major international company commented: 'I would invest there tomorrow if South Africa, exactly as it is today, were in South-East Asia or even Latin America' (Conradie 2001: 44).

Perversely, however, the end of apartheid in some ways added to the gap between South Africa and its rest. Although South Africa was held back by its regional setting, it was able to attract much of the international aid and most of the region's foreign investment, both direct and indirect. Several international companies, which in their attempts to by-pass sanctions had previously established themselves in the small surrounding states, now relocated themselves in South Africa. Seen through the eyes of the neighbours South Africa was benefiting at their expense. For example, Brian Thabang Thoka noted that previously Swaziland had 'enjoyed significant foreign investment', but, after the political change in South Africa, investment 'declined dramatically'. As a result unemployment in Swaziland increased, leading to labour discontent, which in turn led to a political crisis in 1998 as trade unions organised strikes and boycotts against the Swazi government, and demanded constitutional reform limiting the monarch's power and allowing the creation of political parties. When, from across the South African border, Cosatu declared its support for the strikes, the Swazi government angrily accused it of interfering in the affairs of a sovereign state (Thika 1998/9: 43).

The end of apartheid had not removed many of the region's problems. Some were self-inflicted while others were the product of an unjust international system. Economic weaknesses could not simply be spirited away, nor could unstable regimes be transformed overnight, or internal wars brought to a speedy end. In Angola, for instance, the prolonged war persisted, although now without the Cold War dimension or the involvement of South African troops. The fighting now had narrower aims, as the MPLA government (led by President Dos Santos) and the dissident Unita movement (of Jonas Savimbi) struggled for power, but it was no less bitter or bloody for that. Rival armies cut their way across the land, killing and maiming many people (soldiers and civilian), denuding natural riches to purchase weapons, and despoiling the country, leaving an impoverished people many of whom fled as refugees. Pretoria played no part in the fighting. Instead Mandela attempted to persuade the two sides to commit themselves to negotiations. He had little success because the combatants distrusted each other and believed they could gain more by fighting.

A Regional Inheritance

The apartheid years had witnessed not only conflict but also attempts by the white government at regional co-operation. Among these were two major shared schemes. The first was the spectacular Cahora Bassa dam on the Zambezi River, near Tete in Mozambique. The original plans, drawn up by Pretoria and the Portuguese colonial authorities, had been for the dam to provide power for South Africa, through power lines stretching across Mozambique, and to attract up to a million Portuguese settlers into newly irrigated areas. Although an impressive piece of engineering led to the dam being built, its aims went unfulfilled, because of the internal instability and conflict in Mozambique. The Portuguese withdrew before any settlers arrived, and, as in Angola, their withdrawal did not see the end of the fighting. In Mozambique an internal struggle developed between the Frelimo government and the dissident Renamo movement, which the apartheid regime supported as part of its destabilisation policy. As in Angola there was great suffering, with 4 million refugees from a total population of 17 million. Another result was that no power reached South Africa from Cahora Bassa. However, there was a positive outcome during Mandela's presidency. This rested on a political settlement in Mozambique, which brought an end to fighting and greater internal stability, which incidentally led to Cahora Bassa functioning and providing power for South Africa.

The second and larger scheme inherited by Mandela's government was not plagued by conflict. This was the Highlands Water Project in the Lesotho mountains. It was designed to help counter South Africa's chronic water problems, whereby, while it consumes 80 per cent of the total it only has 10 per cent of the region's water resources inside its borders. In the light of that the white government – in co-operation with Lesotho and international financial and construction companies – initiated a major enterprise, to divert part of the headwaters of the Orange River in the Lesotho mountains to serve the Witwatersrand, the most populous and developed part of South Africa. Both South Africa and Lesotho gained from the venture: South Africa from the provision of water and power; Lesotho from the capital expenditure involved, the sale of electricity and water to Pretoria, and the provision of its own power needs. The scheme was enthusiastically endorsed by the new government.

Regional Structures

There were also regional structures in place before the advent of Mandela's government. They fell into two categories – those in which South Africa was dominant; and those from which it was excluded. The first category consisted of the Southern African Customs Union (SACU) and the Rand Monetary Area (RMA). SACU – formed in 1910 and renegotiated in 1969 – was the oldest multilateral organisation in Africa. It comprised South Africa and its most immediate neighbours: Lesotho, Botswana, Swaziland and Namibia. With the exception of Botswana, which opted out of the RMA, it had the same membership as SACU. The two bodies survived the vicissitudes of apartheid because it served the members' interests. As well as reducing the costs and problems of customs control and financial transactions it provided a captive market for South African goods, and for the smaller states the redistributed income was a major source of government revenue. In 1995/6, for instance, it made up half the government revenue in both Lesotho and Swaziland, and 30 per cent in Namibia (Gibb 1998: p 301). The apartheid government's attempts to initiate regional bodies with a wider geographical scope and a range of functions, such as Botha's Constellation of States, ran into the sand. However SACU and the RMA survived. Discussions for further reorganisation of SACU were opened in 1997, but were still incomplete when Mandela retired. One of the factors delaying the revision was Pretoria's negotiations with the EU, which could result in a substantial reduction in customs duties, and hence revenue for the smaller states. Despite that, they were not represented at the negotiations.

The second group of regional bodies – comprising the Front Line States (FLS), the Southern African Development Co-ordination Conference (SADCC), and the Common Market for Eastern and Southern Africa (Comesa – had not only excluded white South Africa, but had sought to counter its influence. The FLS was a loosely organised political/security grouping. It first emerged in the mid 1970s to support the liberation movements against the region's white regimes, which then included Rhodesia and the Portuguese colonies as well as South Africa, and it continued its activities against South Africa alone during the 1980s. Linked to the FLS was the Inter-State Defence and Security Conference (ISDCS), which met regularly and informally at a ministerial and official levels.

SADCC was formed in 1979/80, comprising ten black states. Its aims were to foster economic co-operation among its members, to secure international development aid, and to reduce dependence on South Africa. SADCC had an uneven record. It succeeded in gaining aid from the West, particularly for transport facilities – such as the corridor from Zimbabwe to Beira on the Mozambique coast – but trade between members did not grow, stubbornly remaining at 5 per cent of the total, and it did little to reduce economic dependence on South Africa. Comesa – originally called 'The Preferential Trade Area' (PTA) – was formed in 1981. Like SADCC, with which there was some cross-membership, its main thrust was trade and economic development, but perhaps because of its greater geographical spread – reaching as far north as Ethiopia – it was a looser and less effective organisation.

Inevitably the political revolution in South Africa had a major impact on the regional organisations. It became clear to SADCC members that with apartheid coming to an end, confrontation with South Africa would soon be replaced by co-operation. They rejoiced at the end of apartheid, but realised that new challenges lay ahead. In the past they had lived with a malign giant, now they would be living with a benign one, but a giant nonetheless. They confronted a series of demanding questions. Was a new regional structure required? If so, what would be its form and functions? Should it concentrate on economic co-operation, or should these also cover security and political affairs? Should there be criteria for membership? If so should these cover such matters as democracy and human rights? Finally, SADCC members asked themselves: 'How should we handle the new South Africa?'

Their concern was not that South Africa would impose its will by force, but that consciously or unconsciously, it would establish a form of dominance based on its greater resources and its economic power. Although Pretoria insisted that it had no such ambitions, the neighbours withheld their judgement. Nor did they wait for the political changes in South Africa to be sealed before they acted. In August 1992 a SADCC summit meeting at Windhoek after welcoming developments in South Africa – which they hoped would 'take the region out of an era of conflict and confrontation to one of co-operation; in a climate of peace, security and stability' – then dissolved SADCC and reformed themselves into the Southern African Development Community (SADC). SADC's stated aims covered economic, political and security issues. Its objectives were 'to achieve development and economic growth; evolve common political values, systems and institutions; promote and defend peace and security' (SADC 1995). On the economic front the goal was to move from co-ordination towards integration. Politically members committed themselves to a set of principles, including sovereign equality, democracy, individual human rights, and the rule of law. Finally they looked forward to security co-ordination. In seeking to achieve these ends they decided that SADC's central bureaucracy should be very small, with responsibility for policy areas farmed out to individual member states (Cilliers 1996a: 202).

SADC's unspoken agenda related to South Africa. While one of SADCC's motives had been to keep the old hostile giant at bay, one of SADC's was to tame the new friendly giant. It had negative and positive aspects. The negative recognised that South Africa's presence created an imbalance that threatened the whole structure; the positive anticipated harnessing its strength to the advantage of all. Shortly after the 1994 election, Robert Mugabe told the South African parliament of 'tremendous enthusiasm' for South Africa to join SADC, 'because we believe that South Africa, given its level and size of economic development, will have a positive and major role to play in enhancing its efficacy' (Conradie 2001: 47). What Mugabe did not expose were the fears of other SADC members that Pretoria's presence might adversely affect their interests.

South Africa in the SADC

Mandela's government joined the SADC at the first opportunity, and was allocated responsibility for the Finance and Investment sector, to which was later added the Health sector. At first Pretoria hesitated to take the lead. This was demonstrated in August 1995, at the first SADC summit to be held in South Africa. For those who favoured positive action it was a frustrating experience. Dr Eric Leistner wrote of the government's 'self effacing attitude', and attributed slow progress at the meeting to 'a lack of political will', plus fear of South African dominance and 'petty politicking' (Leistner 1997: 121). However, following that slow start Pretoria became more active when Mandela was made

SADC's chairperson in August 1996. Officials in Pretoria sought to improve SADC's efficiency and effectiveness, based on their belief that the summits were mere talking shops, with an unwritten code of conduct, in which the aims were to gain consensus and demonstrate solidarity rather than make decisions and initiate policy (Sidaway and Gibb 2000: 167). Mandela, from the chair, also tried to introduce more candour and to give the organisation a cutting edge. He even proposed sanctions against members who fell short on their democratic credentials. 'Can we continue', he asked in 1997, 'to give comfort to member states whose actions are diametrically against the values and principles we hold so dear?' (Sampson 1999: 558). His appeal fell on stony ground.

Nor was SADC's sectoral approach a great success. At best the picture was uneven. Some ministers and officials undertook their SADC responsibility conscientiously, but others gave priority to the interests of their own government and/or gave little attention to SADC tasks. There was little that SADC's small central bureaucracy in Gaborone could do about it. One SADC official revealed his frustration. 'One assumes', he said, that before a meeting 'member states have had thorough consultation – but that is not necessarily true.' He complained that even when agreement had been reached between officials, 'the atmosphere become very negative' if attempts were made to implement it against a member's wishes and the officials, who previously had supported it, then followed their ministers in opposing it (Sidaway and Gibb 2000: 168).

Pretoria was not alone in its concern about the SADC's limp performance. As a result the Council of Ministers agreed to a review by external consultants, whose report – 'Review and Rationalisation Study' – was presented in April 1997. It recommended that sectors should not be treated separately, but clustered together, with the officials responsible for each cluster working together. However, the proposals were rejected, because some governments wanted to retain their sectors, and because they were said to be 'South Africa biased' (Bertelmann 1998/9: 186). That reaction characterised the resentment that built up in living with such a powerful partner. Another indication came while Mandela was chairing a SADC summit at Blantyre in 1997. Some colleagues accused him of arrogance, when, after six hours of discussion without agreement, he complained of running behind schedule.

Despite its sluggish ways, SADC made some progress. A number of agreements and protocols were signed. In 1995, for example, there were two major agreements. The first was the launching of a Southern African Power Pool, in which Eskom (South Africa's parastatal power company) led the way, using its technical skills and financial resources. Second was an agreement to share water resources. The future provision of water, as noted above, was a major concern for Pretoria. Already it had experience of co-operation in the field – notably the Lesotho Highlands scheme – and realised that to satisfy its increasing needs it would have to engage in further joint ventures. Following those agreements a trade protocol was signed, which ambitiously anticipated a regional free trade area by 2005.

Bilateral Co-operation

Alongside the multilateral agreements Mandela's government developed co-operative bilateral activities. Those with Mozambique were particularly successful – doubtless aided by the personal link arising from Mandela's growing friendship with Graca Machel, which led to their marriage in July 1998, on Mandela's 80th birthday. However, romance alone would not have been enough had it not been reinforced by other factors. The first of these was a harmony of economic interests between the two states, as in the case of the Cahora Bassa dam, and the use of Maputo as a port for the Witwatersrand. The second was in the shared ideas and values that developed between the two governments. Although Mozambique remained one of the poorest states in the world and was politically fragile, its government abandoned its former Marxist beliefs, and declared support for the 'liberal' values of democracy, good governance and the peaceful settlement of disputes.

The third factor was their similar political experiences in the 1990s. In Mozambique's case negotiations began in Rome in July 1990 to try to end the conflict between the Frelimo government of President Joaquim Chissano and the dissident Renamo movement, led by Afonso Dhlakama (previously supported by the apartheid regime). In October 1992 the negotiations led to the signing of a General Peace Accord, followed by multi-party elections in October 1994. Pretoria supported the election by providing monitors, observers and logistical aid. The result was a victory for Frelimo by 48 per cent against Renamo's 39 per cent, while in the Presidential race Chissano narrowly defeated Dhlakama by 52 per cent to 48 per cent. Following that, further assistance came from Pretoria in the form of training centres to help resettle Mozambique's liberation fighters into civilian life, and the provision of aid when Mozambique endured heavy floods. In Mozambique's case peace survived. With substantial foreign aid – which totalled US$10bn between 1987 and 1997 – the Mozambique economy made progress. Although from a very low base the growth rate was impressive. Between 1987 and 1995 it averaged 6.7 per cent per annum, and it was up to 10 per cent in the late 1990s (Naidu 2001: 20).

Co-operation between Pretoria and Maputo led to a number of agreements, three of which were signed in 1996 – first, to improve cross-border security; second, to co-operate in clearing mines from Mozambique; and third, to improve port facilities at Maputo. The next stage was to mount joint schemes with a mixture of private and public financial backing. The schemes included the building of an aluminium smelter and a casino in Maputo; exploration for offshore oil and gas fields; and development of the Maputo corridor. The 'corridor' was an ambitious scheme to improve transport links along the route from the Witwatersrand to Maputo, where port facilities would be improved, and general development along the route. In implementing the scheme a contract was agreed with an international consortium (Trans Africa) to build a high-quality toll road through north-east South Africa, to link Johannesburg with Maputo. At the opening ceremony the two Presidents signed further agreements, covering trade and agriculture. Finally, the friendship between the two countries led to South Africa's success in promoting Mozambique's membership of the Commonwealth, despite the fact that it had not been part of the British empire.

Bilateral co-operation was not confined to Mozambique. For example, in 1995 Pretoria combined with Zimbabwe and Botswana to reach a diplomatic settlement in Lesotho. Four years later Mandela summoned a meeting to resolve potential conflict in Swaziland where the monarch was challenged by the trade unions. In terms of other ventures Pretoria aided Malawi when, like Mozambique, it suffered from floods. In its relations with Zimbabwe a compromise was reached in August 1996 whereby Pretoria agreed to relax the local contents rule on the import of textiles and clothing. In Angola, South Africa helped with mine clearing operations, it was a member of a regional delegation that visited New York in 1995 to plead for a UN peace mission, and it continued throughout the period to seek a settlement between the warring parties.

Regional Strains and Stresses

Despite Pretoria's efforts regional strains and stresses persisted. In Angola the MPLA and Unita continued their bloody struggle for power. Pretoria was always ready to support peace moves, and from time to time attempted to seize the initiative. In 1995 there was renewed hope with the signing of a ceasefire – the Lusaka Agreement – which had UN support. This was followed by slow, tortuous negotiations, which in April 1997 led to the formation of a Government of National Unity and Reconciliation, drawn from both the MPLA and Unita. However, peace was a fragile plant in Angola. Neither side trusted the other, nor were they committed to unity or reconciliation. By June 1997 sporadic fighting started again, and in 1998 the Unita ministers and deputies were expelled from the government. Again Angola was consumed by civil war. Although the battle lines were constantly shifting the country was virtually split into two, with 'two leaders ensconced in two capitals', fighting each other for power, while the UN was 'wearing itself out trying to maintain an uncertain peace' (Rozes 2001: 17–34).

Pretoria's most testing relationship was with Zimbabwe. Harare may have retained an element of resentment from the days of the liberation struggle when the ANC had allied itself with Joshua Nkomo's ZAPU, and not Mugabe's ZANU(PF). Then, following its independence in 1980, Zimbabwe – led by Mugabe – saw itself as the region's leader in the struggle against apartheid. After 1994, however, that changed as the limelight increasingly fell on South Africa and Mandela. The frustration, tinged with jealousy, this caused in Harare was compounded when Pretoria followed policies and embraced principles that Mugabe opposed. Harare's resentment found a spokesman in Jonathan Moyo, who became a minister in Mugabe's government. Writing in 1998, Moyo complained of South Africa acting arrogantly, as though it had the right to speak for the whole continent, whereas, he wrote, 'South Africa is not Africa and Africa is not South Africa'. South Africans, Moyo continued, had much to learn from the continent, yet they distanced themselves and assumed superiority over the rest. They had, he claimed, alienated other Africans, because many of them, 'black and whites, have negative images of Africa and what it means to be an African'. Moyo complained that on a recent Asian tour Mbeki had concentrated his efforts on promoting white business enterprises. Moyo was also dismissive of Mbeki's renaissance proposal. He claimed that the concept had lost all meaning. It had become a catch-all phrase, which only gained attention because leaders, like Bill Clinton and President Museveni of Uganda, endorsed it to cover a lack of substance in their policies. Mbeki's renaissance, declared Moyo, was no more than a 'little political nonsense' (Moyo 1998).

As well as resenting such pointed criticism, Pretoria was also concerned at the behaviour of Mugabe's government, as it became increasingly authoritarian, and pursued flawed policies that undermined the economy. By 1999 inflation in Zimbabwe had reached 61 per cent, the growth rate was a negative 5 per cent, the gap between rich and poor was increasing, and the IMF had suspended its funding because of Harare's refusal to accept its advice. As a result Mugabe's government faced increasing internal discontent, leading to strikes by trade unions, public protests against rising food prices, and demonstrations by war veterans after the government had plundered their pension fund. Mugabe reacted by trying to suppress most of his critics – whether they were political parties, trade unions, the media or white farmers – but he decided to recruit the war veterans to his side. He granted them a compensation package worth Z$4bn, which had not been budgeted, and so further undermined the country's finances. He followed up by initiating a programme of forced land redistribution in which white-owned farms were given to the veterans, as well as ministers, army officers and prominent party members. Mugabe had never disguised his criticism of the Lancaster House Agreement – by which Zimbabwe had gained independence – claiming that the terms had been imposed by the British. Nor had he hidden his belief that the liberation struggle would not be complete until the land was restored to the indigenous Africans. Therefore, when the courts found against the land seizures Mugabe rode rough-shod over them. When violence was employed both by the veterans to gain land, and by his party thugs against political opponents, he condoned it, and used the police as a tool of the ruling party.

Although the situation in Zimbabwe deteriorated further after his retirement, Mandela and his colleagues were aware of the worsening circumstances there. They knew that Mugabe's government was flouting the principles – human rights, free speech and the rule of law – to which they had committed themselves. They knew that Zimbabwe, which had been regarded as one of Africa's best prospects, now faced economic decline, increasing political instability and international criticism. In 1999 a UN report on human development ranked Zimbabwe 130th from a total of 174 states; and in a global competitive investment report it came 57 from the 59 countries reviewed (Peters 2000). They also knew that fairly or unfairly Mugabe's behaviour was undermining the standing of the whole region; with the danger that other states would be tarred with the same brush, making potential investors and aid donors more cautious than ever. The situation also put direct pressure on South Africa through increased migration (legal and illegal) and declining markets. Mandela, without naming

Mugabe, denounced leaders who 'despise the people who put them in power and want to stay in power for ever. They want to die in power because they have committed crimes' (Pabst 2001: 28).

Viewed from outside Africa, Pretoria seemed to have considerable leverage in the situation. As a land-locked country Zimbabwe depended on South Africa for much of its transport and its power needs, and was in debt for these services. It appeared therefore that Pretoria could exert pressure to bring Harare into line. In the event little pressure was applied, because the government's capacity to act was counter-balanced by a compound of practical, political and ideological constraints operating in the African context. On the practical side Pretoria feared that by taking measures against Zimbabwe – say by slowing down supplies or demanding immediate payment of debts – it would further undermine its faltering economy, leading to more problems for the whole region. Thus it was that, despite unpaid bills, Eskom continued to supply power, and South African trains moved goods backwards and forwards across the border. Political and ideological considerations also came into play. Pretoria did not want to be branded as the region's bully, or accused of breaking the unity of African states. Nor did it want more Nigerian/Saro-Wiwa sagas. In addition many Africans admired Mugabe. For them he was a courageous figure – a veteran of the liberation struggle, an intransigent opponent of apartheid and a leader who was still prepared to redress the sins of colonialism by returning the land to its rightful African owners. His land seizure struck a chord of sympathy across the continent, including South Africa, where the ANC's Secretary-General, Kalema Motlanthe, praised it as an admirable initiative that should be followed elsewhere. The elements in the African equation therefore combined to constrain Pretoria in its relations with Zimbabwe. It moved cautiously because it was anxious to avoid confrontation at home and to bring down criticism from across the continent.

Divisions in the SADC: The Organ and the Congo War

In the Windhoek Declaration, which established the SADC, mention was made of 'providing a framework of co-operation for ... strengthening regional solidarity, peace and security'. In line with that a proposal was made in March 1995 to create a regional security structure, the Association of Southern African States (ASAS). It would have its own administration but report to SADC's Heads of State. Namibia proposed that the chairperson should be elected and serve for two years, but Zimbabwe countered by suggesting that Mugabe – as senior leader – should take the chair, and made no mention of a time limit. Although the ASAS proposal was not implemented as such, in June 1996 the SADC summit agreed to create a new body – 'The Organ for Politics, Defence and Security' (OPDS or 'the Organ'). The agreement stated that the Organ was intended 'to limit, through the use of conflict management and prevention, the prospects of conflict arising', and more generally 'to promote peace and stability'. In its operations it was to seek the peaceful settlement of disputes and only use military intervention when other remedies had been exhausted. It was further charged with the conflicting tasks of respecting the sovereign equality of member states, while observing human rights, democracy and the rule of law (Naidu and Vhuromu 2001/2: 45).

Mugabe became the Organ's first chairperson, but uncertainty persisted about his powers and the Organ's position within the SADC. Mugabe wanted the Organ to operate flexibly (like the old Front Line States); to run in parallel with the SADC with its own sphere of operation, and to be under his control. In contrast Mandela – who chaired the SADC – saw the Organ as a subordinate arm, subject to the SADC summit and its chairperson. The rivalry between two men arose partly from Mugabe's frustration at Mandela's global status, partly because of the ambiguity of SADC's structure, and partly from policy and personality differences. Mugabe envisaged the Organ working like a fire brigade, dealing with emergencies as they arose, whereas Mandela put greater emphasis anticipating problems, of countering potential conflict by preventive diplomacy (Clarkin 1998: 93). The differences also reflected the personalities and values of the two men. Mandela, the democrat, favoured reconciliation, negotiation and peaceful agreement, and he radiated personal magnetism. Mugabe, who was not blessed with an engaging personality, was an autocrat ready to impose his will on others, and favouring a vanguard party intolerant of opposition.

The tensions within the SADC intensified with disputes over the war in the Congo (see Chapter 14). In the short period of optimism following Kabila's victory the DRC was accepted into the SADC. (The Seychelles became a member at the same time.) By admitting the Congo, the SADC had extended its geographical borders deep into central Africa, and brought into its fold a huge state with great potential, but with a history from colonial days to the present of brutality, violence, instability and corruption. Pretoria supported the decision in the belief that it was safer to have a volatile DRC inside rather than outside the organisation; in the hope that membership would bolster internal stability and democracy; and in anticipation that the Congo's rich mineral resources and its river systems could be developed to the benefit of all, especially South Africa. ESCOM, South Africa's Electricity parastatal, was especially keen to harness the power of the mighty Congo River to a regional grid. Pretoria was also reluctance to run against a tide of opinion inside the SADC, which favoured admitting the DRC, with some members hoping that such a large state would help to counterbalance South Africa. Finally, in Jack Spence's view, Pretoria was 'having to recognize that Mandela's reputation was a declining asset in the formulation and conduct of foreign policy' (Spence 1998: 163).

The resumption of fighting in the Congo soon dashed the SADC's hopes and brought the differences between Mandela and Mugabe to a head. The atmosphere at the SADC summit in Blantyre in 1997 became so heated that Mandela threatened to resign from the chair unless the position of the Organ was cleared up. The instinctive response of his colleagues was to set up a committee – drawn from Mozambique, Malawi and Namibia – to investigate the impasse, and meanwhile the operation of the Organ was suspended. The committee had still not reported when Mandela retired. The dispute took a further twist when three SADC states – Zimbabwe, Angola and Namibia – decided to send their troops to support Kabila's government The decision was made in August 1998, at a meeting at Victoria Falls hosted by Mugabe. South Africa was not invited. Although the three governments claimed that they were acting in support of a fellow SADC member, the organisation was so badly split that it was rendered impotent as an instrument of conflict resolution. As the individual members went their ways, the situation was ripe for accusation and counter-accusation. In March 1999, for instance, a Zimbabwe minister asserted that if only South Africa would use its military muscle the war in DRC could quickly be ended. He claimed that Pretoria had reneged on a promise to sell arms to Kabila; whereas it had supplied arms to both sides in the Sudan war (Goncalves 1997: 10–11).

Estimates of Foreign Troops Deployed in DRC by 2000

Angola	2,000 –3,000
Burundi	2,000
Namibia	1,600 –2,000
Rwanda	17,000 –20,000
Uganda	11,000
Zimbabwe	12,000

Source: Cilliers and Malan 2001: 25.

Although the SADC members that sent troops to the DRC claimed that they were responding to an appeal from a fellow SADC state, each had additional motives. Angola had security interests, because Unita had established camps in the DRC, from which it launched attacks. The aim of the Angolan government was to drive Unita from these bases, while supporting the DRC. In the event Angolan artillery and air power played an important part in helping Kabila to survive a military crisis in August 1998. Added to these security concerns, President dos Santos had personal ambitions to be recognised as a regional power broker, which he believed would be helped by Angola's participation in the DRC. Namibia had few direct strategic interests, but acted as an ally of Angola, to whom Njoma and Swapo owed a debt from the liberation struggle. There were also reports that substantial personal 'sweeteners' were on offer from the Congo authorities. Leaders in both Angola and Namibia were reported to have stakes in Angola's national oil company (Sonalgal), which was given the concession to distribute petroleum products within the DRC. Njoma's family was also said to have a stake in a Congo diamond company (Naidoo 2000: 327–36).

Of the three SADC members Zimbabwe set the pace and sent the largest contingent of troops. Yet, it had few if any strategic interests in the DRC, and as a country could ill afford the heavy price of its military involvement. At a time when the national economy was in deep trouble, the war effort was a serious drain on the Zimbabwe treasury, despite an agreement that part of the DRC's mining profits would be used to offset the cost. Estimates of the actual costs were shrouded in a fog of uncertainty, and varied from US$100m to US$300m per year (Pabst 2001). The explanation for the involvement lay in Mugabe's determination to demonstrate Zimbabwe's independent power, and to gain rewards for himself, his family, the army and his closest followers. If the national budget suffered from the intervention, the ruling elite did not. It gained substantial personal rewards. For example, it was reported that Kabila had agreed that a Zimbabwe mining company (Ridgepointe) – in which Mugabe and his family had large stakes – was to take over a number of profitable mines in the DRC.

There were further claims that substantial sums of money were paid directly to Zimbabwe leaders, including army officers. There were reports that the ruling ZANU(PF) party, which had built up a business empire (Zidco Holdings), had subsidiaries in the DRC. Further reports were that Zimbabwe Defence Industries – in which the elite had a large stake – had sold arms to the Kabila regime; and that senior army personnel had profited from diamond and transport concessions, and illegal trading in game trophies (Pabst 2001: 24). If those reports had substance a situation had developed whereby as the internal situation in Zimbabwe deteriorated so the involvement in the DRC became increasingly important to the personal wealth of Mugabe and his inner circle (Bausch 2002: 61).

As the SADC members took their different courses so relations between Mugabe and Mandela continued to deteriorate. When Mugabe claimed that the SADC states had unanimously decided to help Kabila, Mandela publicly reprimanded him for 'inflammatory talk'. On their side Mugabe's supporters accused the South African press and broadcasting media of being under the control of white capitalists, who were determined to demonise Mugabe. They viewed Pretoria's attitude and values as 'un-African', and as a demonstration that it was in the pocket of the West (Campbell 1997: 4; Vale and Maseko 1998a: 3).

Although the SADC was weakened by the DRC dispute it did not disintegrate. The parallel policies of military involvement and seeking negotiations continued. In the short term at least, the military option gained ground. In August 1998, SADC Defence Ministers endorsed the intervention of the three members, and an emergency SADC summit, although calling for a ceasefire, confirmed the legitimacy of Kabila's government. In the following month Mandela surprised everybody by telling a press conference that the SADC had unanimously supported military intervention by its members in the DRC. Surprise it may have been, but it opened the way for a new peace initiative. This was welcomed at a SADC summit in Mauritius, where the Presidents of Zambia, Tanzania and Mozambique were chosen to lead the mediation efforts. The meeting also commended the three belligerents for 'timeously providing troops to assist the Government and people of the DRC' (Cilliers and Shaw: 2001: 27). The peace efforts continued, but so did the fighting, and persisted until the end of Mandela's presidency.

16
Punching Above its Weight

The confusion and contradictions associated with the war in the DRC underlined the problems Pretoria faced in sub Saharan Africa. Even the Madiba magic could fail there, as was illustrated not only by his inability to resolve the DRC conflict, but his differences with Robert Mugabe, and earlier in his failure to carry others with him in the Nigeria/Ken Saro-Wiwa affair. There was no lack of commitment from South Africa. The new government (with the ANC predominant) had come to power flourishing a portfolio of principles in which Africa was a top priority. That apart, there was no escaping the fact that South Africa's interests were interlocked with the rest of the continent – that its present and future were directly linked to the fortunes of its neighbours. Although the apartheid government had behaved in a very different way it too had recognised the importance of the continent. It had offered the carrot, and wielded the stick – the carrot by suggesting schemes for bilateral and regional co-operation; the stick by waging war against its neighbours. It could not ignore them, and so when the regional schemes failed it set out to bring them to heel. Similarly, when de Klerk started along the path of negotiation he too realised the importance of persuading African states to support him.

In addition to Pretoria's own concerns, other international actors – African states, international organisations, and Western states and companies with strong interests in Africa – expected South Africa to contribute to the continent. However, their expectations differed. In broad terms, although the Africans welcomed Pretoria's co-operation, especially in economic development, they wanted it on the basis of equal political status and without interference in their domestic affairs. When, in their eyes, Pretoria overstepped the mark their reaction was to brand it as an arrogant bully, or a tool of the West. The Western states wanted Pretoria to take on the mantle of a strong leader – Africa's economic dynamo and its natural peace keeper – and one that was ready to kick backsides in a continent that for the West 'has virtually been reduced to television images of the emaciated refugee child starving in the arms of an almost lifeless mother' (Chabal 1992: 3). Pretoria's own self image of its continental role sat uneasily between those two views, rejecting the power play implications of the West, but recognising both that its own relative strength set it apart from other African states, and that more than economic co-operation was needed if the continent's problems were to be effectively addressed.

Overall, therefore, the continental picture was mixed. Pretoria's experience in

Africa rammed home the message that an international identity is the product not only of one's own self image, but also the perception of others. There were continental successes for the new government, such as the overspill from the internal settlement, which led to the end of apartheid and gave Pretoria its place in continental bodies, such as the OAU and SADC. Added to these were more specific successes – including co-operation with Mozambique, participation in peace missions, the expansion of trade relations, and improvements in SADC processes. However, alongside the commitment and progress were disappointments and suspicions.

The disappointments included failure to end major conflicts, such as the wars in the DRC and Angola which threatened the continent's stability. The suspicions rested in part on memories of white South Africa's aggressive past. Added to that was its giant status in the continent, which in the eyes of some critics, was used to promote its own interests at the expense of other African states. Finally its endorsement of some Western values led to accusations that it was ready to forfeit African solidarity to curry favour with the rich and powerful, to which was added concern at the continued influence of whites in government and business. Some of this tension arose from Pretoria's wider international roles as a Middle Power and Bridge Builder, in which it was advantageous for it to have a foot in both the First and the Third Worlds. In the African context that could be and was interpreted as having split loyalties.

The Broader Setting

Compared with other states in Africa the new South Africa had an easier entry into the wider international community, where it was greeted with sympathy and enthusiasm. Again that is partly explained by the past. In the years following World War II international criticism of the white government's racist policies had grown into a major moral cause. The end of apartheid was, therefore, seen as the triumph of good over evil, and moreover a triumph in which the international community could share in the glory. Mandela reinforced the point by stating publicly his appreciation of the international effort, and he underlined its continued importance by his extensive foreign travel on his release and as President. The world that Mandela found, however, was very different from the one that had prevailed during his long imprisonment, and the changes had direct implications for South Africa. With the collapse of the Soviet bloc and the end of the Cold War, white fears of a communist onslaught disappeared, the ANC lost its main external support for the armed struggle, and Western ideas and values became dominant. In South Africa the first impact of the external change was to create conditions in which the main protagonists (ANC and the white government) concluded that their interests were better served by negotiation than continued fighting. These views were reinforced by hopes of a New World Order. If the Gulf War was the example of the use of the military in support of those hopes, South Africa's settlement was the best – indeed the only – example of success in terms of peaceful negotiations. In that sense the new South Africa was a child of the changing world order.

Although the international setting was helpful to negotiation, it was no easy task not only to oust a sitting government in that way, but to transform a complete political structure. Indeed, it seems all the more remarkable as other strife torn parts of the world remain strife torn. As Robert Schrire and Daniel Silke wrote: 'In historical terms, it is very rare for the basic inter state relations to change dramatically. It is only somewhat less unusual for the domestic arrangements within a state to change fundamentally' (Schrire/Silke 1997:13). Yet both happened simultaneously for South Africa. It was an extraordinary and demanding situation, calling for ingenuity, flexibility and resilience, and requiring astute and courageous leadership. That was provided by South Africans themselves, with Mandela and de Klerk to the fore, but in doing so they looked to and were given external support. If the new born South Africa was the product of an internal union, the midwife was the international community.

Yet not all was change. The polity had been revolutionised but not the society and the economy, and South Africa's geographical position remained the same, surrounded by a sea of poverty, and in which were currents of instability. The dilemma facing the government was illustrated in its economic policies (RDP and GEAR). As Heather Deegan commented there was a contradiction as the government tried to combine 'a commitment to meeting the population's basic needs and a radical redistribution of wealth', which implied strong state intervention, while at the same time, 'acknowledging and accepting the mechanisms of the market' (Deegan 1999: 128). It was a dilemma that was not fully resolved.

Assessing the government

The new government came in with a bang. Greeted in triumph at home and abroad, it proclaimed its determination to live by principles drawn from the ANC's experience as a liberation movement, and then laced it with elements of prevailing Western values (including the political commitment to democracy, and the economic acceptance of the market). However, like all governments, and especially one in which the majority of ministers were inexperienced in their responsibilities, there were elements of confusion, loss of efficiency, promises which were not fulfilled, and ministers and officials who failed to live up to the challenges, but remained in office.

Those weaknesses led to criticism of the government for its inefficiency, unrealistic ambitions and for failing to lay down a clear foreign policy. Although there was some substance in the criticism, much of it was misplaced. Even in calmer times, the vagaries and uncertainties of international affairs make it impossible for a government to lay down foreign policy in advance. As James Mayall concluded: 'Most countries make up their foreign policy as they go along, mainly because though their interests may remain constant, the circumstances to which they must react are not' (Mayall 2000: 80). Frequently a government finds itself responding to unforeseen events and developments, and having to modify its original intentions and/or give priority to others. Taking account of such factors, foreign policy can often best be understood in retrospect. Frequently it comes about through the accumulation of day-to-day decisions and actions, which may seem distinctive in themselves, but over time create a pattern and direction. As a result a government may be said to have a foreign policy 'orientation' (as opposed to a predetermined policy), which offers a guide to its current and future policy and development.

A further consideration, as noted above in relation to Africa, is that a state's international status and image are dependent not only on its self image, but on external judgements – on the views, values and interests of other states, organisations and the media – both in general terms and in response to individual events. It was this combination of the new South Africa's own aspirations and resources plus external reactions that shaped four main roles that Pretoria had established by 1999 – The Middle Power, The Bridge Builder, The African Power, and The Regional Giant. As also noted above, Mandela's government gained wide spread international sympathy and support, which was illustrated by the enthusiastic welcome of multilateral organisations. However, it was not content to sit back and accept a low key international position. It was active by choice and made its own luck, as was demonstrated by its election to positions of leadership in international organisations, and the trust in which it was held. Yet, inevitably differences arose between Pretoria and other international actors when their interests clashed, as in the trade negotiations with the European Union. The EU simply refused to accept South Africa's assessment of itself as a Third World country. Similarly, there were clashes with the US over Mandela's refusal to cut off contacts with America's 'rogue states' – like Cuba and Libya – which had supported the ANC's liberation struggle; and there were further clashes with some American private companies.

Foreign policy is shaped by the domestic as well as the international setting and events. In a sense it acts as a bridge between the two. Domestic considerations help to shape the values, principles and interests that are pursued abroad, while international influences penetrate the domestic scene. The domestic setting also provides the resources that are available in pursuit of policy aims. In a world of uncertainty each government has to decide its policies, its reactions to events, the order of priority among them, and the resources it is prepared to allocate in trying to achieve its ends. In terms of resources it has to decide on what it has that may be applicable, and whether and how it will commit them in specific circumstances. It may be constrained either by the inappropriateness or inadequacy of the resources available, or by public opinion, or it may simply chose not to commit the resources, either in part or in whole, because it gives priority to other matters. For example, the new South Africa was not prepared to use its armed forces in the same way as its white predecessor. The military intervention in Lesotho was intended to restore an elected government, not to destabilise it, à la Botha. Equally the government justified its relations with powerful states like Indonesia and China, despite their poor human rights record, as the most effective way of influencing them.

Although the new South Africa has been categorised here as 'Middle Power', in terms of quantifiable resources it is not as well endowed as most other Middle Powers. In a sense it confirmed that by its claim to be of the Third World.

South Africa Gains an International Identity: Its International Roles

However, in Mandela's time it was able to play a prominent part in international affairs, and was more influential than its quantifiable resources appeared to warrant. It was not treated as an ordinary state. The reason was that resources are not all quantifiable and the new South Africa was able to compensate for its lack of them by bringing into play additional factors. The first came from the prestige it gained from its negotiated settlement. The second was related to its position in Africa, where in a continent beset by troubles, South Africa was relatively powerful and stable. The third came from the respect it gained from its own activities and its positive contribution to international organisations. Last, but certainly not least, was the remarkable personality of Mandela himself. He achieved an international status that was based on a combination of wisdom, tolerance and humour, laced with strength and determination. Together these factors enabled the new South Africa – in a phrase that Mandela would savour from his youthful days as a boxer – 'to punch above its weight' in international affairs.

References

The following abbreviations are used:
AI: *Africa Insight*, Journal of The Africa Institute, Pretoria
ASR: *African Security Review*, Journal of The South African Institute for Security Studies, Pretoria
DD: Department of Defence
DFA: Department of Foreign Affairs
DHA: Department of Home Affairs
FGD: Foundation for Global Dialogue, Braamfontein, Johannesburg
HA: House of Assembly
NA: National Assembly
RIIA: Royal Institute of International Affairs, London
SAGMC: South African Governemnt Media Circulation
SAIIA: South African Institute of International Affairs, Braamfontein, Johannesburg
SAJIA, *South African Journal of International Affairs*, Journal of SAIIA
SAIRR, South African Institute of Race Relations, *Annual Survey*

Adam, Heribert and Moodley, Kogila (1993) *The Negotiated Revolution*, Jonathan Ball
Adenauer, Konrad Stiftung (1998) *The African Renaissance*, Occasional Paper No. 8.
African Communist, Journal of the South African Communist Party
Ahwireng-Obeng Fred and McGowan Patrick (1999) 'EU– SA Free Trade Arrangements', *SAJIA* 6:2
Alden, Chris (1993) 'From Liberation Movement to Political Party: ANC Foreign Policy in Transition', *SAJIA* 1,1
Alden, Chris (1998) 'China and South Africa: The Dawn of a New Relationship', SAIIA *Yearbook* 1997/8
Alden, Chris (2002) 'The Chrysanthemum and the Protea: Re-inventing Japanese-South African Relations after Apartheid', *African Affairs* 101:404
Alagiah, George (2002) *A Passage to Africa*, Time-Warner
ANC: *ANC Speaks*: *Documents and Statements of the African National Congress* (no publisher, no date)
ANC (1991) *A New Economic Strategy*
ANC (1993) *Foreign Policy in a New Democratic South Africa*
ANC (1994) *Foreign Policy Perspectives in a Democratic South Africa*
ANC (1997) *Developing a Strategic Perspective on South Africa's Foreign Policy*
Anglin, Douglas G (1995) 'International Monitoring of the Transition to Democracy in South Africa: 1992–1994', *African Affairs* 94: 377
Arnold, Guy (2000) *The New South Africa*, Macmillan

Barber, James (1983) 'BOSS in Britain' *African Affairs* 82:328
Barber, James and Barratt, John (1990) *South Africa's Foreign Policy: The Search for Status and Security*, Cambridge University Press
Batchelor, Peter and Dunne, Paul (1998) 'The Restructuring of South Africa's Defence Industry' *ASR* 7/6
Batchelor, Peter, and Willett, Susan (1998) *Disarmament and Defence Industrial Adjustment in South Africa*, Oxford University Press

References

Bausch, Kerry (2002) 'The Crisis of Sovereignty in the Democratic Republic of Congo', Cambridge University MPhil Thesis (unpublished)

Baynham, Simon (1995) 'The Fourth Horseman of the Apocalypse: Drug Trafficking in Africa', *AI* 25:3

Baynham, Simon (1995) *The Nigerian Nexus: International Trade in Drugs in Southern Africa*, SAIIA.

Berman, Eric G. (2002) 'African Regional Organisations' Peace Operations', *ASR* 11, 4

Bertelsmann-Scott, Talitha (1998/9) 'Regional Integration in Southern Africa', SAIIA *Yearbook 1998/9*

Bertelsmann-Scott, Talitha (1999/2000) 'The European Union, South Africa and the Free Trade Association', SAIIA *Yearbook 1999/2000*

Bertelsmann-Scott, Talitha (ed.) (2000) *The EU– SA Agreement*, SAIIA

Bischoff, Paul-Henri, and Southall, Roger (1999) 'The Early Foreign Policy of the Democratic South Africa' in Wright, Stephen (ed.) *African Foreign Policies*, Westview Press

Blumenfeld, Jesmond (1996) *From Icon to Scapegoat? The Experience of South Africa's RDP*, Discussion Paper No. 4, Brunel University

Blumenfeld, Jesmond (1998) *Assessing South Africa's Growth Strategy*, RIIA Briefing Paper No. 49

Blumenfeld, Jesmond (2000) 'The Post-Apartheid Economy: Achievements, Problems and Prospects', in Spence, J.E. (ed.) *After Mandela*, RIIA

Botha, P.W. (1984) 'An Address by the State President', SAIIA Occasional Paper Sept.

Breytenbach, W. (1997) 'Cuito Cuanavale Revisited', *AI* 27, 1

Broderick, Jim (1997) 'US and South Africa: Uncertain Partners in an Uncertain World', *SAIIA Yearbook 1997*

Brown, Chris (2001) 'Selective Humanitarianism. In Defence of Inconsistency', paper presented at Cambridge Seminar

Bull, Hedley (1977) *The Anarchical Society*, Macmillan

Cameron Commission (1995) 'Enquiry Into Alleged Arms Transactions', SA Government

Cameron, Marshall (1998) *To Walk Without Fear: The Global Movement to Ban Landmines*, Oxford University Press, Toronto.

Campbell, Horace (1997) 'SADF Heads at Loggerheads', *Sappho* (Zimbabwe), 10, 12

Campbell, Keith (1986) *ANC: A Soviet Task Force?* Institute for Study of Terrorism, London

Carlsnaes, Walter and Muller, Marie (eds.) (1997) *Change and South African External Relations*, International Thompson Publishing Co.

Chabal, Patrick (1992) *Power in Africa*, Macmillan

Christie, Kenneth (1997) 'Security and Forced Migration in South Africa', *ASR* 6:1

Cilliers, Jakkie (1996a) 'Security in Southern Africa', SAIIA *Yearbook 1996*

Cilliers, Jakkie (1996b) 'Evolving Security Architecture in Southern Africa', *AI* 26, 1

Cilliers, Jakkie and Shaw, Mark (2001) *Peacekeeping in the DRC*, South African Institute for Strategic Studies

Clapham, Christopher (1996) *Africa and the International System*, Cambridge University Press

Clark, Steve (ed.) (1993) *Mandela Speaks*, Pathfinder

Clarkin, John (1998) *Taking the Lead? South Africa's Policy with Regard to Security in Africa*', Cambridge University, MPhil Thesis (unpublished)

Cock, Jacklyn (1996) 'Arms Trade, Human Rights and Foreign Policy', *FGD*, Occasional Paper 6

Coker, Christopher (1986) *The United States and South Africa: Constructive Engagement and its Crisis 1968–1985*, Duke University Press

Commonwealth Eminent Persons Group, (1986) *Mission to South Africa: Findings of the Commonwealth Eminent Persons Group on Southern Africa*, Penguin

Commonwealth Secretariat (1995) *The Millbank Action Programme*

Conradie, Liesl (2001) 'South Africa's Foreign Policy with Specific Reference to its Role in SADC: 1994–2000', Cambridge University, MPhil Thesis (unpublished)

Cooper, Andrew (1997) *In Between Countries: Australia, Canada – Agricultural Trade*, McGill University Press

Cooper, Andrew, Higgott Richard and Nosell Kim (1993) *Relocating Middle Powers*, University of British Columbia Press

Crew, Mary (2000) 'South Africa touched by the Vengeance of Aids', *SAJIA* 7,2

Crocker, Chester (1980/1) 'South Africa: Strategy for Change', *Foreign Affairs* 59/2

Crocker, Chester (1992) *High Noon in Southern Africa: Making Peace in a Tough Neighbourhood*, W.W. Norton and Co.

Curnow, Robyn (2001) 'South Africa and Regional Security' Cambridge University, MPhil Thesis (unpublished)
Custy, Mary and van Wyk, J.J. (1994) 'Japanese-South African Relationship 1985–1992', *Politikon* 21:2

Davenport, T.R.H. (1998) *The Birth of a New South Africa*, Toronto University Press
Deegan, Heather (1999) *South Africa Reborn: Building a New Democracy*, University College of London Press
De Klerk, Willem (1991) *F.W. de Klerk: The Man and his Times*, Jonathan Ball
De Klerk F.W. (1998a) *The Last Trek: A New Beginning*, Macmillan
De Klerk, F.W. (1998b) *South Africa's Road Back to International Acceptance*, Diplomatic Forum, Rand Afrikaans University, Paper 1/1998
Department of Defence, (1996) *White Paper on Defence;* and (1998) *Defence Review*
Department of Foreign Affairs (1996) *South African Foreign Policy Discussion Document;* and (1998) *Thematic Review: Strategic Plans.*
Departments of Foreign Affairs and Defence (1999) White Paper: *South Africa's Participation in International Peace Missions*
De Villers J.W.; Jardine, Roger; and Reiss, Michael (1993) 'Why South Africa Gave up the Bomb', *Foreign Affairs* 72:5
De Waal, Alex (2003) 'How will HIV/AIDS Transform African Governance?' *African Affairs* 102:406
Dietrich, Christian (2001) 'Blood Diamonds', *ASR* 10:3
Du Bois, Kathleen (1997) 'The Illegal Trade in Endangered Species', *ASR* 6:1

Ellis, Stephen (1992) 'Of Elephants and Men: Politics and Nature Conservation', *Journal of Southern African Studies* 20, 1
Ellis, Stephen; and Sechaba, Tsepo (1992) *Comrades Against Apartheid: The ANC and the South African Communist Party in Exile*, James Currey
Ellis, Stephen (1994) 'Mbokolo: Security in ANC Camps, 1961–1990', *African Affairs* 93:371
Ellis, Stephen (1996) 'Africa and International Corruption', *African Affairs* 95, 379:178
Erwin, Alec (1992) 'South Africa's Economy', *African Communist* no. 129
Esterhuysen, P. (1994) *South Africa in Sub-tropical Africa*, Africa Institute, Pretoria
Evans, Graham (2000) 'Thabo Mbeki and Foreign Policy: The View from Khayelistha', Paper presented to Chatham House Study Group, Oct
Evans, Graham and Newham, Jeffrey (1992) *Dictionary of World Politics: A Reference Guide to Concepts, Ideas and Institutions*, Penguin
Evans, L.H. (Rusty) (1993) *South African Foreign Policy and the New World Order*, Institute of Strategic Studies, Pretoria University, Paper 4

FGD (1996) *Through a Glass Darkly: Human Rights Promotion in South Africa's Foreign Policy*, Occasional Paper, Nov. 1996.
Flint, Edward (1998) 'The South African Defence Industry' in Toase, F.H. and Yorke, E.J. (eds.)
Focus: *South African Focus*, SA Government Publication.
Frankel, Philip H. (1984) *Pretoria's Pretorians: Civil-Military Relations in South Africa*, Cambridge University Press.
Friedman Stephen, and Atkinson, Doreen (eds.) (1994) *The Small Miracle. South Africa's Negotiated Settlement* Ravan, Johannesburg
Frost, Mervin (1997) 'Pitfalls on the Moral Highground: Ethics and South African Foreign Policy' in Carlsnaes and Muller (eds.)
Fukuyama, Francis (1992) *The End of History and The Last Man*, Penguin

Games, Diana (2001) 'Export Boom',(2001) *SAIIA Yearbook 2000/1*
Gastrow, Peter (1999) 'Main Trends in the Development of South Africa's Organised Crime', *ASR* 8, 6.
Gelb, Alan and Floyd, Rob (1999) 'The Challenge of Globalisation for Africa', *SAJIA* 6:2
Geldenhuys, Deon (1981) *Foreign Policy Implications of South Africa's Total Onslaught Strategy*, SAIIA
Geldenhuys, Deon (1992) 'The Foreign Factor in South Africa's 1992 Referendum', *Politikon* 19, 3
Geldenhuys, Deon (1995) *The Two China Policy*, University of Witwatersrand, East Asian Project, Paper 6

References

Geldenhuys, Deon (1998) *Foreign Political Engagement: Remaking States in the Post Cold War World*, Macmillan

Gibb, Michael (1998) 'Southern Africa in Transition', *Journal of Modern African Studies* 36:2

Goncalves, Fernando (1997) 'South Africa's Arms Sales', *Sappho* 10, 12

Grundy, Kenneth (1983) *The Rise of the South African Security Establishment* SAIIA Bradlow Paper, No 1

Grundy, Kenneth (1986) *The Militarization of South African Politics*, I.B. Tauris

Grundy, Kenneth (1997) 'Stasis in Transition: United States-South African Relations' in Carlsnaes and Muller (eds.)

Guelke, Adrian (1999) *South Africa in Transition: The Misunderstood Miracle*, I.B. Tauris

Gutteridge, W. (ed) (1996) *South Africa's Defence and Security into 21*st *Century*, Dent, Dartmouth

Hadland, Adrian (2000) 'Interview with Waldo Stumpf', *Mail and Guardian*, 26.2

Hadland, Adrian and Rantao, Jovial (1999) *The Life and Times of Thabo Mbeki*, Zebra Press, Rivonia, SA

Hamill, James and Spence, Jack (1997) 'South Africa and International Organisations' in Carlsnaes and Muller (eds.)

Hartley, Anthony (1993) 'The Clinton Approach: Idealism with Prudence', *World Today* 49, 2

Heinecken, Lindy (2001) 'Living in Terror: The Looming Security Threat to Southern Africa', *ASR* 10, 4

Helmer, John (1999) 'South African– Russian Relations', *SAJIA* 6, 2

Henwood, Roland (1999) 'South African Foreign Policy and International Practice during 1999', *South African Yearbook of Law* 24, 1

Herbst, Jeffrey (1999) 'South Africa and the African Crisis Response Initiative', SAIIA *Yearbook 1998/9.*

Hill, Lloyd B. (1997) 'Democracy and Human Rights: A Paradox for Migration Policy', *AI* 27, 3

Howard, Michael (1977) 'Ethics and Power in International Politics', *International Affairs* 53:3

IMF (2000) 'World Economic Outlook', May

Israel, Mark (1999) *South African Political Exiles in the United Kingdom*, Macmillan

Kane-Berman, John (1993) *Political Violence in South Africa*, SAIRR

Kasrils, Ronnie (1996) 'The Future of South Africa's Defence Industry: The Government's Perspective', in Gutteridge, William (ed.)

Keohane, Robert (1968) 'Lilliputian's Dilemma', *International Organisations* 23, 2

Keesing's (1991) *Contemporary Archives*, Jan.

Kornegay, Francis (2000) *South African–United States Relations at the Turn of a New Century: Retrospectively Looking Forward*', IGB Occasional Paper No. 26

Kotze, Dirk (2000) 'The Political Economy of Development in South Africa', *ASR* 9, 3

Kuhne, W. (1988) 'Is there a New Soviet Approach to South Africa?', *AI* 18, 2

Kuper, Kate (1997) 'Trade Issues in South Africa's Foreign Policy', SAIIA *Yearbook 1997*

Lambrechts, Kato (ed.) (1991) 'Crisis in Lesotho', FGD Dialogue Series 2.

Landsberg, Chris (1994) in Friedman, Steve and Atkinson Doreen (eds.)

Landsberg, Chris (2000) 'South Africa Inc: Mbeki's External Initiative in Africa and the Global South', *AI* 30, 2

Landsberg, Chris and Hlophe, Dumisani (2001) 'The Triple Black Burden: Race, Knowledge Production and South Africa's International Affairs', *SAJIA* 8, 1

Le Billon, Philippe (2001) 'Angola's Political Economy of War; The Role of Oil and Diamonds', *African Affairs* 100, 398

Leistner, Erick (1997) 'Regional Co-operation in Sub-Saharan Africa', *AI* 27, 2

Leysens, Anthony (ed.) (1994) *The Political Economy of South Africa's Relations with the International Monetary Fund and the World Bank*, University of Stellenbosch

Lodge, Tom (1999) *South African Politics since 1994*, David Philip

Maasdorp, Gavin (1998) 'Trade Integration and Economic Development: Southern African Issues' in Petersson, Lennart (ed.) *Post Apartheid South Africa*, Routledge, Kegan and Paul 1998

McDonald, David (ed.) (2000) *On Borders: Perspectives on International Migration in Southern Africa*, St Martin's Press, New York

McDonald, David and Crush, Jonathan (2000) 'Understanding Skilled Migration in Southern Africa', *AI* 30, 2

McGowan, Patrick (1993) 'The "New" South Africa: Ascent and Descent in the World System', *SAJIA* 1, 1

McKinley, D.T. (1997) *The ANC and the Liberation Struggle*, Pluto Press, London

Makgohlo, Stanley (2002) 'South Africa's Relations with Selected SADC States', SAIIA *Yearbook 2001/2*

Mandela, Nelson (1978) *The Struggle is My Life*, International Defence and Aid Fund

Mandela, Nelson (1993) 'South Africa's Future Foreign Policy', *Foreign Affairs* 72, 5

Mandela, Nelson (1994) *Long Walk to Freedom*, Little Brown and Co, New York

Manhire, Tim (2000) 'Drugs in Southern Africa', paper presented at Chatham House, London, July

Mansergh, Nicolas (1963) *Documents and Speeches on British Commonwealth Affairs 1952–1962*, Oxford University Press

Marais, Hein (1998) *South Africa: Limits to Change*, Zed Books

Maxwell Cameron, Lawson R; and Tomlin B (1998) (eds.) *To Walk Without Fear: Global Movement to Ban Landmines*, Oxford University Press, Toronto

Mayall, James (2000) 'South Africa's Role in International Peacekeeping' in Spence (ed.)

Mayibuye: The ANC's Journal

Mazrui, Ali (1979) *Africa's International Relations: The Diplomacy of Dependency and Change*, Heinemann

Meredith, Martin (1997) *Nelson Mandela: a Biography*, Hamish Hamilton

Millar, T. (1992) 'A New World Order', *The World Today*, 48, 1

Mills, Greg (ed.) (1994) *From Pariah to Participant: South Africa's Evolving Foreign Relations*, SAIIA

Mills, Greg (1995) *South Africa in the Global Economy*, SAIIA

Mills, Greg (1996) 'The Two China Policy', SAIIA *Yearbook 1996*

Mills, Greg (1997) 'South Africa's Foreign Policy: Year in Review', SAIIA *Yearbook, 1997*

Mills, Greg (1998) 'South Africa, the United States and Africa', *SAJIA* 6, 1

Mills, Greg (1999) 'South Africa's Foreign Policy after Mandela', SAIIA *Yearbook 1999/2000*

Mills, Greg (2000) *The Wired Model: South Africa, Foreign Policy, and Globalisation*, Tafelberg

Mills, Greg; and Edmonds, Martin (2000) 'SA Defence Industry', British International Studies Association, Conference Paper, Nov.

Minty, Abdul (1996) '"Summation" in *Through a Glass Darkly? Human Rights in South Africa's Foreign Policy*', FDG

Mlambo, Alois (2001) 'Partner or Hegemon? South Africa and its Neighbours', *Yearbook 2000/1* SAIIA

Moore, Candice (2000) 'Migration into South Africa', Rand Afrikaans University, unpublished thesis

Morris, Jan (1999), *Lincoln*, Penguin

Moyo, Jonathan (1998) 'The African Renaissance: A Critical Assessment', *Sappho* 11, 7

Muller, Marie (1996) 'South Africa Crosses the Nuclear Threshold' in Gutteridge (ed.)

Muller, Marie (1997) 'The Institutional Dimension. The Department of Foreign Affairs and Overseas Missions' in Carlsnaes and Muller (eds.)

Muller, Marie (2000) '*Some Thoughts On South Africa's Economic Diplomacy, and the Role of the Department of Foreign Affairs* – IGD Paper 27

NA: *National Assembly Debates*, SA Government Printers

Nahum, Fasil (1992) 'Africa's Contribution to Human Rights', paper presented at a Botwsana Seminar

Naidoo, Sagaren (2000) 'Congo: From Bad to Worse', SAIIA *Yearbook 1999/2000*

Naidu, Sanusha (2001) *Mozambique: a Lasting Peace?* SAIIA Country Reports No 4

Naidu, Sanusha and Vhuromu, Maluta (2001/2) 'Reviewing the Southern African Development Community', SAIIA *Yearbook 2001/2*

Naidu Sanusha (2002) 'Southern Africa: A Review of the Region', SAIIA *Yearbook 2001/2*

Nel, Philip, Taylor, Ian and van der Westhuizen, James (2000) 'Multilateralism in South Africa's Foreign Policy', *Global Governance* 6, 1.

Nerys, John (2000) 'The Campaign Against British Bank Involvement in Apartheid South Africa', *African Affairs* 99, 396

References

Nqakula, Charles (1994) 'Towards a People Driven RDP', *The African Communist*', no. 138, Third Quarter
Northedge, F.S. (1968) *The Foreign Policy of the Powers*, Faber & Faber

Ojo, Olusola (1997) *Understanding Human Rights in Africa*, University of Limburg, Netherlands
Olivier, Gerrit and Geldenhuys, Deon (1997) 'South Africa's Foreign Policy: From Idealism to Pragmatism', *Business and the Contemporary World* IX, 2
Oosthuysen, Glen (1998) *South Africa in the Global Drug Network*, SAIIA

Pabst, Martin (2001) *Zimbabwe at the Crossroads*, Country Reports No. 3, SAIIA
Peters, Beverly (2001) 'Southern Africa: Reviewing the Region', SAIIA *Yearbook, 2000/1*
Peters, Beverly (2000) 'South and Southern Africa' SAIIA *Yearbook 1999/2000*
Pfister, Roger (2002) 'Development Agency and Gendarme: South Africa's Continental Strategy Beyond the Region', Rhodes University, unpublished PhD thesis
Pfister, Roger (2003) 'Gateway to International Victory: the Diplomacy of the ANC in Africa 1960–1994', *The Journal of Modern African Studies* 41, 1
Pienaar, Sara (1997) 'Relations with Central and Eastern Europe' in Carlsnaes and Muller (eds.)

Renwick Robin (1997) *Unconventional Diplomacy in Southern Africa*, Macmillan
Report: *Southern African Report*, Raymond Louw (ed.), Weekly briefing paper, Forest Town, Johannesburg
Rozes Antoine (2001) 'Angolan Deadlock: Chronicle of a War with no Solution', *ASR* 10, 3

SADC (1995) 'Declaration Treaty and Protocol', Gaborone
Sampson, Anthony (1999) *Mandela: The Authorised Biography*, HarperCollins
Schoeman, Maxi (2000) 'South Africa as an Emerging Middle Power', *ASR* 9:3
Schonteich, Martin (1999) 'Age and Aids: South Africa's Crime Time Bomb', *ASR* 8, 4
Schrire, Robert and Silke, Daniel (1997) 'Foreign Policy: The Domestic Context' in Carlsnaes and Muller (eds.)
Schutte, Charles, Shaw, Mark and Solomon, Hussein (1997) 'Public Attitudes Regarding Undocumented Migration', *ASR* 6, 4
Shaw, Mark (1997) 'State Response to Organised Crime in SA', *Transnational Crime* 3, 2
Shaw, Mark (1999) *Crime as Business and Business as Crime: West African Criminal Networks in Southern Africa*, SAIIA
Shaw, Mark (2002) 'West African Criminal Networks in South and Southern Africa', *African Affairs* 101: 404
Shelton, Garth (1998) *South African Arms Sales to North Africa and the Middle East*, FGD, Occasional Paper No. 16
Shelton, Garth (2001) 'South Africa and the Nuclear Non Proliferation Treaty', SAIIA *Yearbook, 2000/1*
Shearer, David (1999) 'Africa's Great War', *Survival* 41, 2
Shubin, Vladimir (1995) 'Reflections on Relations between the Soviet Union/Russian Federation and South Africa: 1980s/1990s', *SA Perspective*, University of the Western Cape
Shubin, Vladimir (1999) *ANC: A View from Moscow*', Mayibuye Books
Sidaway, James and Gibb, Richard (2000) 'SADC, COMESA, SACU: Contradictory Formats for Regional Integration in Southern Africa'
Siddiqui, Rukhsana (1999) *The Globalisation of the South African Political Economy*, Bradlow Paper SAIIA
Simon, David (2000) 'Trading Spaces', *International Affairs* 77, 2
Slovo, Joe (1990) 'Has Socialism Failed?' *African Communist* no. 121
South Africa at a Glance (2000) Eds Inc, Craighall, Johannesburg
Sparks, Allister (1995) *Tomorrow is Another Country*, Heinemann
Spence, J.E. (1988) *The Soviet Union, The Third World and Southern Africa*, Bradlow Paper SAIIA
Spence, J.E. (1995) *Mail and Guardian* 29.5
Spence, J.E. (1998) 'The New South Africa's Foreign Policy' in Toase, F.H. and Yorke, E.J. (eds.)
Spence, J.E (ed.) (2000) *After Mandela: The 1999 South African Elections*, RIIA
Steyn, Pierre D. (1996) 'The Future of South Africa's Defence Industry', in Gutteridge (ed.)

Strauss, Conrad (1997) 'South Africa's Foreign Policy: From Rejection to Respectability', SAIIA *Review* 5, 1 SAIIA June
Stremlau, John (1998/9) 'The United States and South Africa: Masakhama', SAIIA *Yearbook 1998/9*
Stremlau, John (2000) 'US-South Africa Relations: High Rhetoric and Hard Realities', *Yearbook, 1999/2000* SAIIA
Stremlau, John (2001) 'US-South African Relations: Back to the Future', SAIIA *Yearbook 2000/1*
Sunday Independent Johannesburg
Suttner, Raymond (1994) 'Trends in the New World Order – Implications for South Africa', *The African Communist*, no. 138, First Quarter

Talbot, Strobe (1995) 'The New Geopolitics: Defending Democracy in the Post Cold War Era', *The World Today* 51, 1
Taylor, Ian (2001) *Stuck in Middle Gear: South Africa's Post Apartheid Foreign Relations*, Praeger
Taylor, Ian and Williams, Paul (2001) 'South African Foreign Policy and the Great Lakes Crisis' *African Affairs* 100: 399
Thika, Brian Thebang (1998/9) 'South and Southern Africa', SAIIA *Yearbook 1998/9*
Thomas Scott (1994) 'The Diplomacy of Liberation: The ANC in Defence of Sanctions', in Mills (ed.)
Thomas, Scott (1996) *The Diplomacy of Liberation: The Foreign Policy of the ANC Since 1960*, Tauris Academic Studies
Toase, F.H. and Yorke, E.J. (eds.) (1998) *The New South Africa: Prospects for Domestic and International Security*, Macmillan
Turok, Ben (1999) *Beyond the Miracle: Development and Economy in South Africa*, Fair Share, University of the Western Cape

UK House of Commons: Foreign Affairs Committee (1991) *UK Policy Towards South Africa and Other States of the Region*, UK Government Printer
UN (1998) *Report of Secretary General* August 1998

Vale, Peter (1992) in Gavin Maasdorp and Alan Whitside (eds.) *Pressure for Change and Southern Africa*, Macmillan
Vale, Peter and Maseko, Sipho (1998a) *South Africa and the African Renaissance*, FGD Occasional Paper no. 17
Vale, Peter and Maseko, Sipho (1998b) 'The African Renaissance', *International Affairs* 74, 2
Van Aardt, Maxi (1996) 'A Foreign Policy to Die For', *AI* 26, 2
Van der Vliet, Virginia (2001) 'Aids: Losing the New Struggle', *Daedalus* Winter
Van Heerden, Neil (2000) 'Implications for South African Industry', in Bertelsmann-Scott (ed.)
Van Nieuwkerk, Anthoni (1998) *Lesotho in Crisis*, FGD Occasional Paper
Van Nieuwkerk, Anthoni (2001) 'Subregional Collaborative Security: The OAU and SADC', *SAJIA* 8, 2
Venter, Denis (1996) 'Regional Security in Sub-Saharan Africa', *AI* 26, 2
Venter, Denis (1997) 'South Africa and Africa: Relations in a Time of Change', in Carlsnaes and Muller (eds.)

Wakeford, Kevin (2000) 'The EU-SA Agreement – Opportunities and Challenges for Business', in Bertelsmann (ed.)
Waldmeir, Patti (1997), *Anatomy of Revolution*, Viking
Waltz, Kenneth (1979) *Theory of International Politics*, Addison-Wesley
Ward, Alan (1998) 'Changes in the Political Economy of the New South Africa', in Toase, F.H. and Yorke, E.J. (eds.)
Welsh, David (1994) 'Liberals and the Future of the New Democracy in South Africa', *Optima* Oct.
Williams, Paul (2000) 'South Africa's Foreign Policy: Getting Critical?', *Politikon* 27, 1
Williams, Rocky (2000) 'From Peacekeeping to Peacebuilding? South African Policy and Practice in Peace Missions', *SAJIA* 7, 2, Autumn
Wright, Stephen (1999) *African Foreign Policies*, Westview Press

Index